GREAT
BEER
GUIDE

MICHAEL JACKSON

GREAT

BEER

GUIDE

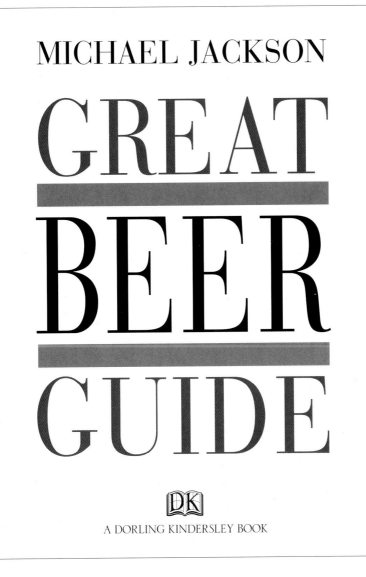

A DORLING KINDERSLEY BOOK

LONDON • NEW YORK
MELBOURNE • MUNICH • DELHI

PRODUCED FOR DORLING KINDERSLEY BY
MARK JOHNSON DAVIES - **DESIGN**
PHIL HUNT - **EDITORIAL**

MANAGING EDITOR	**DTP DESIGNER**
SHARON LUCAS	SONIA CHARBONNIER

SENIOR MANAGING ART EDITOR	**PRODUCTION**
DEREK COOMBES	WENDY PENN

SENIOR ART EDITOR	**US EDITOR**
TIM SCOTT	CHUCK WILLS

RESEARCH CO-ORDINATOR/BEER STYLIST OWEN D. L. BARSTOW

RESEARCH TEAM LARA BREKENFELD, CASEY CLOGG, BRYAN HARRELL,
ANDREE HOFFMANN, GILL LAVERY, BRITTA VETTER, SILKE WAGLER

Published in the United States by DK Publishing, Inc.
375 Hudson Street, New York, New York 10014

Penguin Group

First American Edition, 2000
Reprinted 2004

04 05 10 9 8 7 6 5 4 3 2

DK Publishing, Inc. offers special discounts for bulk purchases for sales promotions or premiums. Specific, large-quantity needs can be met with special editions, including personalized covers, excerpts of existing guides, and corporate imprints. For more information, contact: Special Markets Department, DK Publishing, Inc., 375 Hudson Street, New York, NY 10014. Fax: 212-689-5254

Library of Congress Cataloging-in-Publication Data

Jackson, Michael
    Michael Jackson's great beer guide : the best 500 beers of the world / Michael Jackson.
    p. cm.
    Includes index.
    ISBN 0-7894-5156-5 (alk. paper)
    1. Beer. I. Title: Great beer guide. II. Title.

TP577 J277 2000
663'.42-dc21
                                                     00-024039

AB940
Colour reproduced by Colourscan, Singapore
Printed in Singapore by Star Standard

discover more at
www.dk.com

Contents

GREAT BEER

Many of the world's best-known beers are almost tasteless. Their sales may be huge, but, like many popular products, they are not memorable. To produce a tasteless brew from barley-malt and hops is difficult, but a dubious achievement. These are not great beers. If it tastes like soda-pop with added alcohol, it is not a great beer; it is a means of delivering alcohol to the brain without the intervention of taste.

Great beer has taste. It need not be high in alcohol, but it is full of flavor. Some great beers have only two or three percent alcohol; others have nine or ten. One might be a summer refresher, the other a wintry nightcap. It is their flavor that makes them great.

PILSNER MALT

All great beers have the flavors of barley-malt and hops. Some, like the classic lagers of Munich, lean toward malty sweetness. Others, such as the great Pilsner lagers, are accented to herbal, aromatic hoppiness. Great lagers have a clean malt-and-hop character. Wheat beers have a sharper, more quenching, tang. Some wheat beers taste naturally spicy; others have spices or fruits added. The types of yeasts used to make ales create naturally fruity flavors. Porters and stouts have more toasty, roasty tastes.

All of these flavors, and many more *(see pp.516–17)*, belong in beers of various types. Some beers are richly malty, others almost abrasively hoppy, some acidic in their fruitiness, depending in part on the moment for which they

CHOCOLATE MALT

are intended *(see pp.518–19)*. Some particularly fine beers have a teasing interplay of these elements, seeming to be sweet at one moment and dry the next. These beers seem to offer more flavors each time the glass is raised. This is what is meant by complexity.

A bland beer is boring and not appetizing. A complex beer is satisfying without necessarily being satiating. Nor is it just a question of flavor. A great beer begins with aroma, then comes the texture and flavor, and finally the "finish" (a more elegant word for "aftertaste").

GOLDING HOP

CASCADE HOP

Bland beers have no finish. Drinkers are left wondering whether they just had a beer or simply breathed some wet air (this phrase was coined by Native American writer William Least Heat Moon to describe the experience of drinking "light" beer). Great beers have a long, lingering aftertaste. As with wine, tasters talk of "length."

Wine language can seem pretentious to beer drinkers, but the pleasures of malt and hops are no less varied than those of the grape. Read on, seek out, taste…

Michael Jackson

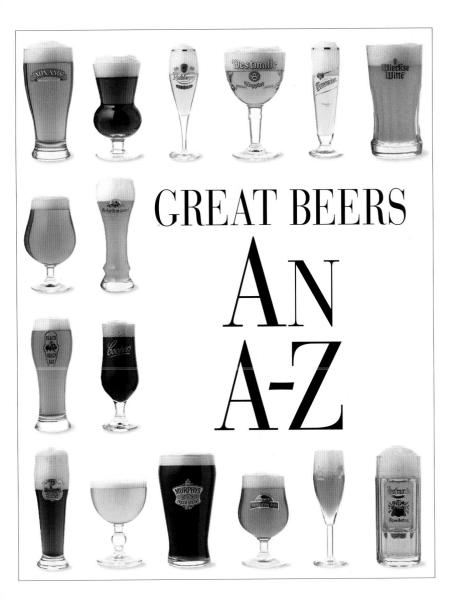

GREAT BEERS

AN
A-Z

A

AASS BOCK

🛡 **REGION OF ORIGIN** Norway, Scandinavia	
🍾 **STYLE** Bock	
% **ALCOHOL CONTENT** 5.2 abw (6.5 abv)	
🍺 **IDEAL SERVING TEMPERATURE** 48° F (9° C)	

To ask for an Aass might embarrass (or amuse) English-speakers. Properly pronounced to rhyme with "horse," Aass means "summit" in Norwegian, and is in this instance a family name. This lager brewery is in an old port town called Drammen, near Oslo. The beer shown here is a dark-brown lager in the strong style known as Bock. It has a sweet, malty aroma, almost like that of licorice toffee, and a very smooth creaminess. At the brewery, the malt meets the mountain water using traditional techniques: a process called double-decoction; an unusually long boil; and five to six months' lagering (cold maturation).

Skål!
This export bottling spells Bock in the German way. In Norway, it might be rendered as Bokkøl, the last syllable being the word for beer.

ADNAMS BROADSIDE

🛡	**REGION OF ORIGIN**	Eastern England, UK
🍺	**STYLE**	Strong Ale
%	**ALCOHOL CONTENT**	5.0 abw (6.3 abv)
🍾	**IDEAL SERVING TEMPERATURE**	50–55° F (10–13° C)

A whiff of grapeshot from British cannon is remembered in the beer called Broadside. The shots were fired against the Dutch during the Battle of Sole Bay in 1672. The seaside town of Southwold, on Sole Bay in Suffolk, is the home of the Adnams brewery. Broadside is an amber-red strong ale with a rocky head; firm, remarkably smooth body; mellow, nutty, malt flavors; a cherrylike fruitiness; and in the finish, enough lingering dryness to make the drinker thirst for another. A draft version of the beer is less strong, at 3.8 abw (4.7 abv).

Explosive brew?
As the label shows, a "broadside" refers to all the cannons on one side of a ship being fired at once.

ADNAMS SUFFOLK STRONG ALE

🛡	**REGION OF ORIGIN**	Eastern England, UK
🍾	**STYLE**	Bitter Ale
%	**ALCOHOL CONTENT**	3.6 abw (4.5 abv)
🥃	**IDEAL SERVING TEMPERATURE**	50–55° F (10–13° C)

The brewery salutes its native county with this beer. Suffolk Strong Ale has a firm, dry, biscuity, malt background, but its more pronounced flavors are drier and spicier. These appetite-sharpening tastes originate from the distinctly resiny and aniseedy variety of hops called Fuggles, which are used generously. This beer is appetizing, soothing, and marginally more potent than modest-strength British pub "session" beers, though not particularly "strong." It scores for flavor, not strength.

Grand view
The label illustrates the brewery as it was in the 1890s. The present site dates from 1660, but there may have been another location as early as 1345.

AECHT SCHLENKERLA RAUCHBIER

🛡 **REGION OF ORIGIN**	Franconia, Bavaria, Germany
🍾 **STYLE**	*Bamberger Rauchbier*
% **ALCOHOL CONTENT**	3.8 abw (4.8 abv)
🍺 **IDEAL SERVING TEMPERATURE**	48° F (9° C)

Aecht is old German for "genuine," Schlenkerla is the name of a famous tavern/brewery in the Bavarian town of Bamberg, and *Rauch* is German for "smoke." This style of beer is made from malt dried over fires of local beechwood. It has a firm smokiness from its aroma through its palate to its clean, dry, long finish. Its aroma and flavors are a shock at first, but this style marries perfectly with smoked ham or sausages.

Cool smoke
The traditional stoneware drinking vessel keeps the beer cool and fresh, but does not display its color.

A

Affligem Nöel Christmas Ale

⬡ **Region of origin**	Flemish Brabant, Belgium
🍺 **Style**	Strong Spiced Ale
% **Alcohol content**	7.2 abw (9.0 abv)
🍶 **Ideal serving temperature**	55° F (13° C)

The Benedictine monastery of Affligem, just to the west of Brussels, was founded in 1074. Like many abbeys, it once made its own beers, but fine ales are now created on its behalf by the De Smedt brewery in the nearby town of Opwijk.

Affligem gives its name to a range of strong ales with a Champagnelike second fermentation in corked bottles. Even its "weakest," the golden "Blond," has 5.2–5.6 abw (6.5–7.0 percent alcohol by volume). There is a stronger, darker "Double" and a yet more potent golden "Triple." All have deliciously rich flavors. The fermentation of very strong beers can create fruity flavors, but Affligem's products are also variously spiced with sweet orange peels, aniseed, and caraway. The Christmas beer is the most luxuriously flavored of them all: a pruney, brandyish brew for after Christmas dinner.

ALASKAN AMBER

🛡	**REGION OF ORIGIN**	Pacific Northwest US
🍾	**STYLE**	*Altbier*
%	**ALCOHOL CONTENT**	4.2 abw (5.25 abv)
🍺	**IDEAL SERVING TEMPERATURE**	48° F (9° C)

Alt means "old," and this style came before lager in Germany. Although it is smoothened by a cold lagering (maturation), it is otherwise more like an English ale. Many European styles of beer were made by immigrants to the United States before Prohibition, and most have recently been revived there by a new generation of small brewers. Geoff Larson was an engineer at an Alaskan goldmine – and a homebrewer. In 1986, he and his wife Marcy established a commercial microbrewery in the state capital, Juneau. They decided to include in their range an *alt*, called simply Alaskan Amber. This unusual style has become their principal product. It has a malty aroma; a slightly oily, clean palate; and a spicy dryness in the finish.

ALASKAN SMOKED PORTER

🛡 **REGION OF ORIGIN** Pacific Northwest US
🍾 **STYLE** Smoked Porter
🍺 **ALCOHOL CONTENT** 4.75 abw (5.9 abv)
🥛 **IDEAL SERVING TEMPERATURE** 50–55° F (10–13° C)

Having first been inspired to revive Alaska's *Altbier (see previous page)*, Geoff and Marcy Larson introduced another hybrid in 1988. This creation, a completely new style of brew, has won a worldwide reputation among beer-lovers, and been much imitated in the US. It is a smoked beer like those of Bamberg, Germany, but not in the form of a lager. Instead, it has the hoppier, yeastier accents of an English porter. The microbrewery is opposite a fish smokery where the malt is smoked over alder. The Smoked Porter is very big and complex. It starts oily, with suggestions of very bitter chocolate and burned fruits, then seems to explode with smokiness.

Fit for a snifter
Bigger, richer beers express their flavor more fully if served in a small glass like a brandy snifter.

ALBA SCOTS PINE ALE

REGION OF ORIGIN	Central Scotland, UK
STYLE	Pine/Spruce Beer
ALCOHOL CONTENT	6.0 abw (7.5 abv)
IDEAL SERVING TEMPERATURE	55° F (13° C)

Bruce Williams used to run a home-brew supply business but then turned to commercial brewing. His first beer was Fraoch Heather Ale *(see p.172)* and with his brother Scott he has gone on to produce other styles. Like their Heather Ale, the Alba uses a flavoring that was employed before hops. This beer uses no hops at all, just pine sprigs and spruce shoots. The explorer Captain Cook made this type of beer when he landed in what is now New Zealand. The tradition is recalled by present-day nonalcoholic brews such as Birch Beer in the US. Alba Scots Pine Ale is aromatic, oily, peppery, and medicinal.

Lumber room
To emphasize the use of local materials, Alba is presented with a pine-log beerholder.

ALFA LENTE BOK

🛡 **REGION OF ORIGIN** Province of Limburg, the Netherlands

🍾 **STYLE** Spring Bock *(Lente Bok)*

% **ALCOHOL CONTENT** 5.2 abw (6.5abv)

🥛 **IDEAL SERVING TEMPERATURE** 48° F (9° C)

The English word "Lent" probably refers to the lengthening days of spring. In Dutch, *lente* means "spring." This seasonal lager is made by the small, old-established Alfa brewery north of Maastricht. This Bock (the Dutch often spell it without the "c") has a beautifully retained head and a textured, dryish, fresh, malt character. It is strong but light-bodied for the style and very drinkable. While Bocks are intended as potent, warming brews for cold weather, their strength and richness can vary according to the season and region. Some places launch their Bock beers in October/November, others in February/March, and some in April/May. Traditionally, Bocks were dark and full-bodied. Today, the May/spring variation may be paler, and lighter in body. Some dark malts (but not all) contribute richness to beer, though there is no connection between the color of a beer and its alcohol content.

Blooming head
It is more than foam. It is a "beautiful bloom," according to the Germans. In the language of brewers, "Brussels lace" is left down the side of the glass.

ALFA MIDZOMER BIER

🛡	**REGION OF ORIGIN** Province of Limburg, the Netherlands
🍾	**STYLE** Spiced Summer Lager
%	**ALCOHOL CONTENT** 3.6 abw (4.5 abv)
🍺	**IDEAL SERVING TEMPERATURE** 48° F (9° C)

Why Alfa? "Because we are the first – the best," said great-grandfather Meens, an enthusiast for ancient Greek. The Meens family dates from the 1600s, and its monastery-like brewery from 1870. Its sandstone spring produces glacial water said to be 6,000 years old. While many breweries make beers especially for summer, Alfa devotes this product specifically to midsummer. Alfa is known for the quality of its spring water, and for its all-malt beers (avoiding the corn and rice often used). Its Midzomer Bier is a softly drinkable all-malt lager, with a modest alcohol content and a spicing of coriander and orange peels to add a refreshing zest. It is lightly grainy, with a perfumy tartness. By bottling it sedimented, the brewery adds a cleansing note, and perhaps some roselike flavors.

Animal farm
The crest on the main label, showing three ducks, represents the Meens family. The neck label shows the three lions of Limburg.

ALFA SUPER DORTMUNDER

🛡 **REGION OF ORIGIN**	Province of Limburg, the Netherlands
🍾 **STYLE**	Strong Dortmunder
⅌ **ALCOHOL CONTENT**	6.0 abw (7.5 abv)
🍺 **IDEAL SERVING TEMPERATURE**	48° F (9° C)

While the city of Dortmund is on Germany's Ruhr River, the nearby Rur River flows into a greater waterway known in Dutch as the Maas. Taking its name from its position as a crossing point on this river is the city of Maastricht, around which are several renowned Dutch breweries. The Dortmunder style of firm-bodied, dryish, medium-strong, golden lager has inspired Dutch brewers such as Alfa and others not far away in Belgium. While the Dortmund brewers take their local style for granted, the Dutch and Belgian brewers make bigger and stronger interpretations. Alfa acknowledges this with the term "Super" Dortmunder. This beer has a delicate, almost vanilla-like aroma (from a heavy, late dose of Tettnanger hops); a light body for such a strong brew; but a creamy texture and taste, reminiscent of fresh, melt-in-the-mouth bread. It is satisfying without being satiating, and perilously drinkable.

AMSTEL HERFSTBOCK

🛡	**REGION OF ORIGIN**	North Brabant, the Netherlands
🍾	**STYLE**	Bock
%	**ALCOHOL CONTENT**	5.6 abw (7.0 abv)
🍺	**IDEAL SERVING TEMPERATURE**	48° F (9° C)

The Amstel brewery used to stand on the river of the same name in Amsterdam a few blocks from Heineken. The bigger company took over its local rival in 1968 and later closed the brewery. The Amstel name has been retained and appears on a variety of styles including the Bock shown here. This is the most characterful brew bearing the Amstel name. It has a licorice-toffee aroma; a malty richness of body; pleasantly medicinal "cough drop" flavors; and a beautifully rounded, perfumy, hoppy finish. The prefix *herfst* has the same root as the English word "harvest," but in Dutch means "autumn." The beer is launched in October, and might be regarded as a late autumn or early winter warmer.

Kick of the goat
"Bock" means goat in many Germanic languages, including Dutch – hence the visual pun on labels and glasses.

ANCHOR LIBERTY ALE

A

	REGION OF ORIGIN West US
	STYLE American Ale
	ALCOHOL CONTENT 4.9 abw (6.1 abv)
	IDEAL SERVING TEMPERATURE 50° F (10° C)

San Francisco's Anchor brewery is famous for its Steam Beer, but the company has several other renowned brews. Among them is Liberty Ale, inspired by English bitter ales and first produced in 1975 as a commemorative brew to mark Paul Revere's 1775 ride to warn the American revolutionaries that the British were coming; thus started the War of Independence. Liberty was brought back as one year's Holiday Ale, and became a regular brew in 1983. It is hugely aromatic, though its bouquet is complex and rounded. The body is surprisingly light, but smooth and oily. The palate develops cleansing, appetizing, ginlike, lemon-rind flavors, and the finish is as dry as a Martini.

Beer bird
A beer commemorating liberty
from colonial rule appropriately
displays the American eagle.

ANCHOR OLD FOGHORN

	REGION OF ORIGIN West US
	STYLE Barley Wine
	ALCOHOL CONTENT 7.0 abw (8.7 abv)
	IDEAL SERVING TEMPERATURE 55° F (13° C)

This brew led the way in the introduction of barley wines by small American brewers in 1975, and is still one of the best. It has a soft, oily, apricot-citrus character in both its big bouquet and juicy palate, and an intense, flowery dryness. While barley wines are by definition malty, American examples balance their richness and sweetness with a heavy dose of hops. Old Foghorn undergoes a process known as dry hopping, where more hops are added during maturation. It sits on hops in the maturation tank for nine or ten months, soaking up their essential oils and aromatic resins. Their sleep-inducing properties make it a restful bedtime beer.

Foggy thinking?
US authorities argue that, as "barley wine" is not really a wine, the term "ale" should be added.

ANCHOR "OUR SPECIAL HOLIDAY ALE"

🛡 **REGION OF ORIGIN**	West US
🍾 **STYLE**	Spiced Ale
% **ALCOHOL CONTENT**	4.4–4.8 abw (5.5–6.0 abv)
🌡 **IDEAL SERVING TEMPERATURE**	55° F (13° C)

Each year, beer lovers anxiously await Anchor's "Holiday" Ale. It is released at Thanksgiving and is available through Chanukah and Christmas until New Year. The Special Holiday Ale is almost always spiced, but the ingredients change each year. In various "vintages" tasters think they have detected allspice, chocolate, cinnamon, cloves, coriander, juniper, licorice, nutmeg, and zest of lemon. Many brewers like to use traditional "Christmas spices." Ingredients like juniper are local in Nordic countries, where earlier pagan societies toasted midwinter, perhaps to assuage the fear that daylight would never return. Among today's brewers, seasonal beers are an opportunity to experiment with new recipes.

Tree of time
Each year's label bears a different image of a tree – in pre-Christian societies the tree had sacred status as a symbol of the winter solstice.

ARCEN HET ELFDE GEBOD

🛡	**REGION OF ORIGIN**	Province of Limburg, The Netherlands
🍶	**STYLE**	Belgian-style Strong Golden Ale
%	**ALCOHOL CONTENT**	5.6 abw (7.0 abv)
📶	**IDEAL SERVING TEMPERATURE**	50° F (10° C)

With, for English-speakers, a threateningly, embarrassingly, or merely appropriate, soft "c", Arcen is a town in The Netherlands. A brewery there that once made Skol lager has gone on to better things with Het Elfde Gebod. This name means "The Eleventh Commandment" – in the Catholic south of Belgium and The Netherlands, they say this commandment is "Remember to eat and drink well." It is sometimes issued in the way Americans say "Enjoy!" Het Elfde Gebod, filtered and more restrained in alcohol than similar brews, has a perfumy apple aroma; some banana and honey notes in the palate; and a teasing interplay of sweetness and dryness. The beer was originally produced by Breda/Oranjeboom, also in the Netherlands.

A

Asahi Stout

🗒	**Region of origin**	Honshu, Japan
🍶	**Style**	Strong Stout
%	**Alcohol content**	6.4 abw (8.0 abv)
🍺	**Ideal serving temperature**	55° F (13° C)

The name Asahi ("rising sun") is used by several Japanese companies, including this large brewery. The production of Western-style beers was introduced to Japan from the 1860s as a result of American, Dutch, and German influences. Asahi traces its history to the 1880s, and produces some traditional styles as well as its big-selling Super Dry light lager. The company's most characterful beer is this strong stout, made in the Irish and British tradition. In the heyday of the export of strong stouts from the British Isles, these brews were matured in wood, in which resided semiwild brewing yeasts called *Brettanomyces*. Such a yeast is still used in Asahi Stout, creating what brewers call a "horse blanket" character. This huge beer is earthy, tarlike, smoky, whiskeyish, and very much a winter warmer.

Sumo stout?
Despite being such a muscular beer, this is remarkably smooth, even by the standards of stouts. In small English type, the label refers to satin smoothness.

AUGUST SCHELL DOPPEL BOCK

🛡 **REGION OF ORIGIN**	Midwest US
🍾 **STYLE**	Double Bock
% **ALCOHOL CONTENT**	5.4 abw (6.8 abv)
🥃 **IDEAL SERVING TEMPERATURE**	48° F (9° C)

Founded in the largely German-American town of New Ulm, Minnesota, in 1860, August Schell is one of the few old-established regional breweries surviving in the US. One of the Schells, from Germany, married a Marti, from Switzerland, and that family still runs the business. It is also one of America's prettiest breweries, in woodland with its own deer park. Schell has in recent years done much to rediscover its heritage. In addition to a tawny, rummy Bock (4.6 abw; 5.8 abv), there is now this well-balanced *doppel* ("double"). It has an appetizing interplay of citric hop and cookielike malt in the aroma; a smooth, medium body; clean, syrupy palate; and an underpinning of dryness and hoppiness in the finish. It contains four malts and two American hop varieties. The beer is available from January to March.

Doppel dose?
"Double" Bock does not mean twice as strong. Generally, a Bock has around 4.8 abw (6.0 abv) and a doppel about 5.6 abw (7.0 abv).

A

AUSTRALIS BENEDICTION

🛡 **REGION OF ORIGIN**	North Island, New Zealand
🍾 **STYLE**	Belgian Abbey Ale
% **ALCOHOL CONTENT**	7.0 abw (8.7 abv)
🍺 **IDEAL SERVING TEMPERATURE**	57° F (14° C)

The name Australis is Latin for "a southern place." Confusingly, the Australis range is made in New Zealand. Young veteran Ben Middlemiss produces these beers at Galbraith's brewpub, in Auckland. They are all flavorsome and complex to a degree scarcely known in either country. All are conditioned (matured) in the bottle. "Ben's Addiction" suggested the name of this particular product, though it is in the Belgian abbey style. Its orangey color is reminiscent of the Trappist classic Orval (see p.348). So is its woody aroma, though Benediction's bouquet is more cedary and aniseedlike. Its palate – medicinal, spicy, herbal, winey – is reminiscent of another Belgian classic, Chimay Cinq Cents (see p.118). Indeed, a yeast believed to have originated at Chimay is used. Benediction has a malt and candy-sugar richness, but finishes bone dry.

AUSTRALIS HODGSON IPA

🛡 **REGION OF ORIGIN**	North Island, New Zealand
🍾 **STYLE**	India Pale Ale
% **ALCOHOL CONTENT**	5.0 abw (6.3 abv)
🥃 **IDEAL SERVING TEMPERATURE**	50–57° F (10–14° C)

Named after the London brewer George Hodgson, who first produced a pale ale in the 1700s, this is a serious attempt to be as traditional as possible. "India Pale Ale" was both strong and hoppy to withstand the sea journey to the thirsty British in the colonies. All three of this Australis series are conditioned in the cask for four months, then bottled, re-yeasted, primed with sugar, and matured for a similar period before being released. They are presented as "real ale" on lees (yeast sediment). This one has an earthy, oily, orange-zest aroma (the hops are New Zealand Goldings); a malt background that is textured and nutty (Maris Otter, from Yorkshire, England), with hints of vanilla pod; and a rooty, peppery finish. With its fresh, assertive flavors and soft but beautifully balanced carbonation, it drinks remarkably like a cask-conditioned draft.

AUSTRALIS ROMANOV BALTIC STOUT

⬡ **REGION OF ORIGIN** North Island, New Zealand

🍾 **STYLE** Baltic/Imperial Stout

% **ALCOHOL CONTENT** 6.24 abw (7.8 abv)

🍺 **IDEAL SERVING TEMPERATURE** 55–64° F (13–18° C)

Before railroads or surfaced roads, it was easier to distribute beer by sea. In the days before pale ales, the London brewers of the early Industrial Revolution exported porters and stouts via the North Sea and the Baltic. The Russian Empress Catherine the Great admired this style of beer, and ordered breweries in St. Petersburg to produce it. Romanov is in this "Imperial" style. It has the aroma and flavor of strong mocha coffee (actually deriving from a high percentage of roast barley and crystal malt). Is the coffee laced with Polish bison-grass vodka, Slivovitz plum brandy, or rum? None of the three, but these flavors are suggested by its powerful alcohol and natural spiciness. One warming flavor glows after the next. The body is tarlike, the finish as smooth as dark toffee. Try it with a chocolate dessert, after dinner, or with a cigar.

Ayinger Altbairisch Dunkel

	Region of origin Upper Bavaria, Germany
	Style Dark Lager
	Alcohol content 4.0 abw (5.0 abv)
	Ideal serving temperature 48° F (9° C)

Munich's best-known "country" beers are made in the nearby village of Aying, comprising little more than a church, maypole, and brewery (with its own restaurant and inn). The village is very typical of Bavaria, especially the counties near the Alps. This region, the Munich basin, grows some of the world's best barley for malting and brewing. Soft water from the Alps makes for gentle beers, and icy mountain caves gave rise to the custom of lagering (cold maturation). The first lagers were made in this area, and were dark. *Altbairisch* means "Old Bavarian." *Dunkel* means "dark." Most Bavarian breweries have a *Dunkel*, and the best are maltier than dark lagers further afield. Ayinger malts its own barley. Its Dunkel is a notably malty example, even slightly buttery, but very clean, and with a good balancing dryness. Malt can seem slightly spicy. This style of beer has enough flavor to accompany food, especially spicy sausages.

AYINGER CELEBRATOR

🛡️ **REGION OF ORIGIN**	Upper Bavaria, Germany
🍺 **STYLE**	Double Bock (*Doppelbock*)
% **ALCOHOL CONTENT**	5.76 abw (7.2 abv)
🍶 **IDEAL SERVING TEMPERATURE**	48° F (9° C)

The name Celebrator could perhaps be applied to any beer, but is especially appropriate to this one. In Germany and some other countries, the extra-strong style of (usually dark) lager known as Double Bock typically has a name ending in -ator. This derives from the first such rich, sustaining beer, made by Paulaner monks as a Lenten "liquid bread," and called Salvator ("Savior"). Ayinger's Double Bock was originally called Fortunator, but was felt to be too clumsy when the beer was exported to the US. The name Celebrator was at first used only in the US market, but is now also employed in Germany. Celebrator has a gentle but appetizing hop aroma; soft, oily, coffeeish, malt flavors; and a punch of figgy, spicy dryness in the finish. It seems to have become markedly drier since Ayinger opened a larger brewery. This style of beer is typically served as a springtime warmer.

AYINGER OKTOBER FEST-MÄRZEN

REGION OF ORIGIN Upper Bavaria, Germany

STYLE *Märzen/Oktoberfest*

ALCOHOL CONTENT 4.6 abw (5.8 abv)

IDEAL SERVING TEMPERATURE 48° F (9° C)

None of the breweries outside Munich's city limits is permitted to have its beer at the Oktoberfest, but many make the style of the season: a medium-strong lager, originally bronze or amber-red in color, and very malty, especially in aroma. The potency derives from the days before refrigeration, when it was impossible to brew in summer – a large batch of beer was brewed in March (*März*) for the summer months. This rich beer could continue to ferment in storage, and the last was consumed at festivals in September and October. Ayinger's example has a gold-to-bronze color, very fresh hop and malt aromas, nutty flavors, and a lightly firm body. The brewery organizes many smaller festivals in the countryside around Munich in the summer and autumn.

B

BACCHUS

REGION OF ORIGIN East Flanders, Belgium

STYLE Flemish Red/Brown

ALCOHOL CONTENT 3.6 abw (4.5 abv)

IDEAL SERVING TEMPERATURE 48–55° F (9–13° C)

In the ultra-refreshing, quenching, sweet-and-sour, winey style of West Flanders *(see Rodenbach, p.386)*. This orgiastically named example is one of several extrovert brands from the Van Honsebrouck brewery, of Ingelmunster, East Flanders. Bacchus has a vinegary bouquet; a touch of caramel; an oaky, woody palate; and a late, light, spritzy acidity. Wood aging is used. Another East Flanders brewery, Van Steenberge, of Ertevelde, has an entrant called Bios, from the Greek word for life. It has a slightly syrupy start and a late, lactic dryness. That beer is subtitled Vlaamse ("Flemish") Bourgogne.

Bacchus and the lion
The black lion of Flanders appears on the label. The brewery's home town was once the seat of the Count of Flanders.

BADGER TANGLEFOOT

🛡	**REGION OF ORIGIN**	West of England, UK
🍺	**STYLE**	Pale Ale
%	**ALCOHOL CONTENT**	4.0 abw (5.0 abv)
🍺	**IDEAL SERVING TEMPERATURE**	55° F (13° C)

Why Badger? "Because it is a prominent local animal," says the managing director of the Hall and Woodhouse brewery, for whom the badger has long been the emblem. Tanglefoot is said to have been named by a salesman who stumbled after sampling a test brew. Despite its name, it is not especially strong, but is full of flavor, balancing the pineapple-like fruitiness of the house yeast with the lemony, resiny, quinine dryness of the hop variety Challenger.

BALTIKA PORTER

REGION OF ORIGIN The Baltic (St Petersburg, Russia)

STYLE Porter/Imperial Stout

ALCOHOL CONTENT 5.6 abw (7.0 abv)

IDEAL SERVING TEMPERATURE 55–64° F (13–18° C)

Although porter-brewing was introduced to St. Petersburg by Catherine the Great, this example dates only from the 1990s. The very large Baltika brewery was established in the last days of the former USSR. As communism faded, the brewery became a joint venture between its employees and the Norwegian Ringnes group. A porter that had only been produced occasionally as a winter special was, in 1995, added as a regular brew. This brew is soft, starting with a cereal-grain sweetness, but in the end proving to be lightly dry, with some whiskeyish notes. A fruitier, winier Imperial Porter is made in St. Petersburg by the Vienna brewery. A firmer, spicier, more warming example comes from Stepan Razin, the city's oldest brewery, founded in 1795. That brewery is named after a 16th-century folk hero. A champion of the people against Tsarist rule, Stepan Razin was martyred by beheading, and his story inspired many drinking songs.

BANKS'S

	REGION OF ORIGIN	West Midlands of England, UK
	STYLE	Mild Ale
	ALCOHOL CONTENT	2.8 abw (3.5 abv)
	IDEAL SERVING TEMPERATURE	50–55° F (10–13 C°)

One of the most famous mild ales in Britain is Banks's. The term "mild" refers to a restrained hop character. A mild ale is, by definition, not bitter, and usually has a lightly sweetish smoothness of malt character. Dark malts are often used, though there are also paler milds. The style is also usually low in alcohol. With its easy drinkability and restorative sweetness, the style was traditionally popular among industrial workers, especially in the foundries of the West Midlands. The Banks's brewery at Wolverhampton built its fortune on mild, but has now dropped the term in favor of the meaningless description "Uniquely Balanced Beer," and an injunction that the ale be served chilled. If the instruction is followed, it will flatten the oily, creamy, nut-toffee maltiness of this delicious, flavorsome brew.

Uniquely balanced?
All brewers seek some balance in their beers. This one is well-balanced, though leaning toward malt, as is appropriate for the style.

BANKS'S ULTIMATE CURRY BEER

REGION OF ORIGIN West Midlands of England

STYLE Pale Ale

ALCOHOL CONTENT 4.25 abw (5.3 abv)

IDEAL SERVING TEMPERATURE 50° F (10° C)

The British love for beer is possibly exceeded by devotion to the foods of the Indian Subcontinent, and the two often share an evening. Unfortunately, most Indian restaurants in Britain offer only bland lagers, where India Pale Ales might be more appropriate. One of the heartlands of "Indian" food in Britain is the West Midlands, home of the Banks's brewery. The company's Ultimate Curry Beer was created in 1998, and has a sunny color with a distinctly crisp, gingery, sherbety flavor. To build this character, four hop varieties are used, including the relatively new First Gold, which is notably citric, perhaps tangerine-like. The beer grew from a competition run by the National Hop Association, who wanted see curry-eaters drinking a beer made with English varieties. Most lagers use Continental European hops.

BASS No.1

🛡 **REGION OF ORIGIN**	Burton, Trent Valley, England, UK
🍾 **STYLE**	Barley Wine
% **ALCOHOL CONTENT**	8.4 abw (10.5 abv)
🍺 **IDEAL SERVING TEMPERATURE**	Store at 55° F (13° C); Serve at 50–55° F (10–13° C)

This may have been the first barley wine to have been widely marketed (around the turn of the century) though that is not the reason for the name – it was produced in Bass's brewhouse Number One. Today, it is made only occasionally but is still commercially available. Its production involves 12 hours' (rather than the usual 90 minutes') boil in the brew-kettle and as many months' maturation in the cask. It is firm, smooth, oily, oaky, and in the late finish very bitter, but strangely addictive. An early advertisement for Bass No.1 claimed that it was recommended by doctors. This was based on an article in the medical journal *The Lancet* in 1909, which described the beer as "nourishing."

Truly the King of Beers…
…says the back label. This hefty ale makes a startling contrast to American Budweiser, which omits the "truly."

B

BASS "OUR FINEST ALE"

🛡 **REGION OF ORIGIN**	Burton, Trent Valley, England, UK
🍾 **STYLE**	Pale Ale
% **ALCOHOL CONTENT**	3.5 abw (4.4 abv)
🍺 **IDEAL SERVING TEMPERATURE**	50–55° F (10–13° C)

Bass is the best-known brewing company in Britain. Its most famous product in its home country is its cask-conditioned ale Draft Bass. Although this draft product has lost considerable character over the years, it does retain a delicacy and complexity, greatly assisted by its two-strain yeast. Being a cask product, this is available only in pubs, but the bottled counterpart in Britain is now offered in a pint bottle. Despite being filtered and pasteurized, the bottled version retains an appetizingly flowery aroma. The palate is crisply hoppy at first, developing a malty, lightly nutty smoothness. A slightly stronger and more floral – but blander – brew called Bass Ale is also produced for the US market. The Belgian version, yet marginally stronger, and fruitier, is made by Artois.

The brand
A symbol branded onto the cask probably gave rise to the Bass red triangle, which in the 1880s became the first registered trademark design in Britain (and perhaps the world).

Bateman's XXXB

🛡 **REGION OF ORIGIN** East Midlands of England, UK

🍾 **STYLE** Bitter Ale

％ **ALCOHOL CONTENT** 3.9 abw (4.8 abv)

🍺 **IDEAL SERVING TEMPERATURE** 50–55° F (10–13° C)

British beer lovers have cherished this old brewery ever since George Bateman and his wife Pat won a battle to ensure its independence. The brewery's products have won many awards. Its XXXB recalls the days before mass literacy, when the strength of a beer was indicated by numerals or symbols branded onto the wooden cask. This beer is not especially strong, but is very full in flavor. It starts malty (the barley variety is Maris Otter) and sweetish, developing some plummy fruitiness, then an aniseedy spiciness, and finally a clean dryness. The aniseed might suggest Fuggles hops, but the variety is actually Goldings.

Local landmark
The trademark is a stylized
depiction of the windmill under
which the brewery stands.

BAVIK KUURNSE WITTE

REGION OF ORIGIN West Flanders, Belgium

STYLE Belgian Strong Wheat Beer

ALCOHOL CONTENT 6.0 abw (7.5 abv)

IDEAL SERVING TEMPERATURE 48–50° F (9–10° C)

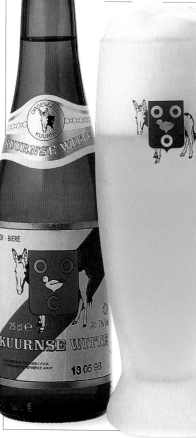

The farming family De Brabandere established its local brewery in Bavikhove, West Flanders, in 1894, and the fourth generation still runs the business. This enterprising company takes pride in tradition and produces a wide range of local and national products *(see also Petrus, pp.362–64)*. These include an unusually strong wheat beer, Kuurnse Witte. This is a local brew for the nearby town of Kuurne, whose self-mocking donkey symbol appears on the label. Such symbols are common in provincial Flanders, whose people sometimes characterize themselves as being stubborn but hard-working. Kuurnse Witte has a lemony, winey, peppery note. The last two characteristics are often present in stronger beers, and arise because the yeast has to work harder during fermentation.

BAVIK WIT BIER/WITTEKERKE

REGION OF ORIGIN	West Flanders, Belgium
STYLE	Belgian Wheat Beer
ALCOHOL CONTENT	4.0 abw (5.0 abv)
IDEAL SERVING TEMPERATURE	48–50° F (9–10° C)

The spiced wheat beers of Belgium traditionally contained a small proportion of oats, and one of the few breweries to persist with this tradition is De Brabandere, of Bavikhove. Oats provide a silky smoothness, and that is evident in this beer. The spicing is typical for the Belgian style of wheat beer: Curaçao orange peels and coriander, but with more emphasis in the latter. The beer is very aromatic, with a clean, teasing, perfumy fruitiness and a faintly herbal tartness. It is light-bodied but beautifully rounded. In Belgium, the term *wit* (white) beer is exploited in a promotional tie-in with a popular television soap opera set in a fictitious village called Wittekerke – the beer is increasingly marketed under this name.

BEAMISH IRISH STOUT

🛡	**REGION OF ORIGIN**	Republic of Ireland
🍶	**STYLE**	Dry Stout
%	**ALCOHOL CONTENT**	3.2 abw (4.0 abv)
🍺	**IDEAL SERVING TEMPERATURE**	50–55° F (10–13° C)

William Beamish was one of two Scottish-Irish Protestant landowners from the north who exported local butter and beef, and in 1792 became involved in brewing. They established a company to make porter, a toasty, near-black style of beer that was then very popular. In such breweries, porter was made in several strengths, which gradually became known as "plain," "stout," and "export." These gave rise to today's classic Irish dry stouts. The brewery is now in the Scottish Courage group. Its principal product is Beamish Stout. It is toasty, with buttery, creamy, and peppery notes in a late, lingering, dry finish.

BELHAVEN 80/- EXPORT ALE

REGION OF ORIGIN	Scottish Borders, UK
STYLE	Scottish Ale
ALCOHOL CONTENT	3.1 abw (3.9 abv)
IDEAL SERVING TEMPERATURE	50–55° F (10–13° C)

A Benedictine monastery on a nearby island is believed to have given rise to this brewery at the harbor hamlet of Belhaven, near Dunbar in Southern Scotland. In Scotland, ratings in shillings were used in the 1800s to indicate tax bands on beer. Today, the terminology survives as a general indication of alcoholic content, though not of specific potencies. The lowest strength beers are identified as 60/– and the highest 90/–. Belhaven 80/– has a full tawny color; a smooth, firm, toasty palate; and a good flavor development, with a faint, jammy, pineapple note from the house yeast.

Haven herald
Scotland's lion is specifically the rampant lion, often seen on a flag with a yellow background.

BELHAVEN WEE HEAVY

REGION OF ORIGIN	South of Scotland, UK
STYLE	Wee Heavy
ALCOHOL CONTENT	5.2 abw (6.5 abv)
IDEAL SERVING TEMPERATURE	55° F (13° C)

A Scottish "heavy" is typically full-bodied but not especially strong, usually at around 3.2 abw (4.0 abv). Stronger beers are sometimes dubbed Wee ("Small") Heavy. This style is similar to a barley wine, but often maltier and darker, and is best known as "Scotch Ale" in some other parts of the world. Belhaven Wee Heavy is oily, creamy, grainy, toasty, nutty (almondy), and fruity. It has all the richness and flavor of a classic Wee Heavy, though it is less strong than some. Despite this, it is headily alcoholic and a good winter brew. Belhaven occasionally produces a stronger (6.4 abw; 8.0 abv) draft-only version under the name 90/–. There is also a less potent (4.8 abw; 6.0 abv) bottled Wee Heavy under the Fowler's name, brewed for the Bass subsidiary Tennent's.

BELLE-VUE KRIEK

⌖ **REGION OF ORIGIN** Brabant, Belgium

🍾 **STYLE** *Kriek-Lambic*

％ **ALCOHOL CONTENT** 4.2 abw (5.2 abv)

🍶 **IDEAL SERVING TEMPERATURE** 47–48° F (8–9° C)

There may once have been a "beautiful view" *(belle-vue)* from the older of this company's two breweries but today, the site, at Molenbeek, is on the edge of Brussels. The nearby town of Lembeek is home to *lambic*, a style of beer containing unmalted wheat fermented with wild yeasts. These yeasts create a winey, sourish flavor that is often moderated by the addition of fruits such as the local dark cherry, known in Flemish as the *kriek*. Belle-Vue's Kriek beer is among the sweeter and more commercial, but still has considerable complexity of flavor. It has an oaky, ironish note, as well as some blackcurrant-like fruitiness.

Taking a tarter view
Belle-Vue is owned by the Belgian national group Interbrew (Artois). An unsweetened bottled beer is offered as Sélection Lambic.

BERLINER BÜRGERBRÄU
BERNAUER SCHWARZBIER

B

	REGION OF ORIGIN Northern Germany/Berlin
	STYLE Black Beer
	ALCOHOL CONTENT 4.1 abw (5.2 abv)
	IDEAL SERVING TEMPERATURE 48° F (9° C)

Historic Bernau, northeast of Berlin, was once famous for its breweries. None survive, but the town's name is saluted by the Berliner Bürgerbräu. This 1869 brewery is still in its original buildings in Köpenick, an old borough of the former East Berlin. During the communist period, it concentrated on a Pilsner-style lager. After reunification, the brewery was acquired by the beer-making Häring family. They have greatly restored the brewery, introducing a wide range of beers, including this *Schwarz* (black) beer. This style of lager, something of a speciality in the former East Germany, typically uses very dark malts to create a bitter-chocolate flavor. Among examples of the style, Bernauer Schwarzbier is the most truly black, with an earthy aroma, an oily, espresso, chocolate-and-rum flavor, and a long, smooth, clingy finish.

Beer with attack
Bernauer Schwarzbier is served at an annual pageant to mark an attack on the town during the wars with the Hussites of Bohemia.

BERLINER BÜRGERBRÄU MAIBOCK

REGION OF ORIGIN	Northern Germany/Berlin
STYLE	May Bock
ALCOHOL CONTENT	5.4 abw (6.8 abv)
IDEAL SERVING TEMPERATURE	48° F (9° C)

Since Germany was reunified, and this traditionalist Berlin brewery privatized, its range of beers has constantly developed. In addition to a dark (*dunkler*) Bock, it has a golden variant for the spring. This Maytime Bock has a creamy aroma; a relatively light body; a faintly buttery malt character; and a grassy, herbal, hop finish. Its crispness of finish is intended to add a refreshing edge to an otherwise hefty, sustaining beer. When winter ends, the beer gardens and lakeside terraces of Berlin soon fill up. Bürgerbräu is on Berlin's biggest lake, the Müggelsee, which is a favorite picnic spot. If the weather is a bit colder, drinkers might opt for a dark Bock. As it moderates, the Maibock comes into season.

BERLINER BÜRGERBRÄU ROTKEHLCHEN

🛡 **REGION OF ORIGIN**	Northern Germany/Berlin
🍾 **STYLE**	Export
⌖ **ALCOHOL CONTENT**	4.25 abw (5.3 abv)
🍺 **IDEAL SERVING TEMPERATURE**	48°F (9°C)

In Germany, each style of brew has its own shape of glass, and even some individual beers have their own drinking vessels (though this is more common in Belgium). In the early days of Berliner Bürgerbräu, the brewery used a red-handled mug for a lager that was broadly in the Export style (traditionally drier than the basic golden lager, but less hoppy than a Pilsner, a fractionally fuller gold than either, and slightly stronger). In asking for this beer in its distinct mug, customers would demand "a robin redbreast" (in German, a *Rotkehlchen*). After the reunification of Berlin and Germany, both the beer and its glass were reintroduced, to mark the 125th anniversary of the brewery. Bürgerbräu had some difficulty in finding a manufacturer that could produce the traditional glass, but eventually found one. The Rotkehlchen beer is smooth and firm in body, but mild in palate, with a restrained bitterness.

BERLINER KINDL WEISSE

🛡	**REGION OF ORIGIN** Northern Germany/Berlin
🍾	**STYLE** *Berliner Weisse*
%	**ALCOHOL CONTENT** 2.0 abw (2.5 abv)
🌡	**IDEAL SERVING TEMPERATURE** 48–54° F (9–12° C)

One of the two principal brewing companies in Berlin is Kindl, founded in 1872, and now part of a national group with Binding of Frankfurt. The brewery is in Neu Kölln where, through a monastic-looking arch, it has a handsome copper brewhouse set into marble tiles. Its classic brew is its Weisse, a wheat beer in the Berlin style. This type of beer is typically low in alcohol and high in refreshing acidity, the latter characteristic introduced in a lactic fermentation. The Weisse, which is most readily available in the summer, is firm, carbonic, and fruity, with a cutting hit of sourness. This type of beer is typically sweetened with a *schuss* (dash) of raspberry syrup or the green essence of the herb *Waldmeister* (woodruff).

The Champagne of the North
That was the verdict of Napoleon's troops on Berliner Weissebier. The oversized Champagne saucer is the typical glass for this style of beer.

BERT GRANT'S FRESH HOP ALE

⬚ **REGION OF ORIGIN** Pacific Northwest US

🍾 **STYLE** Pale Ale

% **ALCOHOL CONTENT** 4.2 abw (5.2 abv)

🍺 **IDEAL SERVING TEMPERATURE** 50–55° F (10–13° C)

Scottish-born Bert Grant is one of the personalities of the American brewing industry. He is one of the country's leading experts on hops, and was a pioneer of both microbreweries and brewpubs in the US. The brewery he founded is in the heart of American hop country, in the Washington State town of Yakima. This particular beer can be made only during the hop harvest. As the name suggests, the hops are used fresh (as fast as 20 minutes after being picked), rather than being dried for preservation. Only the Cascade variety is used. The aromas and flavors in the beer are reminiscent of grass, leaves, garden mint, and perhaps tangerine.

BERT GRANT'S IMPERIAL STOUT

🛡 **REGION OF ORIGIN** Pacific Northwest US

🍾 **STYLE** Imperial Stout

％ **ALCOHOL CONTENT** 4.8 abw (6.0 abv)

🌡 **IDEAL SERVING TEMPERATURE** 50–55° F (10–13° C)

The innovative Bert Grant was the first US brewer to make a strong stout in the style of St. Petersburg. This style, from the 1700s, was introduced in 1982, the year he founded his brewery. Although it is less potent than most Imperial Stouts, it was at the time one of the strongest, tastiest, and biggest-bodied beers in America. Today, some are richer, but Grant's is splendidly flavorsome: chocolatey, roasty, and firmly oily, with some honeyish perfuminess. A robust warmer from the Twin Peaks country across the Cascade Mountains.

B

BERT GRANT'S INDIA PALE ALE

🛡	**REGION OF ORIGIN**	Pacific Northwest US
🍾	**STYLE**	India Pale Ale
%	**ALCOHOL CONTENT**	3.4 abw (4.2 abv)
🍺	**IDEAL SERVING TEMPERATURE**	50–55° F (10–13° C)

The first new-generation brewery in the US to use the term India Pale Ale was Grant's, in Yakima, capital of the Washington State hop-growing region. Grant's thus began the revival of this classically hoppy style. Grant's IPA is unusually pale, with a firm, dry, slender body. It has a great deal of floral hop flavor; a fresh apple fruitiness; and a powerful, lingering, very dry, bitter finish. The hop varieties used are Galena and Cascade, and the beer is said to have 50 units of bitterness.

BERT GRANT'S
PERFECT PORTER

🛡	**REGION OF ORIGIN**	Pacific Northwest US
🍾	**STYLE**	Plain Porter
%	**ALCOHOL CONTENT**	3.2 abw (4.0 abv)
🍺	**IDEAL SERVING TEMPERATURE**	50–55° F (10–13° C)

A biography of brewer Grant was called *The Ale Master*. For a time his beers carried neck labels appearing to take credit for human happiness. His brand-name Perfect Porter is hardly modest, but the alcohol content is. Despite which this beer is astonishingly well-rounded in both body and flavor, with suggestions of cocoa powder, toasted nuts, and a touch of peat.

Looking glass
Bert Grant sees himself every time
he raises a glass of his own beers.
The brewery has a strong image.

BIG ROCK MCNALLY'S EXTRA ALE

🏷️ **REGION OF ORIGIN**	Province of Alberta, Canada
🍾 **STYLE**	Irish Red Ale
📊 **ALCOHOL CONTENT**	5.6 abw (7.0 abv)
🌡️ **IDEAL SERVING TEMPERATURE**	50–55° F (10–13° C)

Ed McNally's forbears left Ireland during the potato famine. He became a successful lawyer and barley farmer in Canada in the 1970s. In 1985 he launched the Big Rock brewery in the foothills of the Rockies, in Calgary. Big Rock has in the past 15 years made an extensive range of products, several quite robust, but McNally reserves his own name for this favorite. His Extra has the malty flavors typical of Irish ales, but is stronger than most. It has a bright amber-red color; a flowery aroma; and a fresh, rich maltiness reminiscent of toasted, buttered raisin bread.

Big Time Bhagwan's Best India Pale Ale

REGION OF ORIGIN Pacific Northwest US

STYLE India Pale Ale

ALCOHOL CONTENT 4.6 abw (5.8 abv)

IDEAL SERVING TEMPERATURE 50–55° F (10–13° C)

Several American breweries use jocular names for their IPAs. Big Time, in Seattle, pays wry tribute to Bhagwan Shree Rajneesh, who established a commune in nearby Oregon in the 1980s. After all, IPA does stand for India Pale Ale, and in this case the name is spelled out in full. This example speaks less of the British Empire than the Pacific Northwest. The beer has the grapefruit-zest American hop aroma typical in many northwestern beers; perfumy, sweet-orange flavors; a light, soft body; and a lemony, stony, appetizingly dry finish.

BIG TIME OLD WOOLY

B

🛡 **REGION OF ORIGIN** Pacific Northwest US

🍾 **STYLE** Barley Wine

％ **ALCOHOL CONTENT** 8.0 abw (10.0 abv)

🌡 **IDEAL SERVING TEMPERATURE** 55° F (13° C)

Mammoths might have been more common in icy Alaska than in rainy Washington State, but the hairy pachyderm makes an appropriate symbol for this big, strong winter warmer. The Big Time pub and brewery in Seattle is noted for beers with extravagant names and flavors to match. This one has beautifully combined aromas and flavors of fragrant hop, grapefruit rind, and layered maltiness. It is smooth, and hoppy enough to be dazingly soporific.

Prehistoric nip
Old Wooly is vintage-dated, and unusual in that it develops with age.

OLD WOOLY
1997
Barleywine Ale
Brewed & Bottled By
BIG TIME BREWING COMPANY
Seattle, Washington
Net Contents 6.3 Fl. Oz.

BITBURGER PREMIUM PILS

🛡 **REGION OF ORIGIN**	Rhineland-Palatinate, Germany
🍾 **STYLE**	Pilsner
% **ALCOHOL CONTENT**	3.7 abw (4.6 abv)
🌡 **IDEAL SERVING TEMPERATURE**	48° F (9° C)

This brewery, in the town of Bitburg, in the Rhineland Palatinate, claims it was the first in Germany to have used the term Pilsner, in 1883. At a time when most breweries were local, Bitburger could distribute by rail: a line had been built to carry cannon from steelworks at Saarbrücken to the Prussian army. Its Pils is very light, soft, and clean. The beer appears at first to be accented toward a clean, sweet maltiness, but finishes with a firm, elegantly rounded, hoppy dryness. Some of the malting barley is grown locally, and so is a proportion of the hops. In early days, the lagering cellars were cooled with ice from the Eifel lakes.

Establishing an identity
The Victorian-looking
"connoisseur" on the label is
an early example of branding.

BLACK SHEEP ALE

B

🛡 **REGION OF ORIGIN** Northern England, UK

🍾 **STYLE** Pale Ale

% **ALCOHOL CONTENT** 3.5 abw (4.4 abv)

🌡 **IDEAL SERVING TEMPERATURE** 55° F (13° C)

The name suggests that this ale might be as happy being served with lamb as with beef. The "black sheep" is Paul Theakston, who fell out with other family members over the sale of the famous brewery that bears their name. He set up on his own as the Black Sheep Brewery in the same tiny town, Masham, North Yorkshire. His ale has aniseedy, cedary, hop aromas and flavors, and a big, dry, smooth, firm maltiness, enhanced by the use of a multistrain yeast and square stone fermenters.

BLACK SHEEP RIGGWELTER

🛡 **REGION OF ORIGIN**	Northern England, UK
🍺 **STYLE**	Old Ale
% **ALCOHOL CONTENT**	4.6 abw (5.7 abv)
🌡 **IDEAL SERVING TEMPERATURE**	50–55° F (10–13° C)

The abbeys that probably brought brewing to the Yorkshire Dales earned their wealth from wool, so the sheep is a powerful symbol in this area. The Black Sheep brewery likes to emphasize this. In Dales dialect, a riggwelter is a sheep that has rolled on to its back and cannot get up again. The term derives from Old Norse, as does the name of the county seat, York (from the Viking settlement *Jorvik*). Drinkers should take care not to be overturned by Riggwelter, an ale of some potency. It has a medium-to-full body, a depth of malty, syrupy, toffeeish flavors, and a minty hop finish.

BLACK SHEEP
YORKSHIRE SQUARE ALE

B

🛡 **REGION OF ORIGIN** Northern England, UK	
🍾 **STYLE** Pale Ale	
% **ALCOHOL CONTENT** 4.0 abw (5.0 abv)	
🍺 **IDEAL SERVING TEMPERATURE** 55° F (13° C)	

Yorkshire Square is the name for a distinctive type of fermentation vessel. Many breweries now have cylindrical, closed fermenters, but some Yorkshire breweries have open squares. Some are made from steel, but the most traditional are made from stone, notably slate. The true Yorkshire Square has two decks, linked by a central porthole. As the brew ferments in the lower deck, it foams into the upper portion, creating a clean, full-bodied, malt-accented brew. Black Sheep Yorkshire Square Ale has a malty aroma, a firm, slightly syrupy body, and a late, herbal (bay leaves?) hoppiness. It is dry, appetizing, and full of flavor.

Square sheep
*The stylized label drawing brings a touch of
wit from an English county whose native
humor tends to be wry rather than rumbustious.*

BLACKSTONE ST CHARLES PORTER

🛡 **REGION OF ORIGIN**	South US
🍾 **STYLE**	Porter
⅛ **ALCOHOL CONTENT**	4.0 abw (5.0 abv)
🍺 **IDEAL SERVING TEMPERATURE**	50–55° F (10–13° C)

New-generation brewery and restaurant established in the mid-1990s in Nashville, Tennessee. The beers were created by star brewer Dave Miller. "Saint" Charles is the son of one of the owners. The porter that takes his name has a firm body and offers the sensation of biting into a praline filled with cream. The richness rounds into bitter chocolate. The beer is smooth, sociable, and dry enough in the finish to demand another round.

BOLTEN UR-ALT

REGION OF ORIGIN Korschenbroich, North Rhine-Westphalia, Germany

STYLE *Altbier*

ALCOHOL CONTENT 3.8 abw (4.7 abv)

IDEAL SERVING TEMPERATURE 48° F (9° C)

A truly "old" brewery, tracing its history to 1266, in Korschenbroich, west of Düsseldorf. Since the 1600s, the brewery, inn, and farm have been owned by the Bolten family. Early beers of the region used peat-smoked malt, were spiced, and were fermented with wild yeast. The term *Altbier* was introduced in the 1890s. The beers had a low carbonation until the postwar period. Bolten Alt has deep, complex, dry, malty flavors. The version called Ur-Alt is unfiltered, more textured, and juicier-tasting.

BOON FRAMBOISE

🛡 **REGION OF ORIGIN** Province of Flemish Brabant, Belgium

🍾 **STYLE** *Framboise/Frambozen-Lambic*

％ **ALCOHOL CONTENT** 5.0 abw (6.2 abv)

🍶 **IDEAL SERVING TEMPERATURE** Store at 50–55° F (10–13° C).
Lightly refrigerate for two or three hours before serving. Serve at 47° F (8° C)

The French *framboise* (raspberry) is preferred on this label to the Flemish *frambozen*. The brewer, though, is Flemish, and he makes his *lambic* beers in Lembeek itself. A brewery dating from the 1600s was due to close in 1977 when young revivalist Frank Boon acquired the business. He now produces a range of lambic beers at a brewery on the banks of the Zenne, the river whose valley helps define the region. The wild yeasts of the valley impart a perfumy, flowery, Chardonnay-like dryness, and oak-aging offers a touch of vanilla, to balance the raspberry-jam sweetness of this fresh, delicate brew. Although the beer is lightly sweetened, a lemony acidity emerges to dry the finish. For every liter (1.76 pints) of beer, 7 oz (200 g) of raspberries are used, and a small proportion of cherries.

Party dress
Champagne bottles, dressed with foil,
offer an elegant presentation for many
Belgian beers, especially lambics.

BOON GEUZE

REGION OF ORIGIN Province of Flemish Brabant, Belgium

STYLE *Gueuze-lambic*

ALCOHOL CONTENT 4.8 abw (6.0 abv)

IDEAL SERVING TEMPERATURE 55° F (13° C)

The shorter spelling of *G(u)euze* is preferred by Frank Boon. Being a gueuze, this beer is a blend of young and old *lambics* that ferments in the bottle, causing carbonation and sparkle. It has great finesse: a soft floweriness of aroma (rhubarb?); a momentary gingery sweetness; and a long, dry, oaky, faintly salty finish. A wonderful beer to serve with blood sausage (black pudding) and applesauce.

BOON KRIEK "MARIAGE PARFAIT"

🛡 **REGION OF ORIGIN** Province of Flemish Brabant, Belgium

🍾 **STYLE** *Kriek-Lambic*

% **ALCOHOL CONTENT** 4.8 abw (6.0 abv)

🍺 **IDEAL SERVING TEMPERATURE** 50–55°F (10–13°C)

A classic example of a cherry beer with real fruity tartness and winey, "dry sherry," toasty complexity, though the precise character will vary from one year to the next. The beer is conditioned on freshly harvested cherries, in wood, in an elaborate regime. Every winter, when the cold weather prevents runaway fermentations, the brewery's blending vessel is used to make one batch of Mariage Parfait. This "Perfect Marriage" is blended from that year's young *lambic* and (in greater proportion) Boon's finest matured brews (18 months to two years). They are then matured in the bottle for up to two years.

B

BORVE ALE

REGION OF ORIGIN Highlands, Northern Scotland, UK

STYLE Strong Scottish Ale

ALCOHOL CONTENT 8.0 abw (10.0 abv)

IDEAL SERVING TEMPERATURE 50–55° F (10–13° C)

A hugely distinctive, characterful, complex beer from a tiny brewery in a former school at the hamlet of Ruthven, near Huntley, in the Grampian mountains. The brewery was founded in the mid-1980s, originally at Borve House on the Hebridean island of Lewis, where Gaelic is still widely spoken. Borve Ale is matured in casks that have previously been used to age first Bourbon and then Scotch whiskey. It emerges with an oaky, "hopsack" aroma; a relatively light but clingy body; orangey flavors; and a big finish that is charcoal-like, peppery, and even salty.

Gaelic ale
The Scottish Gaelic text on the label says "Brought to life on the Isle of Lewis."

BOSCOS FLAMING STONE

🛡	**REGION OF ORIGIN** South US
🍾	**STYLE** Stone Beer
🍾	**ALCOHOL CONTENT** 3.8 abw (4.8 abv)
🍺	**IDEAL SERVING TEMPERATURE** 50° F (10° C)

An American pioneer of Stone Beer. The Boscos brewery and restaurant was opened in 1992, in Germantown, a suburb of Memphis, Tennessee, and has since sprouted a branch in Nashville. The name comes from the Italian for wood. Colorado granite is heated in a wood-burning pizza oven in the making of Boscos Flaming Stone, which is based on a wheat ale. It has a pale color; a toffeeish, nutty palate; and a very late development of a refreshing, slightly sour, smoky dryness. The brewery's several other products include a very flavorsome Scotch Ale, called Isle of Skye, which has won awards in bottle-conditioned form.

BOSTON BEER WORKS
BEANTOWN NUT BROWN ALE

REGION OF ORIGIN	Northeast US
STYLE	Brown Ale
ALCOHOL CONTENT	4.4 abw (5.5 abv)
IDEAL SERVING TEMPERATURE	50° F (10° C)

The "navy" or baked bean, prepared with salt pork or ham and molasses (and on occasion beer), is a traditional dish of maritime Boston, Massachusetts – hence "Beantown." The Boston Beer Works' Nut Brown, being on the sweeter side, might go well with this classically simple dish. The beer starts sweetish, with a cherryish fruitiness, but dries out, with suggestions of cinnamon and cedar. It has a light-to-medium body, smooth texture, and very satisfying flavors. The Boston Beer Works is a brewpub near Fenway Park, home of the Red Sox baseball team.

BOSTON BEER WORKS
BUCKEYE OATMEAL STOUT

🛡 **REGION OF ORIGIN** Northeast US	
🍶 **STYLE** Oatmeal Stout	
% **ALCOHOL CONTENT** 4.4 abw (5.5 abv)	
🍺 **IDEAL SERVING TEMPERATURE** 55° F (13° C)	

The Boston Beer Works is one of an excellent selection of brewpubs that have become tourist attractions in Boston. Among the brewery's very assertive beers is this full-bodied, rich, oily, oatmeal-tasting, marshmallow-like, sweetish stout. In its rotating range of 30 or 40 products, the Beer Works has brewed a wide selection of porter and stout variations. These have included a creamy, peppery Imperial Stout; and a Cherry Stout with semisweet and milk chocolate for Valentine's Day.

BRAINS IPA

REGION OF ORIGIN South Wales, UK

STYLE India Pale Ale

ALCOHOL CONTENT 3.6 abw (4.5 abv)

IDEAL SERVING TEMPERATURE 50–55° F (10–13° C)

The slogan says "It's Brains You Want." The brewery, founded in 1713, was acquired by Samuel and Joseph Brain in 1882, and is still owned by the family. The Cardiff brewery was once in the very center of the city, but production has now moved to a former Bass plant in a more industrial location. Brains' principal beers are known for their maltiness, but its IPA has a hoppy fragrance. It then presents a lightly malty, sweetish background flavor, before returning to the hop in an appetizing finish, with suggestions of orange zest and lemon rind.

Dragon's brew
Many beers in this style have symbols of India on the label, but Brains prefers the red dragon emblem of Wales.

BRAINS SA

🛡 **REGION OF ORIGIN**	South Wales, UK
🍾 **STYLE**	Bitter/Pale Ale
% **ALCOHOL CONTENT**	3.4 abw (4.2 abv)
🍺 **IDEAL SERVING TEMPERATURE**	50–55° F (10–13° C)

Some argue that the name SA derives from the initials of founder Samuel Arthur Brain; in fact, it originally stood for Special Ale. This beer is always known simply by its initials in its home city, where it is regarded with great affection and loyalty. It is subtitled Best Bitter, and is enjoyed as an easy-drinking beer that nonetheless has plenty of satisfying flavors. Like many Welsh beers, it is accented toward maltiness. SA has a spicy aroma; a light, faintly almondy, crystal-malt character, soft on the tongue; and finishes with a late, dry, appetite-tickling fruitiness and hoppiness.

Rugby restorative
Wales' national sport
is intended to be
evoked by the jersey-
like quartered design.

BRAKSPEAR SPECIAL

REGION OF ORIGIN Southern England, UK

STYLE Bitter Ale

ALCOHOL CONTENT 3.4 abw (4.3 abv)

IDEAL SERVING TEMPERATURE 50–55° F (10–13° C)

The name rhymes with Shakespeare, and Brakspear's beers are favored by contemporary British writers John Mortimer (whose *Paradise Postponed* was set in a brewery) and Colin Dexter (creator of the popular fictional detective Inspector Morse). The brewery, tracing its history to 1779, is on the Thames River, in the regatta town of Henley, Oxfordshire. Brakspear Special is beautifully balanced; light, smooth, and drinkable; with a late, lingering bitterness. The "double" fermentation mentioned on the label refers to a traditional system of two vessels. The first encourages the development of complex flavors. The dropping of the brew into the second vessel refines those flavors.

Holy bee
The bee on the label is also a
Papal symbol. A Brakspear
was the only English Pope.

BRAND DUBBELBOCK

B

	REGION OF ORIGIN	Province of Limburg, The Netherlands
	STYLE	Double Bock (*Dubbelbock*)
	ALCOHOL CONTENT	6.0 abw (7.5 abv)
	IDEAL SERVING TEMPERATURE	48° F (9° C)

The oldest brewery in the Netherlands is Brand's, dating from 1341. The Brand family became involved in 1871, and still are – though for 10 years the company has been owned by Heineken. The Brand's brewery has in its range a well-regarded Pilsner-type and three Bock beers. Its *Dubbelbock* (Dutch spelling) has the creaminess and fruity "warming" maltiness of a Lowland Scotch whiskey.

Triple Dutch
In addition to its Double,
Brand's has different
Maytime and year-round
versions of Bock.

BRAND IMPERATOR

🛡 **REGION OF ORIGIN**	Province of Limburg, The Netherlands
🍾 **STYLE**	Bock
％ **ALCOHOL CONTENT**	5.2 abw (6.5 abv)
🥛 **IDEAL SERVING TEMPERATURE**	48° F (9° C)

The name suggests a pre-Lenten Double Bock like the famous German Salvator *(see p.355)*. On the other hand, Salvator's color would better suit a strong brew for May. In recent years, the brewery has added more specialized products for both of those seasons. Imperator is a much longer-established product, available year-round. It is a delicious lager, with the aroma of cream; a big, firm body; fresh, marshmallowy flavors; and hints of maple syrup in a deep, dryish finish.

BRAND OUD BRUIN

| | **REGION OF ORIGIN** Province of Limburg, The Netherlands |
| **STYLE** Old Brown Lager |
| **ALCOHOL CONTENT** 2.8 abw (3.5 abv)) |
| **IDEAL SERVING TEMPERATURE** 46–48° F (8–9° C) |

A smooth and malty interpretation of the Dutch style of sweet, "Old Brown" lager. This example finishes like saccharine-sweetened coffee. (Bring on the cookies?) An antique-style beer seems very appropriate at the Netherlands' oldest brewery. A spiced beer, fermented with wild yeast, was made in the days when the brewery was a brewpub on the Lord of the Manor's estate. When the local clergyman complained that peasants preferred the pub to the pulpit, the brewery was sold to the Brand family.

The Lord's beer
When the Lord of the Manor owned the brewery at Wijlre, near Maastricht, he proclaimed a local monopoly on beer. This is remembered in the text on the neck label.

BRECKENRIDGE AUTUMN ALE

REGION OF ORIGIN Southwest US

STYLE Brown Ale/Old Ale

ALCOHOL CONTENT 5.4 abw (6.8 abv)

IDEAL SERVING TEMPERATURE 50–55° F (10–13° C)

The Rocky Mountain ski resort and former gold-mining town of Breckenridge, Colorado, gained its first brewpub in 1990, probably America's highest, at 9,600 ft (2,926 m). Breckenridge produces a wide range of beers. Its bottled Autumn Ale has a chestnut color; a firm, toffeeish, textured body; and hints of sweet syrup and cocoa. A delicious beer. In 1992, a larger "branch" Breckenridge was added in the Lower Downtown ("LoDo") district of Denver. The handsome, arched, brick facade of the 1928 industrial building reveals a large single-room brewery and pub. Immediately confronted by a sizable (20-barrel) brewhouse in the middle of the public area that is protected by nothing more than a small railing, visitors can feel for a moment that they have entered through the wrong door. The idea is that the guest "shares the experience."

BRICK BOCK

REGION OF ORIGIN	Province of Ontario, Canada
STYLE	Bock
ALCOHOL CONTENT	5.6 abw (7.0 abv)
IDEAL SERVING TEMPERATURE	48° F (9° C)

Jim Brickman founded this sizeable new-generation brewery in the old beer and whiskey town of Waterloo, Ontario, in 1984. Although its Bock recipe has been varied from one year to the next, its typical characteristics include a very malty aroma; a light but firm palate; and a depth of dark-malt flavors, developing licorice, rooty, peaty, burned, whiskeyish notes. The beer is said to be matured for three months.

Seal of strength
Some Brick Bock
bottlings have an
attractive wax seal.

BRIDGEPORT ESB

	REGION OF ORIGIN Pacific Northwest US
	STYLE American Ale/ESB
	ALCOHOL CONTENT 4.6 abw (5.8 abv)
	IDEAL SERVING TEMPERATURE 50–55° F (10–13° C)

The bridges of Portland, Oregon, unite a city framed by the Columbia and Willamette rivers, both flowing from hop regions. BridgePort, founded in 1984 as Columbia River Brewing, is the oldest micropub in this great city of small beers. Its ESB is perfumy and fruity, rounded off by an appetizingly dry, hoppy acidity.

Bridging the Atlantic
Extra Special Bitter has become
a recognized style in the US,
inspired by Fuller's ESB from
London (see p.177).

BridgePort India Pale Ale

🛡 **Region of origin**	Pacific Northwest US
🍶 **Style**	India Pale Ale
◉ **Alcohol content**	4.4 abw (5.5 abv)
▮ **Ideal serving temperature**	50–55° F (10–13° C)

One of the many fruity, dry, bitter India Pale Ales made in the Pacific Northwest. This bottle-conditioned brew from Portland, Oregon has a lemony, grapefruity, resiny aroma; an oily palate, with suggestions of vanilla pod and orange peach sorbet; and a rush of intense minty, woody, cedary bitterness in the finish. No fewer than five hop varieties are used: Cascade, Chinook, Golding, Crystal, and Northwest Ultra.

Initialled ales
In the US, ESB indicates a
well-rounded medium strong
ale, while IPA implies a much
hoppier brother brew.

B

BRIDGEPORT OLD KNUCKLEHEAD

🛡 **REGION OF ORIGIN** Pacific Northwest US

🍺 **STYLE** Barley Wine

％ **ALCOHOL CONTENT** 7.3 abw (9.1 abv)

🍺 **IDEAL SERVING TEMPERATURE** 55° F (13° C)

A celebrated barley wine from the pioneering brewery and pub in Portland, Oregon. An assertive, delicious, juicy maltiness is cut by grassy, peppery hop flavors, and rounded in a warming finish. A bottling is released in November, and each year's label features a different local celebrity. One year, the mayor of Portland was asked if he would like to be the next Knucklehead; "It's a lot better than being Bud," he replied.

Brooklyn Black Chocolate Stout

REGION OF ORIGIN Northeast US

STYLE Chocolate/Imperial Stout

ALCOHOL CONTENT 6.6 abw (8.25 abv)

IDEAL SERVING TEMPERATURE 55° F (13° C)

Brooklyn was once New York's brewing borough, but its last kettle seemed to have been silenced in the 1970s. Then, in 1988, the Brooklyn Brewery company was established. Its robust beers were initially produced under contract upstate, but in 1996 a new brewhouse was unveiled in Brooklyn. The company had begun with an assertive lager and a brown ale, but brewer Garrett Oliver has since created superbly flavorsome brews in a wide range of styles. His own favorite is this strong stout, which achieves an astonishingly chocolatey taste from malt alone. It is a rich beer that is textured, spicy, and fruity. Brooklyn Black Chocolate Stout is a winter seasonal brew, and vintages have varied in strength between the initial 6.6 abw (8.25 abv) and 6.9 abw (8.75 abv).

B

BROUGHTON
BLACK DOUGLAS

REGION OF ORIGIN Scottish Borders, UK

STYLE Scottish Ale

ALCOHOL CONTENT 4.1 abw (5.2 abv)

IDEAL SERVING TEMPERATURE 50–55° F (10–13° C)

This brewery is at Broughton, near Biggar, just north of the English-Scottish border. Established in 1979, it was one of the first new-generation breweries in Scotland. Its bottled beers have become much more widely available

since a change of ownership in 1995. Black Douglas is one of its newer products, available year-round in the bottle, but regarded as a winter brew in its cask-conditioned draft form. It is not quite black, but has a north-of-the-border color and maltiness. Its aroma suggests malted milk, the palate is lightly syrupy, and the finish has the bitterness of dark chocolate. The beer is named after Sir James Douglas, a swarthy man with raven-black hair, who carried the heart of Scottish King Robert the Bruce into battle.

BROUGHTON GREENMANTLE

🛡 **REGION OF ORIGIN** Scottish Borders, UK

🍺 **STYLE** Scottish Ale

⊘ **ALCOHOL CONTENT** 3.1 abw (3.9 abv)

🍺 **IDEAL SERVING TEMPERATURE** 50–55° F (10–13° C)

A literary beer. Broughton was the home of novelist John Buchan, and the brewery's first beer was named in honor of his story *Greenmantle*. The brewery's original partners were members of the Collins publishing family and the Youngers' brewing dynasty. Perhaps reflecting the brewery's location in the Borders, Greenmantle Ale seems to fall stylistically between an English bitter and a Scottish 70/–. It has a hint of Scottish honeyed maltiness in its background but has a more English accent in its medium-amber color, gently oily, flowery hoppiness (one taster suggested nettles), and slightly citric fruity tartness.

BROUGHTON SCOTTISH OATMEAL STOUT

🛡	**REGION OF ORIGIN**	Scottish Borders, UK
🍾	**STYLE**	Oatmeal Stout
%	**ALCOHOL CONTENT**	3.4 abw (4.2 abv)
🍺	**IDEAL SERVING TEMPERATURE**	55° F (13° C)

This style of beer is not specifically Scottish, but the grain is typically associated with the country, so it makes for a happy marriage. David Younger, who helped establish the brewery in 1979, was in his days there known as a lover of stout. In recollection of this, the brewery's stout is labeled with an illustration of his great-grandfather, Robert Younger, also a brewer. In 1844, Robert Younger founded a brewery that bore his name. Yet another Younger, Robert's great-grandfather George, gave his name to a brewery that he founded, in 1770. The stout that honors them is silky and creamy but relatively lean and dry for the style. It also has some flavorsome hints of ginger and pepper. This beer is sold in some markets as Kinmount Willie, after a border reiver (raider) from the Armstrong clan. Kinmount Willie is alleged to have been a forbear of US astronaut Neil Armstrong, a claim that the brewery emphasizes in the American market.

BUDELS ALT

🛡 **REGION OF ORIGIN** Province of North Brabant, the Netherlands

🍺 **STYLE** *Altbier*

% **ALCOHOL CONTENT** 4.8 abw (6.0 abv)

🍺 **IDEAL SERVING TEMPERATURE** 48° F (9° C)

Few European breweries are as eclectic in their beer styles as Budels, of North Brabant in the Netherlands. Its range includes not only a *Kölsch* type but also this *Altbier*, albeit at an alcohol content that is higher than typical. This interpretation has a pale color for the style; fresh spicy hop and fudgy malt in the aroma; lively flavor development, with hints of ginger; and a firm, very dry finish.

Toasting Alt
On this label, the crowned head of Brabant, Jan Primus, is shown as the mythical King of Beer, Gambrinus, alleged inventor of the toast.

BUDELS PAREL KÖLSCH

🛡 **REGION OF ORIGIN**	Province of North Brabant, the Netherlands
🍾 **STYLE**	*Kölsch*-type
% **ALCOHOL CONTENT**	4.8 abw (6.0 abv)
🥛 **IDEAL SERVING TEMPERATURE**	47–48° F (8–9° C)

Not made in the traditional *Altbier* region, or even in Germany, and a little stronger than the original, but broadly in the style of a *Kölsch*. This beer is made across the Dutch frontier, beyond even the border province of Limburg, in the Brabant town of Budel. The enterprising Budels brewery launched it in 1985 as a novel speciality. *Parel* is Dutch for "pearl." The beer has a very good, resiny, hop aroma; a firm, smooth body; a dry palate; a faint hint of raspberry and vanilla fruitiness; and a dry, appetizing finish.

BUDWEISER BUDVAR

🛡 **REGION OF ORIGIN** Bohemia, Czech Republic

🍾 **STYLE** Golden Lager

％ **ALCOHOL CONTENT** 4.0 abw (5.0 abv)

🍺 **IDEAL SERVING TEMPERATURE** 48° F (9° C)

In the Czech Republic, only beers from Pilsen may use the name of that city. While they emphasize the hop, their similar, more southerly rivals from the brewing city of Budweis (also known as České Budějovice) lean towards a light, smooth maltiness. The city, on the Moldau River, began with a monastery and in the 1200s grew as a southern stronghold of the kingdom of Bohemia. Before trademarks, any brew made there would have been described as a "Budweiser" beer. Budweiser Burgerbrau, established in 1795, made the city's first lager in 1853. That brewery still operates. Budweiser Budvar came later, in 1895. By then, the German-American brewer Adolphus Busch was already making a "Budweiser" beer. Several other US brewers have in the past used the term Budweiser to describe their beers, but Busch's exclusive US rights to the name were eventually established beyond doubt. The Czech Budweiser beers are generally more assertive in flavor than their American namesake, but not substantially higher in alcohol.

B

BURRAGORANG BOCK BEER

REGION OF ORIGIN New South Wales, Australia

STYLE Bock

ALCOHOL CONTENT 5.1 abw (6.4 abv)

IDEAL SERVING TEMPERATURE 48° F (9° C)

As the aboriginal-sounding name suggests, this is an Australian beer. It is produced near Burragorang Lake, in Picton, 50 miles (80 km) southwest of Sydney, and is the country's biggest-tasting beer. In 1978, the first application to licence a microbrewery in Australia was made by Geoff Scharer, a fourth-generation Australian from a family who originated from Zurich, Switzerland. In 1987, Scharer finally made beer, advised by the late Otto Binding, Germany's microbrewery pioneer. Made with three malts and German Spalt hops, Burragorang Bock Beer pours with a huge head; has a silky body; a perfumy, appetizing, malt character; suggestions of toffee; and a resiny, hop balance. The brewery also has a very hoppy, Pilsner-style brew.

BURRAGORANG BOCK BEER

Painting by Robin Collier

It's the water
The depiction of the Burragorang Valley on the Burragorang Bock Beer label shows a tract of land owned by the brewery's proprietor. The valley is the main source of Sydney's water. The painting was commissioned by the Water Board from artist Robin Collier.

BURTON BRIDGE BRAMBLE STOUT

🛡	**REGION OF ORIGIN**	Trent Valley, England, UK
🍾	**STYLE**	Dry Stout with Fruit
%	**ALCOHOL CONTENT**	4.0 abw (5.0 abv)
🍺	**IDEAL SERVING TEMPERATURE**	50–55° F (10–13° C)

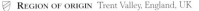

Britain's brewing capital, Burton, has – on Bridge Street – one of the country's livelier new-generation microbreweries, with its own pub. The Burton Bridge Brewery was established in 1982. Its huge range of specialities includes this bottle-conditioned stout primed with the concentrated juice of blackberries ("brambles"). The fruit adds a touch of acidity and earthiness to a stout that is tarlike, burned-tasting, and very big for its alcohol content.

Blackbird brew
When one of the brewery's principals noticed blackbirds eating apples in his garden, he thought they also might enjoy blackberries – hence the image on the label.

B

BURTON BRIDGE
EMPIRE PALE ALE

🛡 **REGION OF ORIGIN** Trent Valley, England, UK
🍾 **STYLE** India Pale Ale
% **ALCOHOL CONTENT** 6.0 abw (7.5 abv)
🥤 **IDEAL SERVING TEMPERATURE** 50–55° F (10–13° C)

Although pale ale is said to have first been produced in London, the style was perfected and made famous by the great breweries of Burton, and helped this town become Britain's beer capital. Though it is small, its central location in the Midlands of England helped. Before rail and road, the beer was shipped by canal to the ports of the Mersey and Humber. The new-generation brewery Burton Bridge has sought to revive the tradition of strong, hoppy IPA in Britain. There is a distinct "hopsack" aroma and taste to this lively, leafy, peppery, orangey, bitter brew.

Batting for beer?
Britain's greatest gifts to India? Today, beer is a less obvious passion there than cricket, a common language, and Parliamentary democracy.

BURTON BRIDGE PORTER

REGION OF ORIGIN	Trent Valley, England, UK
STYLE	Porter
ALCOHOL CONTENT	3.6 abw (4.5 abv)
IDEAL SERVING TEMPERATURE	55° F (13° C)

Today, in the English-speaking world, a porter is usually a lighter-bodied counterpart to dry stout. In Britain, the term porter began to vanish around the time of World War I, and had largely gone by the 1930s, though it lingered far longer in Ireland and never totally disappeared from the United States. Microbreweries reintroduced it to Britain in the late 1970s. Burton Bridge's range includes a fine porter at an easily-drinkable strength. It has a ruby to black color, and a pillowy head. There are hints of crystal sugar in the aroma; smoky, fruity notes; and a sappy dryness in the finish.

BUSH 12%

🛡 **REGION OF ORIGIN** Province of Hainaut, Belgium

🍶 **STYLE** Barley Wine

%️ **ALCOHOL CONTENT** 9.6 abw (12.0 abv)

🍺 **IDEAL SERVING TEMPERATURE** 50° F (10° C)

The strongest beer in Belgium – subject to occasional challenges – is also a classic for its complexity of flavors. "Bush" is an Anglicization of Dubuisson, family name of the brewery's owners. The brewery was liberated by the British at the end of World War I, and the English name later adopted as a tribute. The beer, reminiscent of an English barley wine, has a peachy, creamy aroma; a nutty, chewy palate; and a long, earthy, orange-peel dryness in the finish.

Beating around the Busch
The name has nothing to do with the American Busch. Bush 12% is sold in the US under the name Scaldis.

BUSH DE NOËL

⬦ **REGION OF ORIGIN** Province of Hainaut, Belgium

🍾 **STYLE** Barley Wine

％ **ALCOHOL CONTENT** 9.6 abw (12.0 abv)

🍺 **IDEAL SERVING TEMPERATURE** 50° F (10° C)

The Christmas version of Bush is a variation on the theme, with a fuller nutty maltiness, slightly less bitterness, and a more flowery hop aroma. It is also sometimes offered bottle-conditioned, developing a leaner, oilier body and a yet more flowery flavor and aroma. Yet a further version is Bush Sept. In French, this sounds like *bouchette*, implying a mini mouthful. Only in Belgium could a beer of such a potency (actually, 6.0 abw; 7.5 abv) be deemed small. The drop – in gravity as well as alcohol – diminishes the maltiness, and allows the yeasty floweriness (violets?) to come through, and the minty, peppery hop. There is also added coriander.

CAINS FORMIDABLE ALE

🛡 **REGION OF ORIGIN** Northwest England, UK

🍾 **STYLE** Bitter Ale

%) **ALCOHOL CONTENT** 4.0 abw (5.0 abv)

🍺 **IDEAL SERVING TEMPERATURE** 50–55° F (10–13° C)

The formidable Robert Cain, from Cork, Ireland, founded this Victorian brewery across the water in Liverpool. It is itself a formidable structure. Cain also built some of the city's famously elaborate pubs, several of which are still in operation. After several changes of ownership, the brewery restored the name Cains around 1990.

Formidable Ale, pale in color, seems crisp at first, but builds to a surge of gingery bitterness. The brewery also has the softer, maltier, Traditional Bitter and the darker, richer Dragon Heart. Special brews have included a tawny Chocolate Ale. This smooth, nutty brew was lightly flavored with dark chocolate, and had a violet-like floweriness. Cupid's Ale, soft but dryish, and very lightly flavored with ginseng, has been known to appear around Valentine's Day.

CALEDONIAN DEUCHARS IPA

	REGION OF ORIGIN South of Scotland, UK
	STYLE India Pale Ale
	ALCOHOL CONTENT 3.5 abw (4.4 abv)
	IDEAL SERVING TEMPERATURE 50° F (10° C)

The small Caledonian brewery in Edinburgh produces Scotland's maltiest beers, but this IPA leans in the opposite, hoppy direction appropriate to the style. Robert Deuchar's was an Edinburgh brewery that closed in the 1960s. The name was revived by Caledonian for this one beer in the 1990s. The restoration of an affectionately remembered name was popular, but would the beer itself be accepted? Although IPA is an old style, this interpretation is modern and perhaps American-influenced in its pale color, orange-flower, roselike, intense aroma, firm crispness, and oily hop bitterness. It has proven a great success not only in pubs but also in fashionable bars in the re-emergent Scotland.

CALEDONIAN FLYING SCOTSMAN

REGION OF ORIGIN	South of Scotland, UK
STYLE	Scottish Ale
ALCOHOL CONTENT	3.9 abw (5.1 abv)
IDEAL SERVING TEMPERATURE	50–55° F (10–13° C)

The brewery overlooks the Edinburgh-London Railway. The Flying Scotsman beer is named after a famous train on that route. The ruby-colored brew contains a tiny amount of rye. It is profoundly malty in its aroma and flavors, but very well-rounded, with hints of raisiny spiciness and toasty dryness. There is a yet greater maltiness, but not as much grainy dryness, in the marginally less strong Merman *(see right)* and the more potent Edinburgh Strong Ale.

Kiln trademark
The trademark on the glass depicts the kiln in which grain is dried at the end of malting. Some whiskey distilleries use a similar symbol.

CALEDONIAN MERMAN

REGION OF ORIGIN	South of Scotland, UK
STYLE	Scottish Ale
ALCOHOL CONTENT	3.8 abw (4.8 abv)
IDEAL SERVING TEMPERATURE	50–55° F (10–13° C)

Devotees joke, "Leaves you legless." Merman is not especially strong, but it has the richest, and most typically Scottish, dark malt character of the brews in the Caledonian range. It has a soft-fruit aroma (ripe plums?), layers of clean maltiness in the body, and a long finish, with hints of anis in its balancing hop character. The brewery dates from 1869, and this beer is based on an Export Ale brewed in the 1890s. Caledonian still boils its kettles by direct flame (as opposed to the more usual steam). This "fire-brewing" creates hot spots, and a caramelization that can heighten the malty flavors. Since a management buyout in 1987, Caledonian has been run by a malt expert who formerly worked in the whiskey industry.

Haven of ale
The label is a copy of an 1896 symbol used by the brewery. A rock formation called The Merman helped guide vessels into Leith, Edinburgh's port.

C

CANTILLON GUEUZE-LAMBIC

REGION OF ORIGIN Brabant, Belgium

STYLE *Gueuze-Lambic*

ALCOHOL CONTENT 4.0 abw (5.0 abv)

IDEAL SERVING TEMPERATURE 55° F (13° C)

Not far from the Eurostar train station in Brussels is the Cantillon brewery, something of a working museum. Cantillon welcomes visitors, and sells gift packs of its superb beers. This enterprise is the most assertively traditional producer of *lambic*, the wild-yeast wheat beer of the region. The family is believed to have brewed as early as the 1700s, in the nearby town of Lembeek (from which lambic probably takes its name) before opening the Brussels brewery in the 1930s. Its beers are dry, juicy, lemony, and tart, though not as aggressive as they once were. There are a wide range of versions, each varying according to the years of beer in the blend. The classic *gueuze* (a blend of young and old lambic) is complex, zesty, and Champagnelike.

If a reminder were needed…
Being a long drink, beer can be a pleasure increasingly interrupted. Perhaps appropriately, the Mannekin Pis statue is the emblem of Brussels, a great brewing city.

CANTILLON GUEUZE VIGNERONNE

🛡 **REGION OF ORIGIN** Brabant, Belgium

🍾 **STYLE** Fruit *Lambic*

% **ALCOHOL CONTENT** 4.0 abw (5.0 abv)

🍺 **IDEAL SERVING TEMPERATURE** 47–48° F (8–9° C)

This *gueuze* has an addition of grapes during maturation. It is notably light on the tongue, and very dry, but with a suggestion of grape skins in the aroma; hints of crisp, clovey spiciness, ginger, and honey in the palate (melding with the lemony flavors that are typical of Cantillon); and a touch of dusty tannin in the finish. The early versions of this brew were primed with Muscat grapes grown in Alsace, but a similar variety from Italy has been employed more recently, and seems to have produced fuller flavors. The grapes are added to casks of maturing beer that is already more than 18 months old. The beer remains in the cask for a further six months, and is then blended with a smaller proportion of one-year-old *lambic* before being bottled. The young lambic provides the sugars for further fermentation in the bottle. A version called St. Lamvinus is made with Merlot and Cabernet Franc grapes.

Star beer
The grapes, grain, and hops wrap themselves round the six-pointed star, one of the international symbols of brewing.

C

CANTILLON KRIEK LAMBIC

🛡 **REGION OF ORIGIN** Brabant, Belgium

🍶 **STYLE** Fruit *Lambic*

% **ALCOHOL CONTENT** 4.0 abw (5.0 abv)

🍺 **IDEAL SERVING TEMPERATURE** 47–48° F (8–9° C)

The driest cherry beer in the world is the Cantillon brewery's *Kriek-Lambic*. Newly harvested cherries are added in July or August to beer that is already 18 months to two years old, and the blend is bottled the following winter. About a quarter of the cherries used are the Schaarbeek variety grown in and around that Brussels neighborhood. The rest are from the well-known growing area of St. Truiden in Limburg, to the east of Brussels. The beer is long and complex, with a remarkable unfolding of flavors. It has a huge, perfumy aroma, with some oily, almondy notes from the stones of the fruit. The palate is tart but well-balanced, intense, and winey, with a fresh, Cabernet-like fruitiness that also hints at raspberry. The finish has a tannic, cherry-skin dryness and some fino sherry, vinegarish notes.

CANTILLON ROSÉ DE GAMBRINUS

🛡 **REGION OF ORIGIN**	Brabant, Belgium
🍶 **STYLE**	Fruit *Lambic*
⌖ **ALCOHOL CONTENT**	4.0 abw (5.0 abv)
🍷 **IDEAL SERVING TEMPERATURE**	47–48° F (8–9° C)

It looks like a rosé wine, but has more complexity than most. With its fine, sustained bead, a pink Champagne of the beer world, perhaps? In Belgium, it is typically served in a Champagne flute. Definitely a beer, too – the name Gambrinus derives from Jan Primus ("John the First"), 13th-century ruler of Brabant, who in many parts of the world is the legendary "King of Beer." Several brews in different countries are named after him. This one has a remarkable fruit aroma, carrying through into the palate, with a delicate, lactic acidity gradually developing. It is a blend predominantly of raspberry *lambic (framboise)* with a smaller proportion of cherry lambic *(kriek)*. Some editions have also contained tiny proportions of elderberry, and vanilla pod. An elegant drink with which to greet guests at a party… and one of the world's great beers.

Choose your humor
Is the humor Rabelaisian or Rubenseque?
Some regard the cartoonish label as indecent
or sexist, but it perfectly captures the joie-de-
vivre *under the surface of bourgeois Belgium.*

CARLSBERG 47

🛡 **REGION OF ORIGIN** Denmark

🍾 **STYLE** Vienna-style Lager

%⃝ **ALCOHOL CONTENT** 5.6 abw (7.0 abv)

🥃 **IDEAL SERVING TEMPERATURE** 48° F (9° C)

The Carlsberg brewery was founded in Copenhagen, Denmark, in 1847, and was the first to produce lager in Northern Europe. Yeast selection in the laboratory at Carlsberg led to the isolation of the world's first single-cell culture in 1883. Since then, lager yeasts have been identified as *Carlsbergensis*. Carlsberg 47 was launched on the 125th anniversary of the brewery. With its distinctively full, reddish-amber color, high strength, and deliciously malty, nutty, apricotlike dryness, it is intended to be a reminder of an early style of lager, originally produced in Vienna in the 1840s and later taken up by Carlsberg. Vienna malts are kilned to create an amber color, some aroma, and a nutty flavor.

Royal brew
The crown on the label indicates that Carlsberg supplies beer to the Danish royal family.

CARLSBERG GAMLE

	REGION OF ORIGIN	Denmark
	STYLE	Munich-style Lager
	ALCOHOL CONTENT	3.4 abw (4.3 abv)
	IDEAL SERVING TEMPERATURE	48° F (9° C)

The Danish word for "old" is *gamle*. In this instance, it describes the oldest style of lager. The first lagers, produced in Munich, were dark brown in color. ("Lager" refers to a yeast that requires a slow fermentation and has nothing to do with color.) This dark version is still known as a Munich-style lager. The first ("Old") Carlsberg brewery made beer in this style. Carlsberg Gamle has a dryish, rooty, very slightly coffeeish dryness. Its color is much fuller than its body (the two are not connected). The toasty flavor and mahogany color are typically created by dark Munich malts. These are, though, much milder than the high-roast barley or malt typically used in stouts.

Ecstatic brew?
"Øl" is Danish for beer. It has the same roots as the English "ale." Both may derive from an old Saxon invocation of religious ecstasy.

CARLSBERG GAMMEL PORTER

🛡 **REGION OF ORIGIN** Denmark

🍾 **STYLE** Imperial Stout

％ **ALCOHOL CONTENT** 6.24 abw (7.8 abv)

🍺 **IDEAL SERVING TEMPERATURE** 55–64° F (13–18° C)

The term "porter" was originally used for a wide variety of toasty-tasting dark brews made in Britain with ale yeasts. When strong examples were exported as winter warmers to cold northern countries, brewers there began to make their own porters. In Britain, the bigger-bodied styles of porter came to be known as stout. Those favored in the cold north are dubbed Imperial, after their popularity with the royal Romanovs. "Old Carlsberg Porter," also labelled Imperial Stout, has been made since 1885. It uses a lager yeast, but the resultant cleanness is overlaid with textures and flavors that are densely oily and tarlike, with suggestions of burlap, oak, cedar, and coffee beans. It is tangily dry but also warming.

CARNEGIE STARK PORTER

REGION OF ORIGIN Sweden

STYLE Baltic Porter

ALCOHOL CONTENT 2.8 abw (3.5 abv) and 4.4 abw (5.5 abv)

IDEAL SERVING TEMPERATURE 50–55° F (10–13° C)

A Scot called Carnegie first brewed this beer in the 1830s, in Gothenburg, Sweden (the two countries historically have strong trading links). Doctors traditionally prescribed the porter, enriched with an egg yolk, for nursing mothers. There are two strengths, the lower of which makes more of a "session" beer. The stronger version leans toward being an imperial stout. Carnegie Stark ("Strong") Porter is creamy and licorice-tasting with a long, dry finish. A top-fermenting yeast is used.

Vintage porter
Carnegie is year-dated. Each "vintage" seems slightly different, though the flavors meld with age.

Castelain Ch'ti Brune

🛡 **Region of origin** Northern France

🍾 **Style** *Bière de Garde*

🍺 **Alcohol content** 5.1 abw (6.4 abv) (Both versions)

🍺 **Ideal serving temperature** 50–55° F (10–13° C)

The odd name is an expression from Northern France meaning a coal miner. The brewery is in the former mining village of Bénifontaine, near Lens. Ch'ti Brune has a dark-chocolate color; a rich body; and portlike flavors, with a vanilla-like nuttiness. This is perhaps the beer for a rich lamb stew. Ch'ti Blonde is still quite syrupy, with fresh, fruity, apricot-like aromas and flavors, and a smooth, dryish, nutty-malt finish. Try it with lamb chops cooked pink. Both beers are unpasteurized. A newer, stronger, golden version, Ch'ti Triple (6.0 abw; 7.5abv), has a fragrant, flowery aroma; grassy, cereal-grain flavors; a nuttily smooth body; and a surging, cherrylike frutiness in a quite bitter finish.

CASTLE EDEN SPECIAL ALE

REGION OF ORIGIN Northeast England, UK

STYLE Bitter/Pale Ale

ALCOHOL CONTENT 4.4 abw (5.5 abv)

IDEAL SERVING TEMPERATURE 50–55° F (10–13° C)

Founded as a coaching inn in the village of Castle Eden during the 1700s or before, this English village brewery has fought magnificently to ensure its survival. From the 1820s to the 1960s, it was the Nimmo's brewery, and was then acquired by Whitbread. In 1998, its closure was announced, and a valedictory brew was issued. The brewery was then rescued in a local management buyout, and Special Ale was launched in celebration. It has a richly malty aroma; a firm, dry palate; complex, geraniumlike, English hop flavors; and very great length. Its flavors benefit from lack of pasteurization (it is sterile-filtered). Special Ale is broadly based on a Whitbread brew once exported to the US.

Retro ale
The label has an intentionally 1950s retro look, but the 1820s facade in the illustration has changed little.

CELIS GRAND CRU

REGION OF ORIGIN Southwest US

STYLE Belgian-style Ale

ALCOHOL CONTENT 7.0 abw (8.75 abv)

IDEAL SERVING TEMPERATURE 45–50° F (7–10° C)

Revivalist Pierre Celis created the Hoegaarden brewery in Belgium in the 1960s. In addition to its famous "white" beer, he devised a strong, golden ale, with orange peels and coriander, which he called Grand Cru. After selling Hoegaarden to Interbrew (producers of Stella Artois) when already past retirement age, he moved to Austin, Texas, and started a brewery there, producing a similar range. The Belgian Grand Cru is flowery and dryish, with suggestions of peach and honeydew melon. The American Celis Grand Cru is still spicy (some tasters have found sorrel), but less delicate, more robust, grassier, more citric, and lemony.

CELIS PALE BOCK

🛡	**REGION OF ORIGIN**	Southwest US
🍾	**STYLE**	Strong, spiced, Belgian-style Ale
⅋	**ALCOHOL CONTENT**	3.1 abw (3.9 abv)
🍺	**IDEAL SERVING TEMPERATURE**	45–50° F (7–10° C)

German-American lager breweries in the US continued the Bock tradition even before the beer renaissance of the last 25 years. In late winter or early spring, they made Bocks slightly stronger, and usually darker, than their everyday products. Some of these still exist. In American states with heavy restrictions on alcohol content, a Bock may be scarcely more potent than a regular beer, but perhaps fuller in flavor. In the Texas town of Shiner, originally a Czech settlement, the local brewery has won a following for a very modest "Bock." When the new generation of breweries sprang up, the "Texas Bock" tradition was taken up by Celis, of Austin. Its entry is not truly a Bock at all, but a smooth, lightly toffeeish, well-balanced ale. It has an almost woody dryness in the finish. This beer contains some crystal malt, is hopped in part with Saaz, and fermented with a Whitbread yeast.

CELIS WHITE

REGION OF ORIGIN	Southwest US
STYLE	Belgian-style Wheat Beer
ALCOHOL CONTENT	3.9 abw (4.9 abv)
IDEAL SERVING TEMPERATURE	48–50° F (9–10° C)

Having established and sold the Hoegaarden brewery, Pierre Celis became fascinated by the new appreciation of characterful beers in the United States. That is why he decided to brew there, and to offer a version of his "white" beer. His Celis White is similar to the beer he made in Belgium but perhaps softer, with more fruity acidity, and less flowery. Since a takeover by Miller, the future of the Celis brewery has been the subject of speculation. It is to be hoped that the brewery's future is ensured. The American "white" has also been made under license in Belgium, by De Smedt, producers of the Affligem range.

How it began
The illustration on the label shows Celis (second from the right) as a young man, helping in Hoegaarden's last old "white" beer brewery.

CERES DANSK DORTMUNDER

> **REGION OF ORIGIN** Denmark
>
> **STYLE** Danish Strong Dortmunder Export
>
> **ALCOHOL CONTENT** 6.2 abw (7.7 abv)
>
> **IDEAL SERVING TEMPERATURE** 48° F (9° C)

The mythological Roman goddess of farming and cereal grains, Ceres, gives her name to this brewery in the Danish city of Aarhus. This brewery has a strong "Danish Dortmunder." The beer has a buttery maltiness and some fruitiness. Ceres' other products include a beer flavored with rum and lemon essence, named after the navigator Bering (who died of scurvy); and a peppery, phonetic Stowt. The city of Aarhus also has an unrelated brewpub called St. Clements, situated in a former newspaper printing premises on the town square. It produces a relatively malty unfiltered Pilsner and seasonal specials.

CHARLES WELLS BOMBARDIER

🛡 **REGION OF ORIGIN**	Eastern England, UK
🍾 **STYLE**	Bitter Ale
% **ALCOHOL CONTENT**	3.4 abw (4.3 abv)
🌡 **IDEAL SERVING TEMPERATURE**	50–55° F (10–13° C)

Sizable regional brewery, long established, and still family-run, in Bedford. Its best-known beer evokes the memory of boxer "Bombardier Billy" Wells, British heavyweight champion from 1911 to 1919. This satisfying, smooth, malt-accented beer has a slightly sulfury, rooty aroma; fruity, cherry-pie flavors; and a cookie-like dryness in the finish. It is hopped with Goldings and Challengers. In 2000, the brewery introduced a yeast-sedimented version of Bombardier in a four-pint plastic bottle. This is sold with a bracket to hold the bottle steady, in an inverted position, while the beer conditions overnight – and a simple tapping system. The beer thus dispensed is a close approximation of cask-conditioned draft as served in the pub.

Earlier image
The brewery likes to celebrate awards and events, but the character toasting on the label predates the Bombardier.

CHELSEA OLD TITANIC

🛡	**REGION OF ORIGIN**	Northeast US
🍾	**STYLE**	Barley Wine
%	**ALCOHOL CONTENT**	6.4 abw (8.0 abv)
🍺	**IDEAL SERVING TEMPERATURE**	55° F (13° C)

Had its voyage been completed, the *Titanic* would have docked at Pier 59 on New York's Hudson River. That is now a yacht marina and the site of the Chelsea brewery and pub (this part of town is known as Chelsea). The brewery's barley wine, named with black humor, might be enjoyed with an epic novel, but not one that prompts nightmares. It has a whiskeyish aroma; a malty, warming palate; and a toasty finish.

Not to be iced
Icebergs loom on the label,
but this ale is to be served at
a natural cellar temperature.

C

CHILTERN JOHN HAMPDEN'S ALE

🛡 **REGION OF ORIGIN** South of England, UK

🍾 **STYLE** Bitter Ale

% **ALCOHOL CONTENT** 3.8 abw (4.8 abv)

🍺 **IDEAL SERVING TEMPERATURE** 50–55° F (10–13° C)

Just north of the Chiltern Hills, in Aylesbury, historic county town of Buckinghamshire. The brewery, established in 1980, revived Aylesbury's beer-making tradition after a gap of 40-odd years. The farm-based Chiltern brewery also sells beer-flavored condiments and cheeses, and even hop-based toiletries. John Hampden's Ale is straw-colored, with the aroma of lemons and ginger, and a very dry, cracker-like maltiness. John Hampden was a leading figure in the English Civil War, with which Aylesbury has strong historical associations.

JOHN HAMPDEN'S ALE

550ml ℮   4.8%

The Chiltern Brewery
TERRICK, BUCKINGHAMSHIRE, ENGLAND

Chiltern Three Hundreds Old Ale

🛡	**REGION OF ORIGIN** South of England, UK
🍶	**STYLE** Old Ale
⚗	**ALCOHOL CONTENT** 4.0 abw (5.0 abv)
🍺	**IDEAL SERVING TEMPERATURE** 50–55° F (10–13° C)

A "hundred" was an old measure of land. The Chiltern Hills were divided into three "hundreds," some of which were wooded hiding places for criminals. Stewards were appointed to patrol these areas, and this position still exists, though with neither duties nor salary. Three Hundreds is produced by the Chiltern Brewery, in Aylesbury. Despite its modest alcohol content, it is in style a good example of an old ale. The beer has a fresh, malt aroma; a nutty sweetness, with suggestions of vanilla in the palate; a fine bead, and a lightly fruity, cherryish tartness in the finish. The brewery has a stronger countpart, at 6.8 abw (8.5 abv), called Bodger's Barley Wine.

CHIMAY CINQ CENTS

REGION OF ORIGIN Province of Hainaut, Belgium

STYLE Abbey (Authentic Trappist)

ALCOHOL CONTENT 6.4 abw (8.0 abv)

IDEAL SERVING TEMPERATURE 57° F (14° C);
Serve no colder than 50° F (10° C)

The best-known of the Trappist abbey breweries dates from the mid-1800s. It became known for dark, sweet brews, but in the 1960s decided to add a drier beer to its range. This version was originally known by the white cap on the bottle, but an additional Champagne-style presentation was added to celebrate the 500th anniversary of the nearby town of Chimay. Cinq Cents has a remarkably fluffy body; a light but firm hit of malt; and an intense, late orangey, perfumy, junipery dryness. This beer is a superb aperitif. It also has the acidity to stand up to the pickled trout dish escavèche, popular in the area.

It's a corker
Chimay beers in the original bottles do not seem to gain quite the softness in maturation imparted by this larger, corked version.

CHIMAY GRAND RÉSERVE

🛡 **REGION OF ORIGIN**	Province of Hainaut, Belgium
🍾 **STYLE**	Abbey (Authentic Trappist)
% **ALCOHOL CONTENT**	7.1 abw (9.0 abv)
🍺 **IDEAL SERVING TEMPERATURE**	59–64° F (15–18° C)

The most portlike of all beers is the vintage-dated Grande Réserve. It is the strongest of the three principal brews made by the Trappist monastery of Notre-Dame, at Scourmont, near the town of Chimay (pronounced "she may"), in the far south of Belgium. The port flavors develop if the beer is laid down for five years or more. This aromatic, lively, rich ale has a medium-sweet middle, with gently drier suggestions of thyme, pepper, sandalwood, and nutmeg in the finish. It is a complex classic, and a delight with Roquefort cheese.

CHRISTIAN MERZ SPEZIAL RAUCHBIER

REGION OF ORIGIN	Franconia, Bavaria, Germany
STYLE	*Bamberger Rauchbier*
ALCOHOL CONTENT	4.2 abw (5.3 abv)
IDEAL SERVING TEMPERATURE	48° F (9° C)

The heartland of smoked beer is the German region of Franconia, especially its baroque town of Bamberg, which is dotted with small breweries. Beechwood from nearby forests is used to smoke the malt. The tiny maltings, brewery, pub-restaurant, and small hotel of the Christian Merz family dates from 1536. The bottled *Märzen*-style version of its *Rauchbier* ("Smoked Beer") has a molasses aroma; a clean, dry, creamy palate; and a fragrant smokiness in the big finish. It is perfect with Bavarian smoked ham.

CHRISTOFFEL BLOND

REGION OF ORIGIN	Province of Limburg, the Netherlands
STYLE	Pilsner
ALCOHOL CONTENT	4.0 abw (5.0 abv)
IDEAL SERVING TEMPERATURE	48° F (9° C)

One of the world's hoppiest Pilsner-style beers, made at Roermond, in Dutch Limburg, near the German border. The town's patron saint is St. Christopher. This new-generation brewery was founded in 1986 by Dutch brewer Leo Brand. Its Blond beer has spicy, piney, hop aromas; very lively flavors; and an appetizingly robust bitterness in the finish. In the Netherlands, the term Pils often indicates a bland beer. It is a shame that such a great style is thus abused (and not only in the Netherlands). Worse still that such a fine Pilsner as Christoffel avoids the term for fear of being bracketed with more neutral-tasting beers. In its anxiety not to sound bland, the brewery settles for the vague Blond.

CHRISTOFFEL ROBERTUS

REGION OF ORIGIN Province of Limburg, the Netherlands

STYLE Dark Lager

ALCOHOL CONTENT 4.8 abw (6.0 abv)

IDEAL SERVING TEMPERATURE 50° F (10° C)

As well as its renowned dry, Pilsner-style Blond *(see previous page)*, this Dutch producer of unfiltered, unpasteurized lager has a ruby-colored brew called Robertus: something between a Vienna, a Munich-style dark, and a Bock. The beer is subtitled "Double Malt," though this claim has no specific meaning. The brew has a fresh, grainy aroma; a firm, smooth body; complex, nutty, malty-fruity flavors; and a dryish finish. A novelty variation on this brew is a product called Taboe. (In Dutch, this is pronounced "taboo.") This is flavored with tobacco essence during primary fermentation. The beer has a slight suggestion of cigar smoke: sweet, especially in the aroma, and then dry and leafy.

Climax ESB

REGION OF ORIGIN	Northeast US
STYLE	American Ale/Extra Special Bitter
ALCOHOL CONTENT	4.4 abw (5.5 abv)
IDEAL SERVING TEMPERATURE	50–55° F (10–13° C)

According to one of the principals of this outstanding ale brewery, "the name represents the point of greatest excitement." Climax, one of the first new-generation breweries in New Jersey, was established in Roselle Park, an old railroad town south of Newark, in 1996. Its products are extremely complex and flavorsome, but appetizingly drinkable. They range from a dryish, perfumy cream ale to an India pale ale with a rooty, almost artichoke-like bitterness. Between these two extremes is a fruitier, maltier, clean, soft ESB full of moreish flavors.

COBBOLD IPA

🛡 **REGION OF ORIGIN**	Eastern England, UK
🍾 **STYLE**	India Pale Ale
% **ALCOHOL CONTENT**	3.4 abw (4.2 abv)
🍺 **IDEAL SERVING TEMPERATURE**	50–55° F (10–13° C)

Coastal, barley country brewery, in Ipswich, England. The enterprise was founded by country gentry, and traces its history to 1723, but was reborn as a microbrewery in a management buyout in 1990. The IPA pours with a very well-retained head; has a good English, slightly peppery, hop aroma; a smooth, light body; a light palate, with a touch of clean apple; and a firm hit of dryness in the finish. There is some appetizingly lingering bitterness.

Regal connection
The label shows Cardinal Wolsey, chief minister to King Henry VIII. Wolsey was born in Ipswich. He is shown by Wolsey's Gate, a local landmark.

COOPERS BEST
EXTRA FOOD STOUT

🛡	**REGION OF ORIGIN** South Australia
🍾	**STYLE** Dry Stout
%	**ALCOHOL CONTENT** 5.4 abw (6.8 abv)
🍺	**IDEAL SERVING TEMPERATURE** 50–55° F (10–13° C)

Most Australian breweries have a stout in their range, and the famously traditionalist Coopers, of Adelaide, makes a most characterful example. Coopers Stout is woody, oily, and strong, but very drinkable with the oysters and mussels of the South Seas.

COOPERS SPARKLING ALE

🛡	**REGION OF ORIGIN**	South Australia
🍾	**STYLE**	Golden Ale
%	**ALCOHOL CONTENT**	4.7 abw (5.8 abv)
🍺	**IDEAL SERVING TEMPERATURE**	50° F (10° C)

Thomas Cooper was a Methodist preacher from Yorkshire, England, who emigrated to Australia in 1852 and started a brewery in Adelaide. Coopers is the last of Australia's old-established family breweries. Its Sparkling Ale (which, with its yeast sediment, can in fact be quite cloudy) had a bronze-red color until about 1980. Now, it has a full golden hue. It is quenching, classic, fruity (with suggestions of apples, pears and, especially, bananas), and dry, with a long finish.

Possessive pour?
The packaging is as folksy as the beer. Cooper's is spelled with an apostrophe on the neck, but not on the main label. The barrel in the center is labeled Kensington Brewery after the Adelaide neighborhood.

COTTAGE NORMAN'S CONQUEST

REGION OF ORIGIN West of England, UK

STYLE Barley Wine

ALCOHOL CONTENT 5.6 abw (7.0 abv)

IDEAL SERVING TEMPERATURE Store at 55° F (13° C);
Serve at 50–55° F (10–13° C)

Chris Norman, an airline pilot, took early retirement and started a brewery with his wife Helen in 1993. It was not quite in a cottage, but was initially in a garage at their house at Little Orchard, West Lydford, Somerset. Two years later, their barley wine was judged Champion Beer at the Great British Beer Festival. For a big beer, it is remarkably appetizing, with fresh cinnamon, sultana, and apple aromas. It has a clean, creamy palate and a spicy, peppery, balancing dryness.

COURAGE IMPERIAL RUSSIAN STOUT

🛡 **REGION OF ORIGIN**	London, England, UK
🍾 **STYLE**	Imperial Stout
% **ALCOHOL CONTENT**	8.0 abw (10.0 abv)
🥛 **IDEAL SERVING TEMPERATURE**	55–64° F (13–18° C)

S cottish Courage, the current owner of this label, inherited Imperial Russian Stout from the now-defunct Barclay's brewery, in London. That brewery exported the beer to the Baltic during the time of Empress Catherine II. With her encouragement, British-style porter was introduced to the Russian Empire. Today's Courage Imperial Russian Stout is typically winey, sherryish, raisiny, woody, and sappy. The most recent vintages have been made at Courage's subsidiary brewery, John Smith's, in Tadcaster, Yorkshire. A bottling of Courage Imperial Russian Stout available in Finland in 1999 had the characteristic sherry note, and some coffee, but lacked the typical raisin tinge.

A "Great" beer
Catherine II is mentioned on the label, which is partly rendered in Russian. The beer is a last vestige of a 200-year-old export trade.

CREEMORE SPRINGS PREMIUM LAGER

 **REGION OF ORIGIN** Province of Ontario, Canada
STYLE Golden Lager/Pilsner
ALCOHOL CONTENT 4.0 abw (5.0 abv)
IDEAL SERVING TEMPERATURE 48° F (9° C)

People from Toronto drive a couple of hours north to weekend or ski in the area of Creemore Springs. In 1987, the village's 1890s hardware store was turned into a microbrewery, bringing its water by tanker truck from nearby springs. Its Premium Lager has a deliciously fresh malt aroma; a smooth, clean, textured, lightly nutty body; and an elegant balance of hoppy dryness.

CRISTAL ALKEN

REGION OF ORIGIN	Province of Limburg, Belgium
STYLE	Pilsner
ALCOHOL CONTENT	3.8 abw (4.8 abv)
IDEAL SERVING TEMPERATURE	48° F (9° C)

Names such as "crystal" have been used by several brewers of golden lagers. This particularly fine Pilsner type is brewed in the town of Alken, in the Belgian province of Limburg. It was the first Belgian Pilsner, launched in 1928 (its rival Stella Artois was at the time a Christmas beer). True to its name, Cristal tastes at first almost like spring water; then comes a clean hit of hoppy dryness in the middle; and a refreshing, crisp finish. The beer has lost some bitterness in recent years. In the same period, Alken merged with Maes, and the joint enterprise was then absorbed by Kronenbourg, which in turn was acquired in 2000 by the parent group of Scottish Courage.

CROWN BUCKLEY BROWN ALE

🛡 **REGION OF ORIGIN** South Wales, UK
🍾 **STYLE** Brown Ale
⅋ **ALCOHOL CONTENT** 2.7 abw (3.4 abv)
🥛 **IDEAL SERVING TEMPERATURE** 50–55° F (10–13° C)

The regal name Crown sat oddly on the shoulders of a brewery once devoted entirely to supplying working men's clubs. The Crown brewery, of Pontyclun, South Wales, merged in 1989 with Buckley's, not far away in the tinplate town of Llanelli. Buckley's, once run by a minister of the Wesleyan church, was later acquired by Brains. The name Crown survives in this brown ale, in the traditional dark, sweetish, low-alcohol style rather than the paler, stronger, drier type found in the northeast of England. Crown Buckley Brown Ale is nutty, toasty, and jammy, with a delicate touch of balancing hop dryness.

DALESIDE MOROCCO ALE

REGION OF ORIGIN Northern England, UK

STYLE Spiced Dark Ale

ALCOHOL CONTENT 4.4 abw (5.5 abv)

IDEAL SERVING TEMPERATURE 55° F (13° C)

The original "Morocco" may have been a brown ale named after dark-skinned servants to King Charles II, and introduced by a courtier to Levens Hall, near Kendal, Cumbria. In the 1870s, a "Morocco" beer matured for 21 years was said to have been served at the hall. Another account talks of a drink brought by a returning Crusader. It is more likely that he brought fruits or spices to put in the brew. At one stage, it also contained meat, presumably to provide protein nutrition for the yeast. The current Morocco was created in the mid-1990s. It is a gingery, orangey, marmalady, toasty, cakey ale, made by the Daleside microbrewery in Harrogate, Yorkshire.

MOROCCO
ALE

A STRONG
DARK AND
MYSTERIOUS
ALE BREWED TO
THE ANCIENT
RECIPE HELD
SECRET AT
LEVENS HALL
FOR OVER
300 YEARS

5.5% ABV
℮ 500ML

BREWED & BOTTLED FOR
LEVENS HALL, CUMBRIA
BY THE DALESIDE BREWERY
HARROGATE - ENGLAND

Ale tale
The insignia on the label recalls the links between Levens Hall and the royal family.

DAS FEINE HOFMARK DUNKLE WEISSE

D

🛡 **REGION OF ORIGIN** Bavaria, Germany

🍾 **STYLE** Dark Wheat Beer

% **ALCOHOL CONTENT** 4.5 abw (5.6 abv)

🍺 **IDEAL SERVING TEMPERATURE** 48–54° F (9–12° C)

As the road from the Bavarian city of Nuremberg approaches the Czech border, the family-owned brewery Das Feine Hofmark sits on a hillside at Loifling, near Cham. This brewery uses water from the same quartz-granite bed as that at nearby Pilsen. It is known for its soft golden lagers, but also makes a well-regarded range of wheat beers, using the term *weisse* ("white") even for this *dunkle* ("dark") example. *Naturtrüb* indicates that the haze is natural. The German word *Trüb* is sometimes used by English-speaking brewers, especially in the US, to describe sediment. It has the same origins as the English "turbid," "turbulent," or "troubled." The brewery name reflects aristocratic origins in the 1500s. The Dunkle Weisse has only a light wheat-beer character (a touch of banana-like fruitiness), but a delicious aroma of fresh cream, and dark-malt flavors reminiscent of nut toffee.

D

DAS FEINE HOFMARK ÖKO PREMIUM

REGION OF ORIGIN	Bavaria, Germany
STYLE	Pilsner
ALCOHOL CONTENT	4.5 abw (5.6 abv)
IDEAL SERVING TEMPERATURE	48° F (9° C)

The abbreviation Öko, short for "ecological," identifies this as an organic brew. The beer has a very good, flowery, hop aroma. Its palate is accented toward a soft, creamy maltiness, but this is underpinned by a very gentle, restrained, hoppy dryness and a spritzy finish. It is very similar to the brewery's Würzig Mild golden lager. *Würzig* means "aromatic." In addition to the "mild" version, there is also a Würzig Herb. The second word does not indicate the use of herbs, but simply means a hoppier, drier interpretation, along the lines of a classic Pilsner. In the same family of golden lagers from this brewery is a remarkably smooth, malt-accented version, with a hint of newly-mown hay, made for the London department store Harrods.

DAS FEINE HOFMARK PREMIUM WEISSE

REGION OF ORIGIN	Bavaria, Germany
STYLE	Wheat Beer
ALCOHOL CONTENT	4.5 abw (5.6 abv)
IDEAL SERVING TEMPERATURE	48–54° F (9–12° C)

While the dark malts give a dominant toffee character to the *dunkle* version of this product, the pale partner shown here has none of that rich sweetness. Without the dark malts, the wheat beer character sings through: soft clovey spiciness and lemon in the aroma, and a yet more evident apple, bananalike fruitiness in the palate. This is a light, smooth, soothing, but also refreshing, interpretation of the style. In Germany, all the fruit flavors are caused by the yeast in fermentation, and not by any attention of fruit at the brewery. That would be banned under the German Beer Purity Law; in Belgium, wheat beers normally contain orange peels.

DE KONINCK

REGION OF ORIGIN Province of Antwerp, Belgium

STYLE Belgian Ale

ALCOHOL CONTENT 5.0abv (4.0w)

IDEAL SERVING TEMPERATURE The brewery suggests 45° F (7° C), but the flavors are more evident at a less severe temperature, around 54° F (12° C)

The name of this beer means "king." In this instance, it was the surname of a man who owned a beer garden in Antwerp. The garden has gone, but its brewery survives. Its principal product, known simply as De Koninck, is the much-loved local beer of Antwerp. It is not described on the tap handle or label as an ale, but it certainly is one. As a bottled brew, De Koninck is good, but its fresh, yeasty, dusty, cinnamon-like spiciness is at its best when served on tap. It has a dense head, is subtle, dryish, but beautifully balanced, toasty, soothing, and drinkable. A stronger (6.4 abw; 8.0 abv), spicier, brandyish version is called Cuvée De Koninck.

Ball of malt
When Antwerpers order a bolleke
(little ball), the choice of glass and beer is always understood.

DE LEEUW DORTMUNDER

⊘ **REGION OF ORIGIN** Province of Limburg, the Netherlands

🍷 **STYLE** Strong Dortmunder Export

% **ALCOHOL CONTENT** 5.2 abw (6.5 abv)

🍺 **IDEAL SERVING TEMPERATURE** 48° F (9° C)

The name De Leeuw (as in "Leo") means The Lion, a popular heraldic name for breweries. The old Lion Brewery is in Valkenburg, east of Maastricht, in the Netherlands. The brewery, in one of the few hilly parts of this famously flat country, is particularly proud of its spring water. Maastricht is on the borders of the Netherlands, Belgium, and Germany. Its home province, Limburg, has historical links with all three countries. Several breweries in this area produce golden lagers inspired by the dryish, medium-strong, local style of the German brewing city of Dortmund. Typically, the Dutch "copies" are stronger than the original Dortmunders. De Leeuw's version has an earthy malt aroma; a very full, marshmallowy, toffeeish palate; a very smooth palate indeed; and a medium-dry finish.

DE LEEUW VALKENBURGS WIT

REGION OF ORIGIN Province of Limburg, the Netherlands

STYLE Wheat Beer

ALCOHOL CONTENT 3.8 abw (4.8 abv)

IDEAL SERVING TEMPERATURE 48–50° F (9–10° C)

A German brewer from nearby Aachen founded this enterprise in a former gunpowder factory, powered by a large waterwheel, in the Dutch town of Valkenburg in 1886. The brewery came into Dutch ownership in 1920. Like most breweries in the area, it was for decades known for its lagers, but in 1993 it introduced a wheat beer. Valkenburgs Wit is soft, malty, and gently fruity, with a dryish, gingery finish. It is a sedimented, spiced brew. Beers in broadly this style were brewed in the days when the Netherlands and Belgium were one country. The most typical fruit used as a flavoring – the dry, tart orange from the former Dutch island of Curaçao in the Caribbean – has survived better in liqueurs in the Netherlands and in beers in Belgium.

DE LEEUW WINTER WIT

🛡	**REGION OF ORIGIN**	Province of Limburg, the Netherlands
	STYLE	Belgian-style Wheat Beer
	ALCOHOL CONTENT	4.6 abw (5.8 abv)
	IDEAL SERVING TEMPERATURE	48–50° F (9–10° C)

The revival of wheat beers in The Netherlands and Belgium led to a considerable fashion for the style in the 1990s. Most examples are at a conventional strength, usually around 4.0 abw (5.0 abv), and serve as light, summery refreshers. A handful of breweries have also experimented with fuller-bodied interpetations, with more alcohol and sometimes darker malts, perhaps as a winter brew. Valkenburgs Winter Wit falls into this category. It is notably bigger-bodied than the regular Wit, with a hefty graininess, sweetness, and spiciness and just a touch of the fruity acidity typical in a wheat brew. The perfect beer with Dutch apple pancakes.

DE RIDDER MALTEZER

REGION OF ORIGIN	Province of Limburg, the Netherlands
STYLE	Strong Dortmunder Export
ALCOHOL CONTENT	5.2 abw (6.5 abv)
IDEAL SERVING TEMPERATURE	48° F (9° C)

The brewery's parish church in the Dutch city of Maastricht is St. Martin's, named after one of the Knights Templar (the order which protected pilgrims). Ridder ("rider") means Knight. A suit of armor stands in the conference room of this brewery, and stained glass illustrates heraldic scenes. The business was founded in 1857 by the brewing brothers van Aubel. When there was no successor, in 1982, it was acquired by Heineken. In some countries, Maltezer sounds like a candy; in Dutch, it is intended to imply a robust character in this beer. It has a flowery hop character but also a dryish maltiness in the aroma; a firm, smooth body; butter-toffee malt flavors; and a gentle underpinning of balancing dryness. It is in much the same style as beers made by other Dutch breweries under the designation Dortmunder.

DE RIDDER WIECKSE WITTE

🛡 **REGION OF ORIGIN**	Province of Limburg, the Netherlands
🍾 **STYLE**	Belgian-style Wheat Beer
📊 **ALCOHOL CONTENT**	4.0 abw (5.0 abv)
🥃 **IDEAL SERVING TEMPERATURE**	48–50° F (9–10° C)

A"wick" is a hamlet, village, town, or neighborhood in several languages, often as a suffix to a place-name (for example, Warwick). Hence Wieckse. This *Wieck* refers to the district where the De Ridder brewery stands, on the Left Bank of the Meuse River (in Dutch, *Maas*), in the heart of Maastricht in Dutch Limburg. The city, surrounded by small breweries, is known for its many cafés. In the center, De Ridder is a local landmark. The brewery makes this wheat beer, with melony fruit aromas and flavors, and a dry, gingery, rooty finish. It is a well-regarded example of the style, and would surely be popular outside the Netherlands if it were more widely available.

A cool beer
The back label suggests a serving temperature of 43–46° F (6–8° C), but such cold kills flavor.

DE TROCH CHAPEAU PÊCHE

REGION OF ORIGIN Province of Flemish Brabant, Belgium

STYLE Peach *Lambic*

ALCOHOL CONTENT 2.4 abw (3.0 abv)

IDEAL SERVING TEMPERATURE 8–50° F (9–10° C)

The farmhouse brewery De Troch makes crisp, dry *gueuze-lambic* beers in the Belgian village of Wambeek, in the traditional region of production. It also has a sweeter range, including several tropical fruit flavors, under the name Chapeau. This peach beer is very sweet indeed, though it also has some of the "fresh apple," Chardonnay-like flavors that can be found in lambic beers, and a "fino sherry" dryness in the finish.

DINKEL ACKER VOLKSFEST BIER

🛡 **REGION OF ORIGIN**	Baden-Württemberg, Germany
🍺 **STYLE**	*Märzen/Festbier*
% **ALCOHOL CONTENT**	4.4 abw (5.5 abv)
🍺 **IDEAL SERVING TEMPERATURE**	48° F (9° C)

Around the same time as the Munich Oktoberfest, the other great southern German capital, Stuttgart, has its own "People's Festival" *(Volksfest)*. The city's breweries make special beers for the occasion. The Carl Dinkelacker brewery makes a lively example with a big, malty start and a good hop balance. Dinkelacker is the name of the brewery's founding family, which is still involved. The modern German word *Dinkel* means the grain known in English as spelt; *Acker* means field. Sadly, spelt does not seem to have featured in any products from the brewery. In 1996, Dinkelacker was senior partner in a merger with the Stuttgart suburban brewery Schwaben Bräu. It has a similar *Märzenbier*, with a delicate hop aroma and sweetish malt character.

DOCK STREET GRAND CRU

REGION OF ORIGIN Northeast US

STYLE Flemish "Red Ale"

ALCOHOL CONTENT 6.0 abw (7.5 abv)

IDEAL SERVING TEMPERATURE 50° F (10° C)

The cult television series *Thirtysomething* made frequent reference to Dock Street. This brewpub/brasserie in the center of Philadelphia produces an astonishing 45 styles of beer per year, about a dozen of which are available at any one time. Dock Street intends this occasional Grand Cru as an undisguised tribute to Rodenbach *(see pp.386–88)*. It succeeds magnificently, though it is less aggressively acidic. Dock Street Grand Cru is aged in wine casks. It has firm, stemmy flavors, with a suggestion of sloe gin, and a cherryish, sweet-and-sour finish.

The rival brewpub at the Sansom Street Oyster House once made a tarter, lighter interpetation using a malo-lactic fermentation as in some wines. This is a process in which strong, apple-tasting malic acids are converted to lactic acids to round out the flavors. Such specialities can sometimes be found at a renowned Philadelphia pub called The Standard Tap (2nd and Poplar).

DOCK STREET ILLUMINATOR

🛡 **REGION OF ORIGIN** Northeast US

🍺 **STYLE** Double Bock

% **ALCOHOL CONTENT** 5.8 abw (7.2 abv)

🍺 **IDEAL SERVING TEMPERATURE** 48° F (9° C)

The strong German Lenten lager Paulaner Salvator ("savior") *(see p.355)* has inspired many similar beers with names ending in -ator. Although a German brewer coined Viagrator, the wry twists are more common among new-generation brewers in the United States, with names like Hibernator, Terminator, and Liberator. An enlightening example, Illuminator is a dark amber Double Bock from the Dock Street Brewery in Philadelphia. It is creamy, with vanilla notes and pruney flavors.

Unholy goat
The usual symbol of Bock beer
is the billy goat, a creature
which is often regarded as
being especially carnal.

D

DOCK STREET MILK STOUT

REGION OF ORIGIN Northeast US

STYLE Milk Stout

ALCOHOL CONTENT 3.7 abw (4.6 abv)

IDEAL SERVING TEMPERATURE 55° F (13° C)

This style of stout is delicious with chocolate desserts. Sometimes the term "milk" or "cream" on the label merely indicates a rich sweetness, but in classic examples it has a more specific meaning: lactose, a sugar derived from milk, is used, in addition to the dark, roasty malts employed to make a stout. Lactose, which is not fermentable, adds creaminess of body and flavor. Dock Street Milk Stout is the "real thing" in that it does contain a proportion of lactose. This stout is very smooth indeed, with flavors reminiscent of dark chocolate and fudge.

Dom Kölsch

- **REGION OF ORIGIN** Cologne, North Rhine-Westphalia, Germany
- **STYLE** *Kölschbier*
- **ALCOHOL CONTENT** 3.8 abw (4.8 abv)
- **IDEAL SERVING TEMPERATURE** 48° F (9° C)

The name means cathedral, and that is the trademark of this medium-sized brewery. Dom is on the corner of Tacitus and Goltstein Streets, just south of the center of Cologne. Its Tacitus tavern there was dubbed "the best kitchen in town" by the influential French critics Gault and Millau. Local dishes are offered. The beer is fresh, clean, and well balanced, with a smooth maltiness and lemony, hop dryness.

Slow maturation
Cologne's cathedral was not completed until the 1800s. It is a symbol of the entire city, as well as this beer.

D

DOMUS CON DOMUS

🛡 **REGION OF ORIGIN** Province of Flemish Brabant, Belgium

🍾 **STYLE** Pilsner

% **ALCOHOL CONTENT** 4.0 abw (5.0 abv)

🍺 **IDEAL SERVING TEMPERATURE** 48° F (9° C)

A beer with Domus? The student clientele of the Domus brewery and pub in Leuven, Belgium, is no doubt amused by the sexy pun, but the beer is perfectly serious. It has a flowery, oily, hop aroma; a rich malt background; and a spicy, minty finish. It is very dry indeed and an excellent aperitif. A cheekily assertive Pilsner-style beer made in the shadow of the town's Stella Artois brewery.

Hoppy students
The Catholic University of Leuven,
dating from 1425, and boasting Erasmus
and Mercator among its alumni, awards
doctorates in brewing science.

DOMUS LEUVENDIGE WITTE

🛡 **REGION OF ORIGIN** Province of Flemish Brabant, Belgium

🍾 **STYLE** Belgian Wheat Beer

% **ALCOHOL CONTENT** 4.0 abw (5.0 abv)

🍺 **IDEAL SERVING TEMPERATURE** 48–50° F (9–10° C)

The city of Leuven is the home of Stella Artois, and the biggest brewing center in Belgium. It is east of Brussels, and close to the wheat-growing area. Leuven has its own tradition of wheat beers, upheld by the Domus brewery and pub. Within the Domus range is Leuvendige Witte, with a fresh, orange-cream aroma; a palate surging with lemon-soda flavors; and a spicy, balancing dryness. Leuven is a university city, known for its many student bars, among which Domus is a classic.

DORTMUNDER UNION EXPORT

🛡 **REGION OF ORIGIN**	Dortmund, North Rhine-Westphalia, Germany
🍺 **STYLE**	Dortmunder Export
⅌ **ALCOHOL CONTENT**	4.2 abw (5.3 abv)
🍶 **IDEAL SERVING TEMPERATURE**	48° F (9° C)

Dortmunder Union-Brauerei (DUB) is the best-known of the city's brewing companies. Its Export has a firm, mouth-filling body; a restrained, malty sweetness; and a lightly dry, rounded finish. DUB acquired Dortmunder Ritter, which also has an Export in its range. The two Exports are similar, but the Ritter seems smoother and more assertive. DUB's traditional local rival is Dortmunder Actien-Brauerei (DAB), which has a light-tasting Export and a similar brew under the name of Dortmunder Hansa. DAB has in recent years acquired Dortmunder Kronen, with a clean, soft Export.

Original style
Once, Dortmund's own style was sold far and wide – hence "Export."
Today, the city makes more Pilsner.

Duvel

- **REGION OF ORIGIN** Province of Antwerp, Belgium
- **STYLE** Belgian-style Strong Golden Ale
- **ALCOHOL CONTENT** 6.8 abw (8.5 abv)
- **IDEAL SERVING TEMPERATURE** 50° F (10° C)

When British beers were fashionable in Belgium, the family-owned Moortgat brewery, at Breendonk, north of Brussels, produced a Scottish ale, using McEwan's yeast. The brewery later decided to restyle it, keeping the yeast and ale fermentation, and the high strength, but using pale malts. The beer is hopped with the Styrian Goldings variety and Saaz. A sequence of warm and cold fermentation and maturation lasts for well over three months. "The devil of a beer!" someone in the brewery observed of the first experimental batch, hence the Flemish corruption *Duvel* (pronounced Doov'l). The brew is extremely fragrant, and has flavors reminiscent of orange zest, pear brandy, green apples, and the lightest touch of smooth, stony dryness.

DUYCK JENLAIN

REGION OF ORIGIN Northern France

STYLE *Bière de Garde*

ALCOHOL CONTENT 5.2 abw (6.5 abv)

IDEAL SERVING TEMPERATURE 50–55° F (10 13° C)

The family name Duyck is from the part of Flanders that extends into France, and the farm-style brewery is just across the Belgian border, at the hamlet of Jenlain, south of Valenciennes. This *bière de garde*, made with a top-fermenting ale yeast, and unpasteurized, pours with a huge head and has an attractive, full amber color. It has a smooth, lightly syrupy start, and develops orangey, spicy, dry flavors in the finish. A very good example of the style, and deliciously food-friendly.

EBULUM

🛡 **REGION OF ORIGIN**	South of Scotland, UK
🍾 **STYLE**	Elderberry Ale
⅌ **ALCOHOL CONTENT**	5.2 abw (6.5 abv)
🍺 **IDEAL SERVING TEMPERATURE**	55° F (13° C)

The name seems to have been widely used for a Celtic type of beer produced in Scotland from the ninth century, and flavoured with elderberries and herbs. Ebulum is the most recent among a widely available range of traditional ales produced in Scotland, by the brewing brothers Williams *(see also entries for Alba Scots Pine Ale, p.17, Fraoch Heather Ale, p.172, and Grozet Gooseberry and Wheat Ale, p.201).* Ebulum has a slate-black color and winey, rooty, licorice-like, slightly medicinal flavors against a toffeeish malt background. The suggestion of licorice is a reminder that elderberry is a member of the genus *Sambucus.* The malt character is heightened by the use of roasted grains, including oats as well as barley.

Highland homebrew
The recipe for this Lowland product was based on 16th-century accounts of domestic brewing in the Highlands.

ECHIGO LAND BRAUEREI ABBEY-STYLE TRIPEL

 🛡 **REGION OF ORIGIN** Honshu, Japan

 🍺 **STYLE** Abbey

 ⁒ **ALCOHOL CONTENT** 7.2 abw (9.0 abv)

 🍷 **IDEAL SERVING TEMPERATURE** 50–57° F (10–14° C)

Many "abbey-style" beers have been introduced in the New World in recent years, most of them in the United States. This example is from the Japanese Echigo brewery that looks rather like a church, at Makimachi, in the prefecture of Niigata, a sake region in the northwest of the main island. The Japanese principal is married to a German; hence the term Land Brauerei. This tripel is dark and has the aroma of raspberries; a suggestion of morello cherries in its oily palate; and an intense almondy dryness in the finish.

EKU 28

🛡 **REGION OF ORIGIN** Franconia, Bavaria, Germany

🍶 **STYLE** Double Bock/Strong Lager

🌢 **ALCOHOL CONTENT** 8.8 abw (11.0 abv)

🍶 **IDEAL SERVING TEMPERATURE** 48° F (9° C)

The slogan on the glass says "The strongest beer in the world," but that record changes hands almost annually. Since the glass was printed, the label has been amended to say that the beer is "one of" the most potent. The initials EKU indicate in German the First United Brewery of Kulmbach, a great brewing town. The figure 28 represents the beer's original gravity (in German degrees), not alcohol. A beer with such a high gravity is inevitably syrupy, but its complex, tangerine-like flavors are surprisingly fresh and clean.

ELDRIDGE POPE ROYAL OAK

REGION OF ORIGIN	West of England, UK
STYLE	Pale Ale
ALCOHOL CONTENT	4.0 abw (5.0 abv)
IDEAL SERVING TEMPERATURE	50–55° F (10–13° C)

Sarah Eldridge started a brewery in Dorchester in the 1830s. Her lawyer, Alfred Pope, became involved in 1870. The owning families were later friendly with Dorset poet and novelist Thomas Hardy. A beer commemorating his life was launched in 1968 *(see p.158)*, and in 1996 the brewery was renamed Thomas Hardy after a management buyout. Another period is remembered in the brewery's pale ale Royal Oak. This is named after the large, bushy tree (farther north, in Shropshire) in which King Charles II hid while fleeing the Parliamentarians. The beer has a fruity accent (raspberries, bananas?), but is well-balanced with a slightly syrupy maltiness, rounding into a lightly dry, earthy, hoppy (Goldings) finish.

ELDRIDGE POPE THOMAS HARDY COUNTRY BITTER

REGION OF ORIGIN	West of England, UK
STYLE	Bitter Ale
ALCOHOL CONTENT	3.4 abw (4.2 abv)
IDEAL SERVING TEMPERATURE	50–55° F (10–13° C)

Too much drink is bad, and leads us to the devil, concedes Thomas Hardy's poetically couched text on the label. On the other hand, some people never get the chance to enjoy even a pint, so those of us who do should make the most of it. Having passed to the great pub in the sky in 1928, he never had the opportunity to sample either the bitter or the barley wine named after him. His philosophical verse seems to favor the moderate alcohol of the bitter. It is hop-accented, and its fruitiness reminiscent of apples, with a touch of banana, though it does have a good balance of nutty malt. The hoppy acidity and malty sweetness are also in good equilibrium. A soothing and appetizing brew.

ELDRIDGE POPE
THOMAS HARDY'S ALE

REGION OF ORIGIN	West of England, UK
STYLE	Barley Wine/Old Ale
ALCOHOL CONTENT	9.6 abw (12.0 abv)
IDEAL SERVING TEMPERATURE	Store at 55° F (13° C)

The ultimate book-at-bedtime beer. Thomas Hardy wrote admiringly of the beers brewed in Dorchester by Eldridge Pope. On the 40th anniversary of his death, a festival to celebrate Hardy was held in Dorchester, and this beer launched for the event. It was intended as a one-off, but has since been produced at least once a year, with a vintage date. It is a beer that will mature in the bottle. When young, it can be as rich, creamy, and meaty as beef broth, though this has been less evident in recent bottlings. There may also be applewood smokiness. After about five years, it develops Madeira flavors, and samples at 25 years have proven lean, warming, and elegant.

THOMAS
HARDY'S ALE

THOMAS
HARDY'S ALE
VINTAGE 1997

In 'The Trumpet-Major' Hardy wrote of Dorchester's strong beer "It was of the most beautiful colour that the eye of an artist in beer could desire; full in body, yet brisk as a volcano; piquant, yet without a twang; luminous as an autumn sunset;..."

IMPORTED
FROM
ENGLAND

	REGION OF ORIGIN Eastern England, UK
	STYLE Porter/Dry Stout
	ALCOHOL CONTENT 4.0 abw (5.0 abv)
	IDEAL SERVING TEMPERATURE 50–55° F (10–13° C)

Taste the sea in this porter? It is fermented in part with a yeast recovered from bottles of porter found in an 1825 shipwreck on the bed of the English Channel. When the bottles were opened, some had filled with seawater, but others contained beer, with still-viable yeast. Flag Porter is produced by the Elgood's brewery of Wisbech, Cambridgeshire. The beer is lively and fruity, with woody, sooty, leathery, oily notes. It is perfect with the gamier varieties of oyster.

BREWED BY ELGOODS WISBECH.
FOR VINCEREMOS WINES & SPIRITS LTD. LEEDS

ORIGINAL

FLAG
PORTER
A Rich Dark
Ale

BREWED USING A TRADITIONAL 19TH CENTURY RECIPE. FERMENTED
WITH AN ORIGINAL 1825 YEAST RECOVERED FROM A SHIPWRECK IN
THE ENGLISH CHANNEL. A NATURAL SEDIMENT MAY OCCUR.

EMERSON'S 1812 INDIA PALE ALE

🛡	**REGION OF ORIGIN**	South Island, New Zealand
🍶	**STYLE**	India Pale Ale
⍟	**ALCOHOL CONTENT**	3.9 abw (4.9 abv))
🍺	**IDEAL SERVING TEMPERATURE**	54° F (12° C)

This new-generation brewery is in the New Zealand city of Dunedin. It makes some of New Zealand's best beers. Emerson's 1812 India Pale Ale is very appetizingly aromatic, with a spicy hop bouquet. There is also a great deal of hop flavor, rather than pure bitterness. The hop notes are set against a light, smooth, juicy, malt background. The flavors are beautifully combined, and the finish is fresh, dry, and faintly lemony. The inspiration for the brewery was a visit by George Emerson, a bio-chemist, to Edinburgh in 1983. He traveled with his son Richard, 18 at the time, who later established the business. Richard, who is almost entirely deaf, has nonetheless been a voluble publicist for his products.

ENVILLE ALE

REGION OF ORIGIN Midlands of England, UK

STYLE Honey Ale

ALCOHOL CONTENT 3.6 abw (4.5 abv)

IDEAL SERVING TEMPERATURE 50–55° F (10–13° C)

A drink fermented only from honey would be a mead, but this magical substance has long been used also as an addition to beer. The Mesopotamians may have employed it as a flavoring. Because honey is very fermentable, much of its obvious flavor would quickly vanish, but some traces always remain. In addition to that, the interaction of yeast and honey creates new, flowery, creamy flavors. Honey beers are made in several countries. A beekeeper, Will Constantine-Cort, established the Enville brewery in 1993, on an aristocratic estate near Stourbridge, England. The bees have access to lime trees, chestnut, hawthorn, flowering balsam, and all manner of nectar. Not surprisingly, Enville Ale, the brewery's first product, is distinctly flowery and perfumy.

E

Everards Daredevil

🛡 **REGION OF ORIGIN**	Midlands of England, UK
🍾 **STYLE**	Strong Ale
% **ALCOHOL CONTENT**	5.7 abw (7.1 abv)
🍺 **IDEAL SERVING TEMPERATURE**	50–55° F (10–13° C)

Dare you drink a beer this strong? That is all that Daredevil implies, though it does comply with a tradition of robust, and sometimes military, names from this brewery. Chairman Richard Everard served in the Household Cavalry, and the family traces its history in the city of Leicester to 1507. It first made beer there in 1849, later switched production to Burton, Britain's beer capital, and in the late 1980s opened its present brewery in Leicester. Its beers are full-flavored. Everards Daredevil, introduced in 1993 as a winter beer, is very robust. It has a sweetish, creamy aroma; a big body, which is very mouth-filling; flavors reminiscent of toffee, marmalade, and pepper; and a rather abrupt finish.

The old devils
Devilish images and names on beer labels are universal, from this one to its English neighbor Old Nick; Belgians like Duvel, Lucifer, and Satan; and France's Belzebuth.

EVERARDS TIGER BEST BITTER

⬥ **REGION OF ORIGIN** Midlands of England, UK

⬥ **STYLE** Bitter Ale

⬥ **ALCOHOL CONTENT** 3.6 abw (4.5 abv)

⬥ **IDEAL SERVING TEMPERATURE** 50–55° F (10–13° C)

The Tiger name derives from the Leicestershire Army Regiment that was stationed in India, and came to be known as the Tigers. Everards had simply called its principal beer "bitter" when bigger companies were inventing brand names for theirs, and in the 1970s Tiger was a late entrant to the keg beer market. Soon after, cask-conditioned beers became fashionable and in this form Tiger gained its reputation. The beer, as in a classic Burton ale, has a hint of sulfur on the nose. Its palate is rounded, nutty, and oily, with some orangey flavors and a dry finish. A stronger bitter, Everards' Old Original, has a similar balance and yet greater complexity.

Time for a tiger
Everards' Tiger is a well-known
name among British ales, and has
no connection with the Tiger of
Singapore and Kuala Lumpur.

FARSONS LACTO TRADITIONAL STOUT

🛡 **REGION OF ORIGIN** Malta
🍼 **STYLE** Sweet Stout
⅜ **ALCOHOL CONTENT** 2.7 abw (3.4 abv)
🍺 **IDEAL SERVING TEMPERATURE** 55° F (13° C)

As its name suggests, this stout contains lactose. Lacto Traditional Stout also has added vitamin B. It is a classic example of a beer marketed as a restorative. It is made by Farrugia and Sons ("Farsons"), on the island of Malta, where it is popular among nursing mothers. An important malt in this brew is the dark, sweetish style typically used to make mild ales. Crystal malt is also employed, perhaps contributing to the nutty, polished-oak aroma. The beer is light-bodied, but creamy and smooth, with rich flavors suggesting ginger, dark chocolate, and currants. It has a slightly yogurty finish.

Stout from the sea
The Roman god of the sea,
Neptune, arises from a garland of
malt and hops on Lacto's label.

FISCHERSTUBE UELI REVERENZ

🛡	**REGION OF ORIGIN**	Switzerland
🍾	**STYLE**	*Helles* Lager
%	**ALCOHOL CONTENT**	4.3 abw (5.4 abv)
🍺	**IDEAL SERVING TEMPERATURE**	48° F (9° C)

One of the first new-generation brewpubs in Europe was established at the Fischer café, in Basel, Switzerland, in 1975. The owner is a doctor of medicine, who playfully calls his brewery Jester *(Ueli)*. Among the beers is a *Helles* rather seriously called Reverenz. It is light and malty in its aroma and palate, with some cookielike flavors in the middle and a touch of hoppy tartness in a dryish finish.

FISH TALE MUD SHARK PORTER

REGION OF ORIGIN Pacific Northwest US

STYLE Porter/Stout

ALCOHOL CONTENT 4.4 abw (5.5 abv)

IDEAL SERVING TEMPERATURE 50–55° F (10–13° C)

Coastal name for a brewery founded in Olympia, capital city of Washington State, in 1993. Founder Crayne Horton also offers that his star sign is Pisces and that he once kept fish. The brewery's beers are big and robust. Mud Shark Porter has a peppery aroma, with hints of pears in cream and rich, dark chocolate that are carried through in the palate. The finish is toasty, roasty, and dry.

The beer that got away
The small print above the illustration
on the label brings the fisherman's
boast to the beer-drinker.

FLATLANDER'S EIGHTY SHILLING ALE

🛡 **REGION OF ORIGIN**	Midwest US
🍶 **STYLE**	Scottish Ale
⅍ **ALCOHOL CONTENT**	3.0 abw (3.7 abv)
🍺 **IDEAL SERVING TEMPERATURE**	50–55° F (10–13° C)

People from the Plains states of the US sometimes self-mockingly call themselves flatlanders. This brewery is in a large, Prairie-style restaurant between Chicago and Milwaukee. It is on the Illinois side of the state line with Wisconsin. The town is called Lincolnshire, but despite that English name, the brewery's most noteworthy product is a very authentic Scottish ale: typically full in color and textured in body, with a dryish, very faintly peaty maltiness. Scottish malt is used.

The homespun wisdom…
…of the Plains surrounds the label: "Drink good beer – be kind – tell the truth."

F

FRANKENHEIM ALT

🏞 **REGION OF ORIGIN** Düsseldorf, North Rhine-Westphalia, Germany

🍾 **STYLE** *Altbier*

％ **ALCOHOL CONTENT** 3.8 abw (4.8 abv)

🍺 **IDEAL SERVING TEMPERATURE** 48° F (9° C)

This light, dry, peppery, spicy *Altbier* is from a major privately-owned brewery in Düsseldorf. The brewery dates from the 1870s, and is still in the Frankenheim family. Another family-owned brewery, Diebels, of Issum, produces the biggest-selling Altbier nationally: a smooth, firm, malty example. Other privately-owned breweries specializing in this style include Rhenania (making a sweetish, slightly thick-tasting Altbier) and Gatzweiler (very fruity).

Private pride
"Privatbrauerei" on German beer labels implies that private owners can indulge their pride in making great beer rather than filling the pockets of their shareholders.

FRANZISKANER DUNKEL HEFE-WEISSBIER

🛡 **REGION OF ORIGIN** Munich, Upper Bavaria, Germany

🍶 **STYLE** Dark Wheat Beer

% **ALCOHOL CONTENT** 4.0 abw (5.0 abv)

🍺 **IDEAL SERVING TEMPERATURE**
48–54° F (9–12° C)

A Franciscan abbey brewery in Munich was acquired in 1858–61 by Josef Sedlmayr, whose family owned the Spaten brewery. In 1922, the two enterprises merged. The Franciscan strand in the company's heritage is celebrated by a range of light but tasty wheat beers, including this version. Like several other brewers, Spaten-Franziskaner uses the contradictory conjunction of "dark" and "white" in its name for this style. This brew has a toffeeish malt aroma, and a creamy, grainy palate. It finishes with some spiciness, suggesting cinnamon and pepper.

FREEDOM PILSENER

REGION OF ORIGIN	London, England, UK
STYLE	Pilsner
ALCOHOL CONTENT	4.0 abw (5.0 abv)
IDEAL SERVING TEMPERATURE	48° F (9° C)

Britain being traditionally an ale country, its brewers generally regard lager as a style to be made cheaply for drinkers who want something bland, and who respond less to flavor than heavy advertising. One of the few British lagers made with any stylistic seriousness is Freedom Pilsener, from a London microbrewery established in 1995. This beer has been variable, but at its best has a smooth maltiness and late dry, flowery hoppiness.

FREEMINER TRAFALGAR IPA

	REGION OF ORIGIN West of England, UK
	STYLE India Pale Ale
	ALCOHOL CONTENT 4.5 abw (6.0 abv)
	IDEAL SERVING TEMPERATURE 50–55° F (10–13° C)

The tiny Freeminer microbrewery, founded in 1992, sits between the shafts of a disused iron mine near the village of Coleford, in the Forest of Dean. Goldings hops from nearby Worcestershire impart a fragrant, cedary, lemon-zest note to Trafalgar India Pale Ale, which has a very long, sustained, appetizing, earthy dryness (60 units of bitterness). One of the brewery's earlier beers was called Hop Charmer. The hop-grower, at the splendidly named hamlet of Trumpet, near Much Marcle, was said to charm the climbing plants by playing blues guitar to them.

Britannia brews the waves
India Pale Ale is a maritime
style, and this example
celebrates a famous sea battle
near the Straits of Gibraltar.

F

FRAOCH HEATHER ALE

🛡 **REGION OF ORIGIN** Central Scotland, UK

🍾 **STYLE** Heather Ale

％ **ALCOHOL CONTENT** 4.0 abw (5.0 abv)

🍺 **IDEAL SERVING TEMPERATURE** 55° F (13° C)

The purple heather that warms the mountains of Scotland was a flavoring in the local beers long before hops were used. In the early 1990s, brewers Bruce and Scott Williams restored the tradition with their Fraoch ("heather" in Gaelic) Ale. The beer has a sunny, amber color; a flowery bouquet; a slightly oily body; and a spicy, apple-like, faintly winey finish. The heather is picked in July, and the new season's beer is available in August/September.

Pictish pint?
The hand-thrown ceramic
chalice is intended to
evoke past ceremonies.

FRÜH KÖLSCH

🛡 **REGION OF ORIGIN** North Rhine-Westphalia, Germany

🍾 **STYLE** *Kölschbier*

％ **ALCOHOL CONTENT** 3.8 abw (4.8 abv)

🍺 **IDEAL SERVING TEMPERATURE** 48° F (9° C)

Opposite the cathedral, on a street called Am Hof (after the Archbishop's Court), the turn-of-the-century tavern of P. J. Früh is the best-known destination for visitors wishing to sample *Kölschbier*. The beer was made on the premises until the 1980s, but is now brewed on a separate site, and is bottled for general sale. P. J. Früh is a classic Cologne pub, with the typical standing area jokingly known as the *Schwemme*. When it is crowded, the Schwemme may seem like a swimming bath, but the reference is actually to a place where horses are watered. Deeper into the pub are scrubbed wooden tables, where the beer is enjoyed with snacks of cheese, blood sausage, and pork *Mettwurst*. The beer has a faint strawberry fruitiness of aroma; a creamy malt background; and an elegant balancing dryness of hop.

FULL SAIL ENDEAVOUR AMBER ALE

REGION OF ORIGIN	New South Wales, Australia
STYLE	Amber/Brown Ale
ALCOHOL CONTENT	3.9 abw (4.9 abv)
IDEAL SERVING TEMPERATURE	50–55° F (10–13° C)

Inspired by the original Full Sail microbrewery, in windsurfing country on the Columbia River in Oregon. After working at another brewery in the same state, Bob Wessler decided to move to Australia, where he had family connections, and where the micro movement was still in its early stages. In 1997, he and his partner Jennifer Colosi established the Sydney Harbour Brewery, and called their first beer Full Sail. This robust ale is firm, malt-accented and, after a hint of sweetness, quite dry. Restrained orangey flavors develop, reminiscent of fruit-in-cream (a hint of vanilla?), and there are suggestions of ginger and bitter chocolate in the finish.

FULL SAIL WASSAIL WINTER ALE

🛡 **REGION OF ORIGIN** Northwest US

🍾 **STYLE** Old Ale

% **ALCOHOL CONTENT** 5.3 abw (6.5 abv)

🍺 **IDEAL SERVING TEMPERATURE** 50–55° F (10–13° C)

The original Oregonian Full Sail, founded in 1987, is at Hood River, where the waterway of that name meets the Columbia. There is also an associated brewpub in nearby Portland. One of the original products is a beautifully rounded Amber inspired by Samuel Smith's Pale Ale from Tadcaster, England. A wide range also includes Wassail. Not only is this winter brew a triumphant combination of alliteration and rhyme, it is an awesome ale, pungent and powerful. It has a garnet color, spicy aroma, oily texture, and an intensely dry, sappy, brandyish finish. Full Sail was in 1998 acquired from its founding partners in a buyout by its employees.

FULLER'S 1845 STRONG ALE

REGION OF ORIGIN London, England, UK

STYLE Strong Ale

ALCOHOL CONTENT 5.1 abw (6.3 abv)

IDEAL SERVING TEMPERATURE 55° F (13° C)

In some parts of the world, the ales of the Fuller's brewery have a cult following for their big flavors and superb balance. Within Britain, much of the beer is sold very locally, in the suburbs around the brewery on the road from London's Heathrow airport. Fuller's 1845 was launched in 1995 to commemorate the 150th anniversary of the company. Having live yeast in the bottle, it will condition (mature) for several months, becoming rounder in flavor. It has a sherbety, orangey aroma; a smooth, liqueurlike body; faintly chocolatey, toasty malt flavors; and a crisp, very dry finish. For a relatively strong ale, it is perilously easy to drink.

Newsflash
The corner flash on the label announces this beer's award as Britain's bottle-conditioned beer of the year for 1998–99.

FULLER'S ESB

	REGION OF ORIGIN London, England, UK
	STYLE Strong Bitter
	ALCOHOL CONTENT On draft: 4.4 abw (5.5 abv); In bottle: 5.9 abv (4.7 abw)
	IDEAL SERVING TEMPERATURE 50–55° F (10–13° C)

This famous beer was launched as Winter Bitter in 1969, and renamed ESB (Extra Special Bitter) in 1971, when it became a year-round brew. For a short time, another brewery in England used the same term, but today in Britain ESB is specifically a Fuller's brand name. Such is the renown of this beer in the United States that many micro-brewers there use the term ESB to denote a style, indicating a strong bitter (fuller in color, maltier, fruitier, and less hoppy than an IPA). The original from Fuller's is malt accented, but with a robust balance of hop bitterness, the two flavors held together by honeyish esters from the house yeast. It is a world classic.

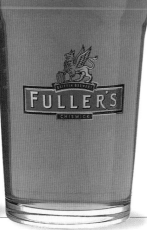

The Fuller flavor
Fuller's ESB is best known as a cask-conditioned (unpasteurized) draft. Pasteurization can reduce flavor and texture so bottled versions are brewed stronger.

FULLER'S LONDON PRIDE

🏷 **REGION OF ORIGIN** London, England, UK

🍾 **STYLE** Bitter Ale

% **ALCOHOL CONTENT** On draft: 3.2 abw (4.1 abv); In bottle: 3.8 abw (4.7 abv)

🍺 **IDEAL SERVING TEMPERATURE** 50–55° F (10–13° C)

Like many British breweries, Fuller's has several examples of bitter. The low-strength, summery Chiswick Bitter (named after the brewery's neighborhood) is refreshingly flowery in its hop character. This is a typically English approach: a beer that is full of flavor but light in body and alcohol, so that several pints can be consumed over the course of an evening. In the middle comes London Pride, with beautifully combined flavors of light, smoothly nutty malt, crisply bitter hop, and faintly honeyish yeast. This is a more satisfying, soothing bitter. Drinkers wanting a little more punch, and perhaps only one pint, opt for the Extra Special Bitter *(see previous page)*.

GAFFEL KÖLSCH

REGION OF ORIGIN	Cologne, Germany
STYLE	*Kölsch*
ALCOHOL CONTENT	3.8 abw (4.8 abv)
IDEAL SERVING TEMPERATURE	48° F (9° C)

The name Gaffel is used here to celebrate the rise of medieval guilds as a precursor of democracy. This respected brewery in Cologne, Germany, traces its history to a brewpub in 1302, and has been in the present family since 1908. This brewery is in the heart of town, just behind the train station. The principal of the company has a remarkable personal museum of steins, glasses, and advertising, but this can be seen only by arrangement. Gaffel has a handsome tavern in the Old Town, at 20–22 Alter Markt. It specializes in *Kölsch*, the city's own delicate, golden style of ale. Gaffel Kölsch has a faint fruitiness in aroma; a light but firm, drily nutty palate; and a crisply flowery, hoppy finish.

GAMBRINUS BÍLÉ

G

🛡 **REGION OF ORIGIN**	Pilsen, Bohemia, Czech Republic
🍾 **STYLE**	*Hefeweizen*
% **ALCOHOL CONTENT**	4.0 abw (5.1 abv)
🍺 **IDEAL SERVING TEMPERATURE**	48–54° F (9–12° C)

The name Gambrinus is a corruption of Jan Primus (Jean, first Duke of Brabant, *c*.1251–95). He was born in Burgundy, and ruled what is now largely Belgium, but he is celebrated in many countries as the legendary King of Beer. Through marriage between royal houses, one of his descendants was the King of Bohemia, the Czech state in which the city of Pilsen stands. The Gambrinus brewery was founded in 1869, in Pilsen. Around the time of World War I, it moved to a site adjoining Pilsner Urquell. Like its neighbor, Gambrinus is known for a beer in the Pilsner style. In recent years, it has added this perfumy, peachy, tart, light wheat beer.

Welcome back, wheat
On the label, the word Bilé means
"white." In the distant past, Bohemia
was especially known for wheat beers.
When golden lagers were developed in
the 1840s, wheat beers vanished. Now
Gambrinus has revived the style.

GAMBRINUS PILSNER

🛡 **REGION OF ORIGIN**	Pilsen, Bohemia, Czech Republic
🍷 **STYLE**	Pilsner
% **ALCOHOL CONTENT**	4.0 abw (5.0 abv)
🍺 **IDEAL SERVING TEMPERATURE**	48° F (9° C)

In the Czech Republic, only a brewery in the city may term itself a Pilsner. The original Pilsner Urquell (see p.366), a now-defunct enterprise called World Brew, and Gambrinus were built next to each other on a valley rising from the city center. The Napoleonic arch of Pilsner Urquell and the imposing gateway to Gambrinus are along the same stretch of road. In its home country, Gambrinus is very popular as a reasonably hoppy lager that is neither as big nor as assertive as Pilsner Urquell, but broadly similar in style. Recent bottlings, labelled in German as Gambrinus "Helles Export Lager From Pilsen," have had a spicy aroma; a lightly creamy palate; and a leafy, minty hop in the finish.

GAMBRINUS PURKMISTR

G

🛡 **REGION OF ORIGIN**	Pilsen/Domazlice, Bohemia, Czech Republic
🍾 **STYLE**	Dark Lager
% **ALCOHOL CONTENT**	3.8 abw (4.7 abv)
🍶 **IDEAL SERVING TEMPERATURE**	48° F (9° C)

This beer was first made at a very old local brewery in Domazlice, south of Pilsen and near the German border. That brewery was founded in 1341, but closed in 1996, and production switched to Gambrinus. The word *Purkmistr* is the Czech counterpart to the German *Burgermeister*, meaning "Mayor." The beer is a dark lager. Czech dark lagers tend to have a fuller color and a softer, richer flavor than those from across the German border, where the style originates. The Czech brews are perhaps like earlier interpretations from Germany, as remembered in the style now known as *Schwarz* black beer. Export bottlings of Purkmistr use the German phrase *Das Echte Schwarz-Bier aus Böhmen* ("the real black beer of Bohemia"). This beer has an aniseed aroma; flavors reminiscent of figs and grainy coffee; a light but smooth body; and a note of bitter chocolate in the finish. A soothing brew or a lightish after-dinner beer.

GARDE KÖLSCH

🏵 **REGION OF ORIGIN** Dormagen, North Rhine-Westphalia, Germany

🍶 **STYLE** *Kölschbier*

％ **ALCOHOL CONTENT** 3.8 abw (4.8 abv)

🍺 **IDEAL SERVING TEMPERATURE** 48° F (9° C)

The first golden beer in the region, a heavier parent to today's *Kölsch*, is said to have been brewed by Garde in 1898. Today's Garde Kölsch is very soft and fresh, with a light, clean, dessert-apple fruitiness and a dry finish. It is a very good example of the style, and one of the fullest in flavor. In Cologne, the beer can be found on draft at the Bei d'r Tant in Cäcilienstrasse. Garde Kölsch is popular on the town's north side. The brewery is north of the city, at Dormagen, in the direction of Düsseldorf.

Guarding the style
Garde, named after the German Imperial
Guard, stands at the perimeter of the defined
Kölsch-producing region.

GEARY'S PALE ALE

🛡 **REGION OF ORIGIN** Northeast US

🍾 **STYLE** Pale Ale

% **ALCOHOL CONTENT** 3.6 abw (4.5 abv)

🍺 **IDEAL SERVING TEMPERATURE** 50–55° F (10–13° C)

Among American pale ales, this is an East Coast classic from one of the early new-generation brewers. It has big, assertive flavours, in a muscular balance, with a crisply appetizing finish. The beer starts smooth and firmly malty; develops some rounded, orangey fruitiness; and finishes with clean, dry, tingly hop flavors. The brewery was established in Portland, in the lobster state of Maine, in 1986. David Geary, an American, developed his skills at Ringwood, England; Greenmantle, Scotland; and various other British breweries.

GILDEN KÖLSCH

🛡 **REGION OF ORIGIN** Cologne, North Rhine-Westphalia, Germany

🍾 **STYLE** *Kölschbier*

% **ALCOHOL CONTENT** 3.8 abw (4.8 abv)

🍺 **IDEAL SERVING TEMPERATURE** 9°C (48°F)

Very flowery in aroma – an attribute of a good *Kölsch*. The palate is light, sherbety, and slightly winey. This beer is made by the Bergische Löwen brewery, in Mülheim, across the river from the city center of Cologne. This brewery is owned by the national group Brau und Brunnen. The brewery also produces Sion Kölsch, which seems maltier, with a pear-brandy fruitiness and a late hop dryness. Sion has a tavern in the city center, in a street called Unter Taschenmacher.

Gilding the glass
Gilden takes its name from a trade guild. Today's Association of Brewers in Cologne protects the Kölsch style and its region of production.

GINDER ALE

🛡 **REGION OF ORIGIN**	Province of Flemish Brabant, Belgium
🍶 **STYLE**	Belgian Ale
% **ALCOHOL CONTENT**	4.1 abw (5.1 abv)
🍺 **IDEAL SERVING TEMPERATURE**	50° F (10° C)

Not "ginger": the man who created this beer was called Van Ginderachter. It is a lively, appetizing beer with apple-brandy flavors deriving from a distinct yeast. Ginder Ale is made by the same company as Stella Artois, in the brewing city of Leuven. The same company, Interbrew, also makes the smooth, anise-tinged Horse Ale and the sherbety, faintly smoky Vieux Temps *(see p.481)*.

GOLDEN HILL EXMOOR GOLD

	REGION OF ORIGIN West of England, UK
	STYLE Golden Ale
	ALCOHOL CONTENT 4.0 abw (5.0 abv)
	IDEAL SERVING TEMPERATURE 50° F (10° C)

At Wiveliscombe, Somerset, a brewery that had been closed for 20 years was brought back to life in 1980. Six years later, the brewery pioneered golden ales in Britain. This beer is made with only one variety of barley: Pipkin, malted in the next county, at Newton Abbot, Devon. The beer is fresh-tasting, firm, creamy, dryish, with a hint of dessert apples.

Single malt
Behind the bottle, a back
label refers to the use of
just one malt.

GORDON BIERSCH MÄRZEN

🛡 **REGION OF ORIGIN** California, US

🍾 **STYLE** *Märzen-Oktoberfest* Lager

％ **ALCOHOL CONTENT** 4.6 abw (5.8 abv)

🍺 **IDEAL SERVING TEMPERATURE** 48° F (9° C)

Some of the best beer-friendly food in the United States is found in the small chain of brewery-restaurants founded in California (initially in Palo Alto), in 1988 by Dan Gordon and Dean Biersch. Despite his beery name, Biersch is the restaurateur. Gordon is one of the few Americans to have graduated in brewing at Weihenstephan, Bavaria. Their Märzen has a good bronze-red colour; a light but smooth body; a spicy, fruity, malt character; and a dry, whiskyish finish.

GORDON HIGHLAND SCOTCH ALE

REGION OF ORIGIN Southern Scotland, UK

STYLE Strong Scottish Ale

ALCOHOL CONTENT 6.9 abw (8.6 abv)

IDEAL SERVING TEMPERATURE 50–55° F (10–13° C)

The Christmas beer under the Gordon name *(see p.190)* has this year-round counterpart with a marginally less hefty alcohol content but a big, fresh, rich maltiness and toasty balance. Both are made for the Belgian market by Scottish Courage. A similar beer, slightly less strong (5.8 abw; 7.3 abv) but with all the richness of a fruit-filled chocolate praline, was launched in the British market in 1998 under the name McEwan's No. 1 Champion Ale.

GORDON XMAS

🛡 **REGION OF ORIGIN**	Southern Scotland, UK
🍾 **STYLE**	Strong Scottish Ale
% **ALCOHOL CONTENT**	7.0 abw (8.8 abv)
🍺 **IDEAL SERVING TEMPERATURE**	55° F (13° C)

Scotland may celebrate Christmas less than New Year, but as a cold northern country, it has a use for the rich and warming ales that were introduced to Belgium by British regiments in two world wars. Scottish Courage brews this beer in Edinburgh for the Belgian market. It is a ruby-to-black ale, pouring with a mountainous head. It has a clean, sweet maltiness, but finishes with a toasty dryness. Much the same brew is made for France under the name Douglas.

Gose Ohne Bedenken

🛡	**REGION OF ORIGIN** Lower Saxony, Germany
🍾	**STYLE** *Gose*
%	**ALCOHOL CONTENT** 3.8 abw (4.8 abv)
🌡	**IDEAL SERVING TEMPERATURE** 48–50° F (9–10° C)

The German town of Goslar, Lower Saxony, is said to have given its name to this style of wheat beer, which was once popular in Leipzig. The style has recently been revived by that city's Ohne Bedenken taproom and beer garden. *Gose* is a wheat beer, lightly spiced with salt. It is also flavored with coriander, and emerges with a citric palate. Traditionally, it is matured in flasks with a narrow neck, so that the yeasty head creates a natural bung to foster carbonation. The beer is typically served with a local version of Camembert cheese, sometimes with a digestif of *Allasch*, an almond-flavored version of the caraway liqueur *Kümmel*.

GOUDEN CAROLUS

🛡 **REGION OF ORIGIN**	Province of Antwerp, Belgium
🍶 **STYLE**	Strong Brown Ale
⊗ **ALCOHOL CONTENT**	6.0 abw (7.5 abv)
🍺 **IDEAL SERVING TEMPERATURE**	55°F (13° C)

The name means "Golden Charles," in a blend of Flemish and Latin. Its origins are in the Holy Roman Empire. It could refer to Charlemagne (742–814), who ruled Europe from Aix-la-Chapelle (Aachen), not far away. Or, more likely, to Charles V (1500–58), who grew up in Malines (Mechelen), where the brewery stands. Part of the brewery is in the premises of a former *beguinage* (religious sisterhood), dating from the 1400s. The business, under the name Het Anker ("The Anchor"), has been run by one family since the 1870s, but production has been irregular in recent years. Gouden Carolus is a Flemish strong brown ale, spiced with orange peels and coriander. At its best, it starts with suggestions of toffee, orange, and passion fruit, then becomes quite tart, and finishes with a spicy, cedary character. Look out for old editions conditioned in the bottle. Delicious with chocolate.

GRANITE BREWERY PECULIAR

🛡 **REGION OF ORIGIN** Nova Scotia, Canada

🍾 **STYLE** Old Ale/Strong Ale

% **ALCOHOL CONTENT** 4.5 abw (5.6 abv)

🍺 **IDEAL SERVING TEMPERATURE** 50–55° F (10–13° C)

Inspired by Theakston's Old Peculier (see p.451), but opting for a more conventional spelling, this Canadian beer is similar in style but slightly paler in color and lighter in body. It pours with a lively, bubbly head; has a fresh, minty, hop aroma; very nutty, creamy, toffeeish, satisfying flavors; and an appetizing, leafy dryness in the finish. The beer was first made in the Granite brewpub in rocky Nova Scotia. That brewery was established in 1985. There are now two granite breweries there, in Halifax, and a third in Toronto, Ontario.

Rock solid
The first Granite brewery was in a building of that stone, but the name is metaphorical. "We wanted a business as solid as rock," says one of the founders.

G

GREAT LAKES DORTMUNDER GOLD

🛡	**REGION OF ORIGIN**	Midwest US
🍾	**STYLE**	Dortmunder Export
(%)	**ALCOHOL CONTENT**	4.5 abw (5.6 abv)
🥛	**IDEAL SERVING TEMPERATURE**	48° F (9° C)

The Great Lakes microbrewery and brewpub (2516 Market St.) was founded in 1988 in the city of Cleveland, Ohio, on Lake Erie. The pub, in the former Market Tavern, has bullet holes from the days of Eliot Ness, who was Cleveland's grandly titled Director of Public Safety. He is said to have frequented the original tavern. The present brewpub is known for big, malty beers. Its Dortmunder has a very full color and body for the style, though its grainy dryness and touch of newly mown hay are exemplary. In general, the most robust interpretations of the Dortmunder Export style are today found in the US.

Gold label
The beer's label brandishes a gold medal won at the Great American Beer Festival, which is held each October in Denver, Colorado. No beer festival anywhere in the world has as many brews or styles.

GREAT LAKES THE EDMUND FITZGERALD PORTER

🛡	**REGION OF ORIGIN**	Midwest US
🍷	**STYLE**	Strong Porter
%	**ALCOHOL CONTENT**	5.0 abw (6.25 abv)
🍺	**IDEAL SERVING TEMPERATURE**	48° F (9° C)

During restoration work at the Great Lakes pub and brewery, a sign from the 1920s or earlier was exposed announcing, "Kennett Ales and Porter on Draft, for Family and Medicinal Purposes." Today's pub makes no such claims for its porter, but its restaurant does use this big, rich brew in a chocolate cake. The beer is smooth, creamy, jammy, and toasty, with a coffeeish dryness. Very well-balanced, and remarkably drinkable for its strength. It was named for a vessel that sank on Lake Superior and was memorialized in a song by Gordon Lightfoot called "The Wreck of the Edmund Fitzgerald."

GREAT LAKES THE ELIOT NESS

REGION OF ORIGIN	Midwest US
STYLE	Vienna Lager
ALCOHOL CONTENT	4.5 abw (5.6 abv)
IDEAL SERVING TEMPERATURE	48° F (9° C)

Gang-buster Eliot Ness, Cleveland's Director of Public Safety, inspired the television series and movie *The Untouchables*. The city's Great Lakes brewery and pub, proud of its bullet holes from those days, honors Eliot Ness with a very serious Vienna-style lager. This beer is rich, creamy, and malty, in both aroma and palate, with a late balance of whiskeyish oakiness and tingling acidity. A big Midwestern beer, to go with a Chicago-style deep-dish pizza, or focaccia bread.

GREENE KING ABBOT ALE

REGION OF ORIGIN	Eastern England, UK
STYLE	Pale Ale
ALCOHOL CONTENT	4.0 abw (5.0 abv)
IDEAL SERVING TEMPERATURE	50–55° F (10–13° C)

The brewery is in the town of Bury St. Edmunds, Suffolk. Edmund was the King of Anglia (from which the word "England" originates). He was murdered by Vikings, and buried at the site of what became a powerful abbey. The brewery, next to the home of the last abbot, dates from at least the 1700s. The Greene family became involved some time after 1799. Sons of the family have included a famously liberal governor of the BBC, and the novelist Graham Greene, who visited the brewery on his 80th birthday. Abbot Ale has a hoppy aroma; a firm, dry palate, with lightly spicy, perfumy, hop flavors; and a long, dry, appetizing finish.

Aristocratic ale
When the beer was introduced in 1955, an artist created an imaginary abbot. His model was an old portrait of Herbert Henry Asquith, first Earl of Oxford, who seems to have had no connection with beer or abbeys.

GREENE KING STRONG SUFFOLK

REGION OF ORIGIN	Eastern England, UK
STYLE	Old Ale
ALCOHOL CONTENT	4.8 abw (6.0 abv)
IDEAL SERVING TEMPERATURE	50–55° F (10–13° C)

Many English breweries once aged beer in wooden tuns, blending old and new to achieve equilibrium. Greene King is the last to do so with this speciality, which deserves to be much better known in its home country. The key ingredient is a strong ale matured in ceiling-high wooden tuns for between one and five years. The beer is less sour than its European counterparts, but iron-tasting, sappy, peppery, and winey. It has been served at dinners of the local brewers' guild with pickled herrings. It is also good with blue cheese, especially English Stilton.

King's influence
When King Henry VIII "dissolved" the abbeys in the 1500s, the monks of St. Edmunds hid in tunnels that probably gave rise to the cellars in which the beer is today matured.

GROLSCH BAZUIN

🛡	**REGION OF ORIGIN**	Eastern Netherlands
🍺	**STYLE**	Spiced Ale
%	**ALCOHOL CONTENT**	5.2 abw (6.5 abv)
🍶	**IDEAL SERVING TEMPERATURE**	48° F (9° C)

The Grolsch brewery, with its distinctive swing-top bottle, takes its name from its home town, originally called Grolle (now Groenlo), in The Netherlands. Grolsch, which traces its history to 1676, has breweries in Groenlo and Enschede. Its well-known principal product is a lightly hoppy Pilsner-style beer, but it also has a range of specialities. Although similar to the English "bassoon" (derived from "bass sound"), the Dutch *bazuin* means trumpet or trombone. Perhaps this is a very resonant beer. It is intended to evoke the first brews from Grolle. The recipe includes cardamom, cinnamon, clove, ginger, licorice, mace, nutmeg, and pimento. The beer is toffeeish, with pronounced licorice, developing to a lemony acidity and a warming, spicy finish that is dry and bitter. A wonderful bedtime brew.

GROLSCH WINTERVORST

REGION OF ORIGIN	Eastern Netherlands
STYLE	Spiced Ale
ALCOHOL CONTENT	6.0 abw (7.5 abv)
IDEAL SERVING TEMPERATURE	48° F (10° C)

The name of this beer means "Winter Frost." It is a distinctive and flavorsome strong ale in a "Four Seasons" range from this Dutch brewer Grolsch. Wintervorst is spiced with clover, honey, and orange peel. It pours with a big, rocky, well-retained head; an aromatic, malty bouquet; rich, sweet, appetizing, licorice-like flavors; a lightly oily, soothing, smooth body; and a gently herbal, flowery finish.

Vorst of both worlds
"Frost" and "first" sound as similar in Dutch as in English. The wintry king (the "first" person) on the label and glass depicts this wordplay.

GROZET GOOSEBERRY & WHEAT ALE

🛡 **REGION OF ORIGIN** Central Scotland, UK

🍾 **STYLE** Gooseberry Ale

％ **ALCOHOL CONTENT** 4.0 abw (5.0 abv)

🍺 **IDEAL SERVING TEMPERATURE** 55° F (13° C)

The name is Scottish for gooseberry. The use of this ingredient in beer was mentioned by Robert Burns, Sir Walter Scott, and James Hogg, the shepherd who became a narrative poet. Revivalist brewers Bruce and Scott Williams introduced their gooseberry beer in 1996. Its basis is a brew of 20 percent wheat and 80 percent barley malt and it is flavored with bog myrtle and meadowsweet. The beer is perfumy and spritzy, with a tangy suggestion of gooseberry skins. Like the Williams' elderberry, heather, and pine brews, it is produced in Strathaven, near Glasgow, and in Alloa. The beer is available in September.

*Ploughman's pint?
...or a shepherd's lunch?
The gooseberry beer is
offered with a leather
drinking vessel.*

GUERNSEY MILK STOUT

REGION OF ORIGIN Guernsey, Channel Islands

STYLE Sweet Stout

ALCOHOL CONTENT 2.6 abw (3.3 abv)

IDEAL SERVING TEMPERATURE 55° F (13° C)

After World War II, "Milk Stout" was a popular colloquialism. The UK Ministry of Food eventually deemed it misleading, but such legislation does not apply on the Channel Islands. With their reputation for dairy cattle, it seems appropriate that they still have a Milk Stout. Disappointingly, this does not contain lactose. It nonetheless has a deliciously creamy flavor, drying in a chewy, licorice-toffee finish.

Polo pint
The trademark of the brewery is a polo pony, reflecting a past owner's enthusiasm.

GUEUZE GIRARDIN

🛡 **REGION OF ORIGIN** Province of Flemish Brabant, Belgium

🍶 **STYLE** *Gueuze-lambic*

% **ALCOHOL CONTENT** 4.0 abw (5.0 abv)

🍺 **IDEAL SERVING TEMPERATURE** 55° F (13° C)

An aristocrat's estate brewery that passed into the hands of the Girardin family several generations ago. This diligent family runs the brewery with no staff, and even grows its own wheat. The brewery, at St. Ulriks Kapelle, in the traditional region of *gueuze* production, still has a mill that grinds the grain between stones. Gueuze Girardin is elegant, lean and complex; perfumy and dry; with unfolding flavors of cedar, hay, and acacia honey.

Vintage years
The brewery dates from 1845, and has been in the family since 1882. Three years in the bottle makes for a classic.

GUINNESS EXTRA STOUT

REGION OF ORIGIN Republic of Ireland

STYLE Dry Stout

ALCOHOL CONTENT 3.4 abw (4.2 abv)

IDEAL SERVING TEMPERATURE 50–55° F (10–13° C)

The world's most famous dry stout. Arthur Guinness was a country brewer in Ireland before setting up in Dublin in 1759. It was originally an ale brewery, but began to make porter in the 1770s. During World War I, fuel restrictions made it difficult for British maltsters to roast their grains, but this was still permitted in Ireland. "Plain Porter" was dropped in the 1970s and, despite a brief revival of that style in the 1990s, Guinness is best known in both Ireland and Britain for its Extra Stout. The bottled version sold in Ireland best highlights the oaky-seeming dryness that is distinctive to Guinness. The creamier draft counterpart is nitrogenated. There are many other versions in different parts of the world, notably the 7.5 percent Dublin-brewed Foreign Extra Stout, which is very slightly soured so that its richness will not be cloying.

GULPENER DORT

REGION OF ORIGIN Province of Limburg, the Netherlands

STYLE Dutch Strong Dortmunder Export

ALCOHOL CONTENT 5.2 abw (6.5 abv)

IDEAL SERVING TEMPERATURE 48° F (9° C)

The village of Gulpen is south of Maastricht, in the Netherlands, but close to Belgium and Germany. The Gulpener brewery's products include this Dort, a shorter but darker and stronger echo of the German style. It has a marshmallowy maltiness, balanced by a leafy hop finish. Nearby, De Leeuw has a slightly drier Dortmunder *(see p.137)*; Alfa a creamy Super Dortmunder *(see p.20)*, even stronger; and De Ridder the well-balanced Maltezer *(see p.140)*.

GULPENER KORENWOLF

REGION OF ORIGIN Province of Limburg, the Netherlands

STYLE Belgian-style Wheat Beer

ALCOHOL CONTENT 4.0 abw (5.0 abv)

IDEAL SERVING TEMPERATURE 48–50° F (9–10° C)

A "grain wolf" is a hamster, a creature that gathers grain in summer and stores it for the winter. The Dutch, living in a tiny and physically vulnerable country, have an affection for all that is small, industrious, and prudent. Korenwolf is a Belgian-style wheat beer with an earthy perfume and a big, fruity attack. It is full of flavor: refreshing, satisfying, and appetizing. The beer is made by the respected Gulpener brewery, near the city of Maastricht.

HACKER-PSCHORR ALT MUNICH DARK

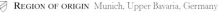

🛡 **REGION OF ORIGIN** Munich, Upper Bavaria, Germany

🍾 **STYLE** Munich Dark Lager

% **ALCOHOL CONTENT** 4.2 abw (5.2 abv)

🍺 **IDEAL SERVING TEMPERATURE** 48° F (9° C)

Composer Richard Strauss was the son of Josephine Pschorr, and he dedicated his most famous work, *Der Rosenkavalier*, to the brewing family that financed him. Hacker-Pschorr's "Old" Munich Dark has a creamy aroma and flavor, with notes of cinnamon, and a lightly syrupy body. Try it with veal sausages.

Hacked off
Hacker-Pschorr has its own range of products, though it has long been owned by Paulaner, and in recent years ceased to operate its own brewery.

HAECHT WITBIER

REGION OF ORIGIN	Province of Flemish Brabant, Belgium
STYLE	Belgian Wheat Beer
ALCOHOL CONTENT	3.8 abw (4.8 abv)
IDEAL SERVING TEMPERATURE	48–50° F (9–10° C)

The older spelling of the village of Haecht, between Brussels, Leuven, and Mechelen. This company began as a dairy in the 1800s, and later added a brewery. It uses a magnificently restored 1930s brewhouse. The company is best known for its Pilsner-style beer. It also produces this dry, grainy, Belgian white, which in aroma and flavor emphasizes the wheat rather than the fruit and spices.

HAIR OF THE DOG ADAM

🛡	**REGION OF ORIGIN** Pacific Northwest US
🍾	**STYLE** *Adam Bier*
%	**ALCOHOL CONTENT** 8.0 abw (10.0 abv)
🥛	**IDEAL SERVING TEMPERATURE** 50–57° F (10–14° C)

The bulldog on the label is intended to communicate character and this tiny brewery, in Portland, Oregon, specializes in extremely robust and unusual beers. *Adam Bier* was a style produced in Dortmund in the days when the city made strong, top-fermenting, dark brews. King Frederick William IV of Prussia is said to have guzzled a large tankard on a hot day and been rendered unconscious for more than 24 hours. There is little information on the original Adam Bier, so this is a free interpretation. It is syrupy, with suggestions of hocolate, roasted ppers, and peat. ottle-conditioned beer ishing complexity.

H

HALE'S HARVEST ALE

REGION OF ORIGIN Pacific Northwest US

STYLE Strong Ale

ALCOHOL CONTENT 3.6 abw (4.5 abv)

IDEAL SERVING TEMPERATURE 50–55° F (10–13° C)

Inspired by a brief spell in 1981, working as an "apprentice" at near-namesake Gale's brewery in Hampshire, England, young American Mike Hale fired his own kettles in Washington State in 1983. He now has an English-accented microbrewery in Spokane and a brewpub in the Seattle suburb of Fremont. His Harvest Ale has the aroma of fruit gums; a juicy palate; and a clean apple note in a dry, perfumy finish.

Hale and hearty
"Rich, robust and distinctive…as brisk
and refreshing as a fall morning," says
Hale's publicity material.

HALE'S SPECIAL BITTER

🛡 **REGION OF ORIGIN** Pacific Northwest US

🍾 **STYLE** English Bitter

％ **ALCOHOL CONTENT** 3.8 abw (4.7 abv)

🥛 **IDEAL SERVING TEMPERATURE** 50–55° F (10–13° C)

Apart from some well-regarded seasonal brews, Mike Hale makes a solid range of regulars at his microbreweries in Seattle and Spokane, Washington. Hale's Special Bitter has a big, rocky head and is dark reddish-amber. It is full of flavor: malty and rounded, with fruity notes reminiscent of glacé cherries and candied peel. It has a spritzy, dry finish. Its initials, HSB, are shared with a similar beer made by Hale's inspiration, Gale's, in Horndean, near Portsmouth, England.

Hale's and Gale's
The stylized tankard forms a letter
"H". Is the initial in HSB for
Hale's or Horndean?

HALLERTAU AUER PILS

REGION OF ORIGIN Upper Bavaria, Germany

STYLE Pilsner

ALCOHOL CONTENT 3.9 abw (4.9 abv)

IDEAL SERVING TEMPERATURE 48° F (9° C)

Germany's best-known hop-growing region is the Hallertau, just to the north of Munich. In the heart of the region, in the village of Au, there has been a brewery on the estate of the aristocratic Beck von Peccoz family since 1590. This *Schloss* (castle or, in this instance, château) brewery produces a lively, bubbly Pilsner, with a fresh aroma; textured malt character; and well-combined flavors of leafy, dry hop. A hop-country classic.

Less majesty
This is the classic label and glass, but younger drinkers are wooed with a version called Becco.

Hansa Urbock

REGION OF ORIGIN Namibia, Southern Africa

STYLE May Bock

ALCOHOL CONTENT 4.8 abw (6.0 abv)

IDEAL SERVING TEMPERATURE 48° F (9° C)

The company name is an old German word for a guild of merchants. "Ur" means "original." This traditional May Bock is made in the former German Southwest Africa, now known as Namibia. It is surely the most remote example of the style. Hansa Urbock, made according to the German Beer Purity Law, has a bright, tawny color; a sweet toffee aroma and flavor; a smooth, medium body; and a brandyish finish. Hansa has some far lighter beers in its range of ten products. Its flagship Windhoek Lager has only 3.2 abw (4.0 abv), but is hoppier than most standard beers in Southern Africa. The company uses the slogan, "Naturally brewed, in the German tradition." The enterprise dates from 1920, and has breweries in Windhoek and Swakopmund. It brews Holsten under licence.

HARVEYS 1859 PORTER

REGION OF ORIGIN South of England, UK

STYLE Porter/Stout

ALCOHOL CONTENT 3.8 abw (4.8 abv)

IDEAL SERVING TEMPERATURE 50–55° F (10–13° C)

A traditional brewery in the old river port of Lewes, East Sussex. The business dates from the 1700s, and the timbered brewery from the following century. Reintroduced in 1993, this porter is based on an 1859 recipe and uses traditional brown malt. The beer has hopsack and cedar in the aroma; medicinal, bitter chocolate notes in the palate; and a powerful, roasty dryness in the finish.

Best bottlings
Harveys 1859 Porter occasionally
appears in bottle-conditioned
form. This is less stable but
can develop great complexity.

Harveys Tom Paine Strong Pale Ale

🛡 **Region of origin**	South of England, UK
🍾 **Style**	Pale Ale
% **Alcohol content**	4.4 abw (5.5 abv)
🥂 **Ideal serving temperature**	50–55° F (10–13° C)

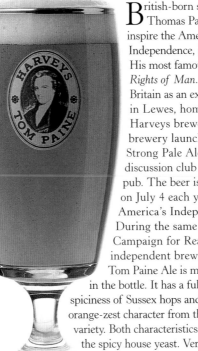

British-born social commentator Thomas Paine helped to inspire the American War of Independence, in which he fought. His most famous work was *The Rights of Man*. While working in Britain as an excise officer, he lived in Lewes, home town of the Harveys brewery. In 1990, the brewery launched Tom Paine Strong Pale Ale for a political discussion club that met in a local pub. The beer is released on draft on July 4 each year to celebrate America's Independence Day. During the same month, the Campaign for Real Ale celebrates independent breweries in Britain. Tom Paine Ale is more widely available in the bottle. It has a full flavor, with the soft spiciness of Sussex hops and a marked fresh orange-zest character from the Styrian Goldings variety. Both characteristics are heightened by the spicy house yeast. Very appetizing.

H

HB Mai-Bock

REGION OF ORIGIN	Munich, Upper Bavaria, Germany
STYLE	May Bock *(Maibock)*
ALCOHOL CONTENT	5.8 abw (7.2 abv)
IDEAL SERVING TEMPERATURE	48° F (9° C)

The initials stand for Hofbräuhaus: the Royal Court Brewery. The beer hall, the world's most famous pub, still functions, on a small square called the Platzl in the center of Munich; the brewery is on the edge of town. The State of Bavaria owns both brewery and beer hall. The beer claims on its label to be Munich's oldest Bock, though that is not strictly true of this Maytime version. It is a fine beer nonetheless, huge in its malt aromas, nutty flavors, and peppery, warming finish.

Hidden depths
Behind the stoneware,
the beer has a deep
reddish color.

HB OKTOBERFESTBIER

REGION OF ORIGIN	Munich, Upper Bavaria, Germany
STYLE	*Märzen/Oktoberfest*
ALCOHOL CONTENT	4.6 abw (5.7 abv)
IDEAL SERVING TEMPERATURE	48° F (9° C)

HB – the Hofbräuhaus – takes a special interest in a festival that began with the wedding of the Crown Prince. Its label illustrates the horses and drays that take part in the procession to "Queen Theresia's Meadows." Its Oktoberfestbier forms a head of Alpine proportions, and has a creamy, malty spiciness reminiscent of licorice or aniseed.

Beautiful bloom
One result of all-malt beers
is a solid foam, prized as
a "beautiful bloom."

HB SCHWARZE WEISSE

🛡 **REGION OF ORIGIN** Munich, Upper Bavaria, Germany

🍺 **STYLE** Dark Wheat Beer

% **ALCOHOL CONTENT** 4.1 abw (5.1 abv)

🍷 **IDEAL SERVING TEMPERATURE** 48–54° F (9–12° C)

The royal family of Bavaria maintained a monopoly on the brewing of wheat beers from the 1600s to the early 1800s. The Hofbräuhaus (Royal Court Brewery) of Munich once specialized in the style. It has promoted its own examples since the revival of interest in wheat beers in the late 1970s. This one is very lively, with spicy (licorice-like), chewy malt flavors; molasses toffee in the middle; and a grainy, slightly tannic (green apple) finish.

Black is beautiful
There was always a dark version, but now it has been deepened to "black" (Schwarze) in the interests of fashion.

HEINEKEN KYLIAN

🛡 **REGION OF ORIGIN**	The Netherlands/France
🍾 **STYLE**	Irish Red Ale
% **ALCOHOL CONTENT**	5.2 abw (6.5 abv)
🍺 **IDEAL SERVING TEMPERATURE**	50° F (10° C)

A beer of complicated parentage. First came the Irish George Killian Lett's Ruby Ale, followed by the version from Pelforth *(see p.359)*, and then the French brewery became part of the Dutch-based Heineken group. The Dutch launched Kylian, which seems a little different in character. It starts quite austere, with a firm, clean maltiness but, as it warms, has a good flavor development toward a restrained fruitiness and nutty sweetness. It is very drinkable. Try it in winter before a Dutch pea soup with ham.

HEINEKEN OUD BRUIN

🏷	**REGION OF ORIGIN**	Province of North Brabant, the Netherlands
🍶	**STYLE**	Old Brown Lager
%	**ALCOHOL CONTENT**	2.0 abw (2.5 abv)
🍺	**IDEAL SERVING TEMPERATURE**	46–48° F (8–9° C)

The most international of beer makers traces its history to 1592, to a brewery in the center of Amsterdam, the site of which is now a famous steak restaurant. The first Heineken became involved with the brewery in 1863, at which time white beer, *faro* (a sweetened beer broadly in the *gueuze* type), old brown, ale, and porter were being produced. Lager brewing of dark brown beers began in 1869 and today's yeast culture was introduced in 1886. Heineken still makes a conventional, dryish, dark lager, mainly for export to the US, but also has the quite different sweeter type in its home market. This Oud Bruin has a coffeeish aroma; a slightly licorice-like palate; and, as with most examples, a sweet finish.

Secret smile
When the current typography of the word Heineken was designed, the shape of the letter "e" was intended to be subliminally reminiscent of a smile.

Heineken Tarwebok

> ⊘ **REGION OF ORIGIN** Province of North Brabant, the Netherlands
>
> 🍾 **STYLE** Wheat Bock
>
> % **ALCOHOL CONTENT** 5.2 abw (6.5 abv)
>
> 🌡 **IDEAL SERVING TEMPERATURE** 48–50° F (9–10° C)

One of the most distinctive, flavorsome, and complex beers made by Heineken is this wheat Bock. No fewer than four types of barley malt are used, along with 17 percent wheat (*Tarwe*, in Dutch) malt. The result is a silky-smooth beer, with suggestions of cream, coffee, chocolate, prunes, and rum. This Dutch interpretation of the style does not have the phenol smokiness or bubble-gum flavors that might be found in a typical German *Weizenbock*.

New Amsterdam
In an amusing, if bold, campaign, this beer was advertised partly in Dutch in New York.

HELLERS WIESS

REGION OF ORIGIN Cologne, North Rhine-Westphalia, Germany

STYLE *Kölschbier*

ALCOHOL CONTENT 3.6 abw (4.5 abv)

IDEAL SERVING TEMPERATURE 48° F (9° C)

In premises that formerly housed a distillery making a bitter liqueur, this new-generation brewpub, dating from the 1980s, is something of a maverick in Cologne's brewing industry. Hubert Heller makes a beer called Ur-Wiess, this term implying a "meadow" beer as served at festivals. In this case, that means an unfiltered beer. This perfumy, fruity brew, with a good hop bitterness, is also served in filtered form as *Kölsch*, in which version the malt emerges more clearly and the hop is slightly subdued. By definition, *Kölschbier* is filtered.

Where flavors meld
Some brewers put barley and
hops on the label. The two meet
in the kettle, as shown here.

HERRENHÄUSER PREMIUM PILSENER

🏷 **REGION OF ORIGIN** Lower Saxony, Germany
🍺 **STYLE** Pilsner
% **ALCOHOL CONTENT** 3.9 abw (4.9 abv)
🌡 **IDEAL SERVING TEMPERATURE** 48° F (9° C)

The city of Hanover and its surroundings are often associated with Korn Schnapps and Steinhäger gin rather than beer. Sometimes, a shot of liquor and a small beer are consumed simultaneously, in a one-handed move that requires dexterity as well as bravado. This is called "a little one" (a *Lüttje Lage*), and is especially associated with festival times. The beers are often light, clean, dryish Pilsners. The Hanover brewery Gilde has a couple of flowery examples. Its smaller local rival Herrenhäuser has the slightly more robust Premium Pilsener shown here, with a light, grassy aroma; a creamy, malty body; and crisply hoppy, appetizing dryness.

HERRENHÄUSER WEIZEN BIER

REGION OF ORIGIN
Lower Saxony, Germany

STYLE *Hefeweizen*

ALCOHOL CONTENT 4.4 abw (5.5 abv)

IDEAL SERVING TEMPERATURE
48–54° F (9–12° C)

A newish product from this Hanover brewery. Its home state of Lower Saxony may in the distant past have produced sourer, more northern styles of wheat beer, but this brew is broadly in the southern style. It has a sweetish, lighty spicy aroma; a smooth, faintly syrupy palate; and a lightly tart finish. A field of wheat is vividly depicted on the label.

HERRNBRÄU
HEFE-WEISSBIER DUNKEL

REGION OF ORIGIN Upper Bavaria, Germany

STYLE Dark Wheat Beer

ALCOHOL CONTENT 4.2 abw (5.3 abv)

IDEAL SERVING TEMPERATURE 48–54° F (9–12° C)

The German Beer Purity Law was first announced by Duke Wilhelm IV, in 1516, in Ingolstadt, now the home of the Herrnbräu brewery. At one stage it was an offense for a brewer in the town to fail to meet his quotas. The penalty was to make 10,000 bricks, a task that must have been very onerous, but surely increased demand for beer without boosting supply. At one stage, a "Beer Street" was built to fetch supplies from nearby Kelheim. Today's dark wheat beer has a nutty sweetness, chocolatey flavors, and a flowery, "violets" dryness.

A masterpiece…
…of old Bavarian brewing art, says the bottom line of the label.

HERTOG JAN
GRAND PRESTIGE

🛡	**REGION OF ORIGIN**	Province of Limburg, the Netherlands
🍾	**STYLE**	Barley Wine
%	**ALCOHOL CONTENT**	8.0 abw (10.0 abv)
🥃	**IDEAL SERVING TEMPERATURE**	55° F (13° C)

The word *Hertog* means duke, and the name Jan recollects the Jan who ruled Flanders and Brabant. This strong Dutch ale is broadly in the style of a barley wine. It was an early speciality after the 1980s' revival of the Arcen brewery, in the Limburg town of the same name. The beer has a dense head; a garnet color; a spicy malt aroma; a surprisingly light, soft body; and a sweetish, very slightly meaty, portlike finish.

HIGHGATE & WALSALL OLD ALE

🛡 **REGION OF ORIGIN**	Central England, UK
🍶 **STYLE**	Old Ale
% **ALCOHOL CONTENT**	4.1 abw (5.1 abv)
🍺 **IDEAL SERVING TEMPERATURE**	50–55° F (10–13° C)

The most famous of specialized mild ale producers is this 100-year-old English brewery in the West Midlands, owned for decades by Bass, but now independent. A beer that is only gently hopped, and malt-accented, like a mild, but made with a little more alcohol, is one classic approach to an old ale or winter warmer. This November and December brew is a fine example. It has a hint of passion fruit in the bouquet; touches of iron, oak, and well-done toast in the palate; and a toffee-like, comforting finish.

How high?
Nothing to do with London's famous literary "village" of Highgate. This one is in the town of Walsall.

HOEGAARDEN SPECIALE

🛡	**REGION OF ORIGIN**	Province of Flemish Brabant, Belgium
🍾	**STYLE**	Belgian Wheat Beer
%	**ALCOHOL CONTENT**	4.5 abw (5.6 abv)
🍺	**IDEAL SERVING TEMPERATURE**	48–50° F (9–10° C)

While the regular Hoegaarden *(see right)* is often regarded as a summer refresher, a slightly stronger, maltier, creamier version for winter was launched under the name Speciale in 1995. While Hoegaarden Witbier is made from equal proportions of raw wheat and malted barley, Hoegaarden Speciale has 55 percent malted barley. Some of this malt is made by the process in which the natural sugars of the barley are encouraged to crystallize. A nutty flavor is imparted to beer by crystal malts. The proportions of coriander and orange are the same in both beers, but the citric character seems to be accentuated by the greater maltiness of the Speciale.

HOEGAARDEN WITBIER

	REGION OF ORIGIN Province of Flemish Brabant, Belgium
	STYLE Belgian Wheat Beer
	ALCOHOL CONTENT 4.0 abw (5.0 abv)
	IDEAL SERVING TEMPERATURE 48–50° F (9–10° C)

The town of Hoegaarden, east of Brussels, is in the heart of wheat-growing country and once had over 30 breweries making the local wheat beer. The last closed in the 1950s, when traditional brews were being driven out by lagers, but in the 1960s enthusiast Pierre Celis revived the style. As a teenager, he had helped make the beer at the last brewery. That inspired his hazy brew, spiced with coriander seeds and Curaçao orange peels. He expected it to appeal to local drinkers, but it actually found a new audience worldwide. His brewery was a great success and was acquired by the Interbrew group in the 1980s. Hoegaarden is perfumy and spicy in aroma, with a fruity palate and a honeyish background.

Why "white"?
The term "white" denotes a wheat beer in Belgium, Germany, and several other countries.

HOEPFNER BLUE STAR

	REGION OF ORIGIN Baden-Württemberg, Germany
	STYLE Smoked *Altbier*
	ALCOHOL CONTENT 4.4 abw (5.5 abv)
	IDEAL SERVING TEMPERATURE 48° F (9° C)

The Hoepfner who founded this brewery, in Karlsruhe, Germany, was a priest. The company is now in the sixth generation of the family. It was established in 1798, and is in an 1898 building that looks like a baronial castle. Despite its long history, it is one of the most innovative breweries in Germany. The beer shown was first brewed in 1996, on New Year's Eve, a very important day for the Scots. It does not identify itself as being Scottish in style, but is in character very similar to the various whiskey-malt brews. The beer contains a proportion of beech-smoked malt, and has a subtly sappy dryness in the finish. It is oily, malty, and lightly nutty, with a touch of flowery elegance. It is made with an *Altbier* yeast. Halfway between Düsseldorf and Dundee?

Dancing the blues away
A six-pack of Blue Star has different images on each label. The theme is "dancing under the stars."

HOEPFNER GOLDKÖPFLE

🏷️ **REGION OF ORIGIN** Baden-Württemberg, Germany

🍾 **STYLE** Export

％ **ALCOHOL CONTENT** 4.5 abw (5.6 abv)

🌡️ **IDEAL SERVING TEMPERATURE** 48° F (9° C)

Among its golden lagers, the Hoepfner brewery of Karlsruhe produces a Pilsner and three variations on the Export theme. The brew called simply Export has a deliciously fresh aroma (newly-baked, crusty bread?); a smooth, malty body; a spicy palate; and a delicate, balancing dryness in the finish. The "super-premium" version shown here is slightly higher in alcohol and fuller in flavors. Although it is billed as being "mild," it does have some oily, soothing, hop flavors. There is also an unfiltered Export, called Hoepfner Kräusen Hefetrüb.

No small beer
The word Köpfle is a diminutive for
head, in the southern German region
of Baden. This golden beer pours with
a fine head, but not a small one.

HOEPFNER JUBELBIER

REGION OF ORIGIN Baden-Württemberg, Germany

STYLE Vienna

ALCOHOL CONTENT 4.5 abw (5.6 abv)

IDEAL SERVING TEMPERATURE 48° F (9° C)

The remarkable ornate label on this beer was originally designed for a brew to celebrate the Duke of Baden's golden anniversary in 1906. A half-full bottle of that beer was found by chance in 1982, when the brewery was planning a special edition to celebrate the 75th birthday of the father of the company's current principal. This Jubelbier, still in production, is a bronze lager in broadly the Vienna or *Märzen-Oktoberfest* style. It starts with a nutty malt character, and is very smooth indeed, but has a light, spritzy dryness in the finish.

A toast to father
The fine "beading" of bubbles is clearly visible in the glass – evidence of the spritziness that characterizes the finish. Despite its full color, it is quite Champagnelike.

HOEPFNER PILSNER

REGION OF ORIGIN Baden-Württemberg, Germany

STYLE Pilsner

ALCOHOL CONTENT 3.8 abw (4.8 abv)

IDEAL SERVING TEMPERATURE 48° F (9° C)

The family name derives from "hop farmer." The Karlsruhe brewery's Pilsner contains four varieties of hop (Perle, Hallertau-Hersbruck, Tettnang, and Saaz). Despite a hefty 37 units of bitterness, the beer is not aggressively dry. The emphasis on aroma hopping makes for a mint-cream character, enhanced by the marshmallowy softness of the malt. The brewery has its own maltings. It also has its own yeast strain, uses open fermenters, and is lagered in horizontal vessels rather than the more common upright cylinders. All of these elements make for a gentle, complex, classic Pilsner. At the brewery tap, the Pilsner has occasionally been served in a beer cocktail with the vermouth-like aperitif Amer-Picon, which is popular across the border in Alsace.

HOOK NORTON OLD HOOKY

🛡 **REGION OF ORIGIN** South/Midlands of England, UK

🍾 **STYLE** Old Ale/Bitter

% **ALCOHOL CONTENT** 3.7 abw (4.6 abv)

🍺 **IDEAL SERVING TEMPERATURE** 50–55° F (10–13° C)

A steam engine is still used at the brewery of Hook Norton, in Banbury, Oxfordshire. Hook Norton occupies a tower brewery dating from 1899 – the raw materials start at the top and gradually combine into beer as they flow by gravity into the cellars. Its best-known beer is Old Hooky, which has an appetizing fresh-shortbread, malt aroma and flavor; a creaminess and fruitiness reminiscent of bananas and strawberries; and a late, balancing dryness in its subtly leafy hop character. Despite its name, it is less of an old ale than a medium-strong, malt-accented bitter.

Baby grand
The label shows a drawing of the tiny brewery, accurate in style, but exaggerated in size.

HOPBACK SUMMER LIGHTNING

🛡 **REGION OF ORIGIN** Western England, UK

🍶 **STYLE** Summer Ale

% **ALCOHOL CONTENT** 4.0 abw (5.0 abv)

🍺 **IDEAL SERVING TEMPERATURE** Just above 50° F (10° C)

After the hops have been boiled in the brew, the leafy cones have to be removed, using a vessel called a hopback. The Hop Back brewery, in Salisbury, England, dates from 1987. Soon after its foundation, it launched Summer Lightning, initially for a beer festival but then as a regular product. At the time, the color was unusually sunny for a British ale. The beer may be light, crisp, and dry, but it is full of subtle flavors: the sweetness of Maris Otter barley malt from Wiltshire, the fragrance of East Kent Golding hops, and the very delicate, banana-like fruitiness of the house yeast.

HOPBACK THUNDERSTORM

🛡 **REGION OF ORIGIN** Western England, UK

🍺 **STYLE** Wheat Ale

% **ALCOHOL CONTENT** 4.0 abw (5.0 abv)

🌡 **IDEAL SERVING TEMPERATURE** Store at 50–58° F (10–14° C);
Serve at 50° F (10° C)

Having been very successful with a seasonal beer called Summer Lightning, this Salisbury brewery in 1997 paid its further respects to the unpredictability of British weather by adding a wheat ale identified as Thunderstorm. This bottle-conditioned beer is made with 50 percent wheat and hopped entirely with the variety Progress. It has a light but firm, juicy malt background; the faintest hint of banana yeastiness; long, very dry, lemon-zest and juniper hop flavors; and a crisp finish.

Nectar of the Gods
The ancient Roman god of drink, Bacchus, appears on all of this brewer's labels.

HOPF DUNKLE WEISSE

REGION OF ORIGIN Upper Bavaria, Germany

STYLE Dark Wheat Beer

ALCOHOL CONTENT 4.0 abw (5.0 abv)

IDEAL SERVING TEMPERATURE
48–54° F (9–12° C)

Hans Hopf, owner of this brewery, almost certainly owes his surname to the hop plant. As chance would have it, he specializes in wheat beer, a style that is usually only lightly hopped. His Dunkle Weisse has a hint of hop in the bouquet, along with some fresh pear and banana. It is a lively beer, firm and smooth, with a restrained dryness, and a quenching, refreshing finish. The brewery is in Miesbach, approximately 35 miles (56 km) south of the city of Munich. It has in recent years produced several unusual variations on the wheat beer theme, including one inspired by the *Eisbock* tradition. It is one of the few German breweries to be innovative in matters of beer style. (Another is its coincidental near-namesake Hopfner.)

HOUGAERDSE DAS

🗒 **REGION OF ORIGIN**	Province of Flemish Brabant, Belgium
🍶 **STYLE**	Spiced Belgian Ale
⅏ **ALCOHOL CONTENT**	4.0 abv (5.0 abw)
🍺 **IDEAL SERVING TEMPERATURE**	48–50° F (9–10° C)

The town of Hoegaarden is close to the invisible frontier between Belgium's two languages: Flemish and French. Over the years, spellings of the town's name have varied, and this revivalist beer has deliberately opted for an "antique" version. Between the two world wars, a brewery in the town produced an amber ale (probably spiced) called DAS, perhaps one of several Belgian brews intended to sound like the British Bass. That brewery has long gone, but the name was reintroduced by the brewers of Hoegaarden White *(see p.229)* in 1996. The new Hougaerdse DAS is an aromatic, juicy, fruity (apples?), bottle-conditioned amber ale. It is brewed from Pilsner and crystal malt, and spiced with Curaçao orange peels and coriander. The brew is fermented with a yeast also used in the famously fruity, complex Ginder Ale, made by the same parent company.

HÜBSCH
SUDWERK HELLES

🛡 **REGION OF ORIGIN** California, US

🍾 **STYLE** *Helles* Lager

％ **ALCOHOL CONTENT** 3.9 abw (4.9 abv)

🍺 **IDEAL SERVING TEMPERATURE** 48° F (9° C)

One of the best German-style breweries in the United States. Hübsch is a family name of one of the founders; *Sudwerk* is from the German for a brewhouse. This is a brewpub and micro in Davis, in northern California. Sudwerk makes a wide range of German styles, including this firm, smooth *Helles*, with a textured, malty start and a clean, crisp smack of hops.

Drinking in the study
The Sudwerk beers are made in
Davis, home of California's wine
university. The subject of beermaking
is also studied at the college.

HULL MILD

🛡 **REGION OF ORIGIN** Northeast England, UK

🍾 **STYLE** Mild Ale

% **ALCOHOL CONTENT** 2.6 abw (3.3 abv)

🍺 **IDEAL SERVING TEMPERATURE** 50–55° F (10–13° C)

A claim to fame among beer lovers, especially in North America: the original brewery, in the Yorkshire fishing and port city of Hull, employed Peter Austin, who later used its distinctively fruity yeast in new-generation breweries throughout the US and Canada. The brewery closed in the 1970s, but the name was resurrected by a microbrewery in 1989. The micro uses the same yeast to make this smooth, toasty, chocolatey, fruity, winey mild.

Huyghe Delirium Tremens

🥖	**REGION OF ORIGIN** Province of East Flanders, Belgium
🍾	**STYLE** Belgian-style Strong Golden Ale
%	**ALCOHOL CONTENT** 7.2 abw (9.0 abv)
🍺	**IDEAL SERVING TEMPERATURE** 50° F (10° C)

Flippant names such as Delirium Tremens reflect the Belgian spirit of "eat, drink, and be merry." The name once resulted in the beer being banned from the United States. For the American market, it was given the name Mateen, after an early Flemish brewer. The beer employs Saaz and Styrian hops, and is fermented with three yeasts (in a two-stage fermentation and bottle-conditioning). It has a very fruity aroma, reminiscent of plums or gooseberries; a sweetish palate; and a lot of warming alcohol in a rather abrupt finish. In 1999, a dark-brown brother brew called Delirium Nocturnum was launched. That beer, made with five malts, is smooth, rich, and perfumy. These beers are among a very wide range made by Huyghe, an old-established brewery at Melle, near Ghent.

H

HUYGHE FLORISGAARDEN WITBIER

REGION OF ORIGIN Province of East Flanders, Belgium

STYLE Belgian Wheat Beer

ALCOHOL CONTENT 2.8 abw (3.5 abv)

IDEAL SERVING TEMPERATURE 48–50° F (9–10° C)

Flower garden? The second word was no doubt inspired by Hoegaarden, the blossoming of which scattered seeds all over Belgium and beyond. The Huyghe brewery, near Ghent, produces this light, sweetish *Witbier*. The same brew is used as the base for a range of Florisgaarden fruit beers, made with essences or extract. One with peach, apricot, and mango is called Ninkeberry. The brewery's technical consultant has children called Floris and Ninke. They no doubt enjoy another of the Florisgaarden range, flavored with chocolate and called Floris Chocolat.

ICENI FOUR GRAINS

🛡 **REGION OF ORIGIN** Eastern England, UK

🍾 **STYLE** Ale

% **ALCOHOL CONTENT** 3.4 abw (4.2 abv)

🍺 **IDEAL SERVING TEMPERATURE** 50–55° F (10–13° C)

The name refers to the tribes led by Queen Boadicea in her battles against the Roman colonization of what is now England. The Iceni heartland was the region now known as East Anglia, especially the county of Norfolk. The microbrewery Iceni is in Ickburgh, north of Thetford, Norfolk. It was founded in 1995, and has a colorful range of beers, several with Celtic names. The four grains in this example are barley, wheat, rye, and oats. The brewery regards each grain as a building-block of flavor. The bottle-conditioned beer has a minty, orangey aroma; a smooth, dry, grainy, oily palate; and a lift in the finish from light, hoppy acidity.

Fit for a queen
The brewery's logo features Queen Boadicea in her chariot. The bigger illustration reminds purchasers that beer is a wholegrain product.

ICENI

FOUR GRAINS

500 MLe

4.2% ABV

"Rye, Wheat Barley & Oats to build in the Flavour"

BOTTLE CONDITIONED BEER AND MAY CONTAIN SOME SEDIMENT. A NATURAL DEPOSIT FROM THE BOTTLE FERMENTATION PROCESS. POUR CAREFULLY TO ENSURE A CLEAR GLASS OF BEER.

I

IM FÜCHSCHEN ALT

⬚ **REGION OF ORIGIN** Düsseldorf, North Rhine-Westphalia, Germany

STYLE *Altbier*

ALCOHOL CONTENT 3.6 abw (4.5 abv)

IDEAL SERVING TEMPERATURE 48° F (9° C)

The name means "The Fox Cub." This is one of the rightly renowned brewpubs in the Old Town of Düsseldorf. Its *Alt*, also a favorite among lovers of the style, is a well-balanced but hoppy interpretation. It has a creamy malt character; a restrained, pearlike fruitiness; and a hoppy acidity in the dry finish.

The brewery, a classic of its type, stands like a miniature industrial building behind the tavern. Inside, customers share scrubbed tables, and the beer accompanies a hearty menu. The house speciality is *Eisbein:* boiled knuckle of pork.

Foxed?
The fox looks thirsty, but this hoppy beer makes customers famously hungry.

INDEPENDENCE FRANKLINFEST

REGION OF ORIGIN	Northeast US
STYLE	*Märzen-Oktoberfest* Lager
ALCOHOL CONTENT	4.4 abw (5.5 abv)
IDEAL SERVING TEMPERATURE	48° F (9° C)

In Philadelphia in 1776, the statesman and scientist Benjamin Franklin helped draft the Declaration of Independence of the American colonies from Britain. The Independence brewery was founded in the same city 219 years later, initially making an ale. Soon afterward, the brewery launched its Franklinfest lager. This has a full bronze color; a depth of malt aroma and spicy flavor; a light but remarkably smooth drinkability; and a clean, sweet finish.

Declared drinker
Benjamin Franklin himself left a
recipe for spruce beer and orders for
half-barrels of ale.

ISAAC BIRRA BIANCA

REGION OF ORIGIN Italy

STYLE Belgian-style Wheat Beer

ALCOHOL CONTENT 4.0 abw (5.0 abv)

IDEAL SERVING TEMPERATURE 48–50° F (9–10° C)

A Champagne bottle for a Belgian-style "white" wheat beer from Italy. The brewery is in the town of Piozzo, in the province of Cuneo, not far from Turin. It is in a pub, called Le Baladin ("The Balladeer" or "Troubadour"). The owner's wife originates from the border region of Belgium and France, and the beer Isaac is named after the couple's son. The playful notion is that a wheat beer is innocent enough for children. This example is aromatized with coriander and the juice of grapefruit and oranges (rather than the peels of the latter, which are more usual). In the finished product, the flavors are more reminiscent of sweet lemons. A secondary fermentation in the bottle is with Champagne yeast. This feature, and the resultant toasty creaminess, are further justification for that elegant bottle.

Jeanne d'Arc Ambre des Flandres

⚜ **Region of origin** Northern France

🍾 **Style** *Bière de Garde*

% **Alcohol content** 5.1 abw (6.4 abv)

▯ **Ideal serving temperature** 50–55° F (10–13° C)

Joan of Arc was born not far away, in the Champagne region. The brewery that honors her was established in 1898 by a family with the Flemish name van Damme. It is hidden in a side street in Ronchin, near Lille. Ambre des Flandres is bottom-fermenting, but in the style of a *bière de garde*. It has a peppery start and a grainy, figgy palate, with a big, dry finish. A very good beer with food, especially the lamb and leek dishes of the region.

JEANNE D'ARC BELZEBUTH

🛡 **REGION OF ORIGIN** Northern France

🍾 **STYLE** Belgian-style Strong Golden Ale

🅰 **ALCOHOL CONTENT** 12.0 abw (15.0 abv)

🍺 **IDEAL SERVING TEMPERATURE** 50° F (10° C)

Beelzebub is from the ancient Greek and Hebrew for the Devil, or his alternate the "Lord of the Flies." He is graphically shown on the label of this beer, from a French brewery with the combustible name Jeanne d'Arc. This immensely strong, bright beer is said to be all-malt (that is, not to contain other sugars). It is smooth, almost fluffy, starting candyish, with peppery alcohol flavors perhaps contributing to a spicy, surprising dryness. Belzebuth is less thick than might be expected at its strength, but is very heady.

Potent brew
Beelzebub protected his followers from
flies... but he derived his name from
Baal, early Semitic god of fertility.

JEANNE D'ARC GRAIN D'ORGE

REGION OF ORIGIN	Northern France
STYLE	*Bière de Garde*
ALCOHOL CONTENT	6.4 abw (8.0 abv)
IDEAL SERVING TEMPERATURE	50–55° F (10–13° C)

Despite its golden color, this beer does contain a small proportion of Vienna malt, imparting a very slight nuttiness. As its name ("barley grain") suggests, it is a distinctly malt-accented beer, but with a good hop balance. The hops include Styrians, with their distinctive orange-zest character, and the camomile-tinged Saaz, as well as the more resiny Brewer's Gold (from Flanders). A further element of flavor, the slightly smoky character of the house yeast, is more apparent in this beer than the brewery's other products. This is because the yeast (top-fermenting) has to work harder to create the relatively high alcohol content. Stylistically, it is a French *bière de garde* with a Flemish accent.

JENNINGS COCKER HOOP

REGION OF ORIGIN Northwest England, UK

STYLE Bitter Ale

ALCOHOL CONTENT 3.8 abw (4.8 abv)

IDEAL SERVING TEMPERATURE 50–55° F (10–13° C)

Far northern brewery, in Cockermouth, near the English Lakes. Apart from being a pun on the location, the name is a reference to drinking. The beer's back label suggests that the cock (tap) and hoop were both parts of the barrel. Cocker Hoop rolls smoothly over the tongue, at first nutty, then lightly orangey and perfumy, and finally hoppy and grassy. A summery, sociable ale with lots of character. Despite its far-flung location, the brewery's products are widely available.

Jever Pilsener

REGION OF ORIGIN Northern Germany

STYLE Pilsner

ALCOHOL CONTENT 3.9 abw (4.9 abv)

IDEAL SERVING TEMPERATURE 48° F (9° C)

The partially moated town of Jever (pronounced "yayver") is a base for tourism on Germany's Frisian coast. Friesland is a region that also straddles Denmark and the Netherlands. The people of Friesland are reputed to have a taste for food and drink with strong flavors. Jever Pilsener is famous among beer lovers worldwide for its bitterness. It pours with the blossoming head favored on German Pilsners, and has a tingling, almost rough dryness on the tongue. The brewery is extremely modern, like those of many other Pilsner producers in Germany, though it does have some turn-of-the-century buildings. Since it was acquired by the national group Brau und Brunnen, Jever Pilsener seems to have diminished slightly in character, but its dryness still makes it a wonderful aperitif.

Jopen Bok Bier

REGION OF ORIGIN Province of North Holland, the Netherlands

STYLE Top-fermenting Bock

ALCOHOL CONTENT 4.4 abw (5.5 abv)

IDEAL SERVING TEMPERATURE 48° F (9° C)

The word *Jopen* was used in Haarlem, once a great brewing city in the Netherlands, to describe a size of beer barrel. This unusual "four-grain" beer is made from barley, wheat, rye (all malted), and raw oats, and is top-fermented and bottle-conditioned. Although developed in Haarlem, it is produced at the Schaapskooi Abbey brewery. To experience its fragrant, orangey aroma is like biting into the fruit itself. The beer is lightly syrupy and malty in the palate, with spicy, dry flavors (but no spices are used).

JOPEN HAARLEMS HOPPENBIER

🛡 **REGION OF ORIGIN** Province of North Holland, the Netherlands

🍴 **STYLE** Spiced Ale

％ **ALCOHOL CONTENT** 5.2 abw (6.5 abv)

🍶 **IDEAL SERVING TEMPERATURE** 55° F (13° C)

The grainy flavors of beer were balanced with fruits, herbs, and spices long before the hop came into use. When it did, it was proclaimed as an innovation. The first hopped beer in the historic brewing city of Haarlem is believed to have been made in 1501. This *hoppenbier* was revived in 1994 for a festival commemorating the 750th anniversary of the city. It is brewed from barley and wheat (both malted) and oats, and hopped with Kent Goldings and Styrians. There are no spices. The beer has a citric aroma; an oaty creaminess; a spicy palate that becomes fruity and then tart; and a sherbety, talclike, scenty finish, dry and clinging.

K

KALTENBERG KÖNIG LUDWIG DUNKEL

REGION OF ORIGIN Bavaria, Germany
STYLE Dark Lager
ALCOHOL CONTENT 4.0 abw (5.1 abv)
IDEAL SERVING TEMPERATURE 48° F (9° C)

Many Celtic sites have given rise to breweries. Translating as "Celtic Hill," Kaltenberg is near Munich. There has been a castle on the hilltop since at least the 1200s, and probably long before. The present castle dates from 1670 but was remodeled in neo-Gothic style in 1848. In the cellar of the castle, Prince Luitpold of Bavaria operates a renowned brewery, specializing in various styles of dark beer. The brew dedicated to his ancestor King Ludwig is light-bodied but smooth and textured, with suggestions of coffee and figs. The beer is served at a jousting tournament at the castle each July.

KALTENBERG RITTERBOCK

REGION OF ORIGIN	Bavaria, Germany
STYLE	Double Bock
ALCOHOL CONTENT	6.2 abw (7.7 abv)
IDEAL SERVING TEMPERATURE	48° F (9° C)

Although Bock beer originated in the north of Germany (in Einbeck, Lower Saxony), it was popularized in the south, in the royal court brewhouse built by Duke Wilhelm V of Bavaria at the end of the 1500s. Prince Luitpold, who brews near Munich at the castle of Kaltenberg, is among the Duke's descendants. One of his beers is Kaltenberg Ritterbock, available during Lent. It is light-bodied for the style, but with a delicious bitter-chocolate praline character.

Ritter means "rider"
The castle's popular jousting tournament is held over three weekends each July in an arena that seats 10,000 spectators.

KASTEEL BIER

REGION OF ORIGIN Province of West Flanders, Belgium

STYLE Barley Wine

ALCOHOL CONTENT 8.8 abw (11.0 abv)

IDEAL SERVING TEMPERATURE 53–55° F (12–13° C)

Also known as Bière du Chateau. The castle, or château, is a moated mansion dating from 1736, at Ingelmunster, in West Flanders. The site was once occupied by the Duke of Flanders. The cellars are now used to bottle-age, for 6–12 weeks, Kasteel Bier, which is brewed nearby by Van Honsebrouck. This extraordinarily powerful beer begins with malt-loaf richness, developing to notes of dried fruit and port, drying to a burlaplike finish. It is made with three malts, dark candy sugar, a dry-hopping of Kent Goldings, and its own yeast. A golden counterpart, called Kasteel Tripel, has suggestions of vanilla, coriander, and citrus. There is also a more vanilla-like golden version.

KILKENNY IRISH BEER

	REGION OF ORIGIN Republic of Ireland
	STYLE Irish Red Ale
	ALCOHOL CONTENT 4.0 abw (5.0 abv)
	IDEAL SERVING TEMPERATURE 48–50° F (9–10° C)

The town of Kilkenny overlooks the largely intact 13th-century abbey church of St. Francis. Encircling the church is a brewery established in 1710 by John Smithwick and, since 1965, owned by Guinness. Under the Smithwick's name, the brewery produces a toffeeish, buttery ale with a touch of burned toast in the finish (3.2 abw; 4.0 abv). This is primarily sold in Ireland. Elsewhere in the world, a slightly stronger, drier, nuttier interpretation is sold as Kilkenny Irish Beer.

Irish red
The reddish cast of Irish ales like Kilkenny, evolved into an element of style.

KING & BARNES FESTIVE ALE

▨ **REGION OF ORIGIN** South of England, UK

🍶 **STYLE** Pale Ale

⅋ **ALCOHOL CONTENT** 4.25 abw (5.3 abv)

🍺 **IDEAL SERVING TEMPERATURE** 58° F (15° C)

Some world-class bottle-conditioned beers have emerged in recent times from King & Barnes, an enterprise tracing its history back 200 years. Meanwhile, takeover bids have called into question the future of the brewery, in Horsham, Sussex. The brewery emphasizes the Maris Otter variety of barley; Goldings hops, in the form of blossoms; and the house two-strain yeast. There are a total of four malts and three varieties of hops in Festive. The beer was first brewed for the post-war Festival of Britain in 1951, and launched as a bottle-conditioned product in 1992. It has an herbal, rooty, hop aroma; a juicy, nutty, faintly chocolatey, malt background; and a dessert-apple, roselike perfuminess in its long finish.

KING & BARNES RYE BEER

🛡	**REGION OF ORIGIN**	South of England, UK
🍾	**STYLE**	Rye Ale/Brown Ale
%	**ALCOHOL CONTENT**	4.4 abw (5.5 abv)
🍺	**IDEAL SERVING TEMPERATURE**	58° F (15° C)

Rye is a grain with an appetizingly bittersweet, fruity, spicy, sometimes minty character. The grain is first baked into bread, then infused, to make Kvass, a beerlike drink native to Russia. Rye is also used in the Finnish brew Sahti. In 1988, the German brewery Thurn und Taxis launched a rye variation on a wheat beer, and in the following decade King and Barnes, of Horsham, took up the theme with a rye ale in Britain. This beer has also been offered under the name Coppercast, reflecting the tinge of color the grain imparts. It is a deliciously oily brew, with suggestions of passion fruit. The beer world's answer to a rye-based vodka from Poland? More like a rye whiskey from Pennsylvania.

KING & BARNES WHEAT MASH

REGION OF ORIGIN South of England, UK

STYLE Wheat Ale

ALCOHOL CONTENT 3.6 abw (4.5 abv)

IDEAL SERVING TEMPERATURE 50–58° F (10–14° C)

Among the rotating range of seasonal beers from King and Barnes, of Horsham, the Wheat Mash is usually released in April, as a refresher for late spring and early summer. The term "mash" refers to the blending of the grains with the brewing water. This beer contains 40 percent wheat (the remainder being barley malt), is hopped with the Goldings variety, and fermented with the brewery's clean, dry, two-strain ale yeast. The result is a brew that is firm, grainy, and as crisp as a cracker, with a late, wheaty, lemony, perfumy tartness.

KLOSTER IRSEER
ABT'S TRUNK

🛡 **REGION OF ORIGIN** Swabia, Bavaria, Germany

🍾 **STYLE** Extra-strong Lager/Double Bock

％ **ALCOHOL CONTENT** 9.6 abw (12.0 abv)

🍺 **IDEAL SERVING TEMPERATURE** 48° F (9° C)

The Abbot may well have got drunk on this very strong lager. The brewery is in a handsome former monastery, at Irsee, in southern Germany. The beer is surprisingly light-bodied for its strength, with an oily maltiness and vanilla-like, oaky, whiskeyish notes. The brewery also has a restaurant, small hotel, crafts gallery, and pottery. Handmade stoneware flasks are sometimes used to package the beer. The packaging here seems to have an even more personal style.

Kneitinger Bock

REGION OF ORIGIN Regensburg, Bavaria, Germany

STYLE Bock

ALCOHOL CONTENT 4.8 abw (6.0 abv)

IDEAL SERVING TEMPERATURE 48° F (9° C)

A charitable foundation benefiting orphans and sick children has operated this family brewery, in the town of Regensburg, Bavaria, since the death, in 1991, of the last Kneitinger. The brewery dates from 1530, and had been in the Kneitinger family since 1876. The brewery and its adjoining original inn are a listed landmark. The inn taps the first cask of a new Bock on the first Thursday in October. Kneitinger Bock is very rich and layered in its complex malt character, with a faint smokiness.

Faith, hop, and charity
The charitable Kneitinger is just one of Regensburg's breweries. Others include Bischofshof, which is owned by a seminary.

KOFF JOULUOLUT

K

🛡 **REGION OF ORIGIN** Finland

🍶 **STYLE** Vienna Lager

％ **ALCOHOL CONTENT** 3.7 abw (4.6 abv)

🍺 **IDEAL SERVING TEMPERATURE** 48° F (9° C)

A Russian founded the Sinebrychoff brewery, oldest in the Nordic countries, in 1819. The brewery, often abbreviated to Koff, in 1987 introduced a lager in the amber-red, malt-accented Vienna style, as a Christmas beer. This example is on the pale side for the style, with a firm, clean, nutty maltiness. The word *Joulu* has the same origin as "Yule." The Finnish word for beer (of any style) is *olut*. The word itself shares a root with the English "ale."

Santa…
…has an office in the north of Finland. His local Christmas beer is made not by Koff but by Lapin Kulta ("Lapp Gold").

K

KÖNIG PILSENER

REGION OF ORIGIN North Rhine-Westphalia, Germany

STYLE Pilsner

ALCOHOL CONTENT 3.8 abw (4.9 abv)

IDEAL SERVING TEMPERATURE 48° F (9° C)

One of the more familiar Pilsner lagers in Germany, König is brewed in the city of Duisburg, a large inland port where the Rhine and Ruhr meet. Although Duisburg is well known for its art museum and zoo, its image as a big city in the heart of a coal-and-steel area may have in the past contributed to the popularity of a Pilsner that was robust for the style. As attitudes have changed, the beer has become milder in flavor and lighter in body. It still has a good malt character, but with more softness. The hop is gentler, but still offers a lingering, lightly tart, dryness. The name means "king," but the brewery is not dedicated to a monarch. König is the name of the founding family. The brewery, founded in 1858 by Theodor König, remained in the family for five generations. In the year 2000, it became part of the Holsten group.

KÖNIGSBACHER PILS

REGION OF ORIGIN North Rhine-Westphalia, Germany

STYLE Pilsner

ALCOHOL CONTENT 3.7 abw (4.8 abv)

IDEAL SERVING TEMPERATURE 48° F (9° C)

While *König* means "King," a *Bach* is, like the northern English "beck," a small river, or creek. Königsbacher is in the historic town of Coblenz, at the meeting point of two larger rivers, the Rhine and Mosel. Königsbacher Pils is a good, straightforward example of the style. It has a fresh, dry, hoppy bouquet; a firm body; and a sustained bitterness in the finish. A newer, unfiltered counterpart is named after the noise of the fizz escaping when the cap is released: Zischke. This beer, available only in hand-filled 5.28-pt (3-liter) bottles, has a fuller color; a sherbety aroma; a light but smooth body; a slightly tart, lemony taste; and a dry finish.

KÖSTRITZER SCHWARZBIER

🛡	**REGION OF ORIGIN**	Thuringia, Germany
🍶	**STYLE**	Black Beer
%	**ALCOHOL CONTENT**	3.8 abw (4.8 abv)
🍺	**IDEAL SERVING TEMPERATURE**	48° F (9° C)

The most famous black beer of all, made in Bad Köstritz, Thuringia. Beer was made in the castles of two local aristocrats between the 1500s and 1600s, and won a wider reputation in the 1700s. The aristocrats' emblems survived on the town's 1907 brewery, which made the local style throughout the communist period. This black brew has a spicy aroma hinting at red peppers, figs, and bitter chocolate. The same character emerges in big, expressive, smooth, long, dry, well-combined flavors. Since the reunification of Germany, the brewery has been owned by Bitburger.

Bad Köstritz…
…was once a spa town. Its black beer nourished Goethe when he was ill. Now it leads a fashion in Germany for extra-dark lagers.

KÜPPERS KÖLSCH

REGION OF ORIGIN Cologne, North Rhine-Westphalia, Germany

STYLE *Kölschbier*

ALCOHOL CONTENT 3.8 abw (4.8 abv)

IDEAL SERVING TEMPERATURE 48° F (9° C)

One of the few *Kölsch* beers to be found on occasion in export markets. Gustav Küpper brewed in the city in the 1800s, but the Kölsch and the present brewery date from the 1960s. It is a large brewery, on the banks of the Rhine. With a relatively "new" Kölsch to promote, Küppers emphasized heritage by establishing at the brewery an excellent museum of beer advertising. The brewery also has a restaurant serving local dishes. The beer is flowery, perfumy, and sweetish.

Coopering the barrel
Like the English word "cooper," Küpper probably means "barrel-maker," but in an old dialect of the Rhine. The modern German word, Küfer, is more often understood as "cellarman." A barrel-maker is a Fassbinder ("vat-binder").

L'ABBAYE DES ROCS
BLANCHE DES HONNELLES

🛡️ **REGION OF ORIGIN** Province of Hainaut, Belgium

🍾 **STYLE** Belgian Wheat Beer

⊗ **ALCOHOL CONTENT** 4.8 abw (6.0 abv)

🥛 **IDEAL SERVING TEMPERATURE** 48–50° F (9–10° C)

In the French-speaking part of Belgium, "white" wheat beers are identified by the word *blanche*. This example is made by a brewery named after a farm that was once a monastery. The brewery is near Montignies-sur-Roc, between Mons, Belgium, and Valenciennes, France. Montignies-sur-Roc is on two small rivers called the Honnelles. Blanche des Honnelles is fuller in color and stronger than most wheat beers, with marmalady and very honeyish flavours. The brewery, now well-established, began as a weekend venture in the domestic garage of a local tax official. He even used a brewkettle to decorate his lawn. The brewery's best-known product is a fruity, spicy (anis?) strong ale called simply Abbaye des Rocs.

LA CHOULETTE AMBRÉE

🛡 **REGION OF ORIGIN** Northern France

🍾 **STYLE** *Bière de Garde*

％ **ALCOHOL CONTENT** 6.0 abw (7.5 abv)

🍺 **IDEAL SERVING TEMPERATURE** 50–55° F (10–13° C)

Ambrée is the principal beer from the La Choulette brewery, run by husband and wife Alain and Martine Dhaussy, at Hordain, near Valenciennes. It pours with a big head and is very aromatic; has a spicy, aniseedy aroma and palate; and a slightly oily texture. It is a very good example of the style, and is an excellent beer with spicy foods. In addition to a *framboise* version *(see p.271)* and its Sans Culottes *(see p.270)*, the brewery also makes a stronger gold beer called Brassin Robespierre.

Artisanal…
…is a term beloved of French and Belgian brewers. It implies a hand-crafted or farmhouse product.

L

LA CHOULETTE BIÈRE DES SANS CULOTTES

	REGION OF ORIGIN Northern France
	STYLE *Bière de Garde*
	ALCOHOL CONTENT 5.6 abw (7.0 abv)
	IDEAL SERVING TEMPERATURE 50° F (10° C)

Without culottes? This wryly refers to the ragged-trousered poor of the French Revolution. Among the events leading up to the Revolution was a beer tax. Sans Culottes is golden, with a toasty, yeasty, Champagnelike aroma, and a similar "house character" to the Ambrée: oily and aniseedy, but less rich in spiciness and body, with a drier, elegantly bitter finish.

La Choulette Framboise

🏷	**REGION OF ORIGIN** Northern France
🍾	**STYLE** *Bière de Garde*, with fruit
%	**ALCOHOL CONTENT** 5.6 abw (7.0 abv)
🍺	**IDEAL SERVING TEMPERATURE** 50° F (10° C)

The name refers to a northern French game that was an antecedent of lacrosse. La Choulette is a farmhouse brewery, founded in 1885, at Hordain, south of Valenciennes. The basic La Choulette is a strong, amber brew in the local style known as *bière de garde*. It is the basis for the *framboise*, which is made with natural raspberry extract. This ruby-colored brew has an almost blackberryish aroma and a hint of cherry brandy in a smooth, cleanly nutty, dryish palate.

Towering brew
This beer is brewed in Ostrevant, a small region centered on Valenciennes. The landmark tower of Ostrevant is a 12th-century fortification.

LA TRAPPE QUADRUPEL

REGION OF ORIGIN Province of North Brabant, the Netherlands

STYLE Abbey

ALCOHOL CONTENT 8.0 abw (10.0 abv)

IDEAL SERVING TEMPERATURE 50–57° F (10–14° C)

The abbey at La Trappe, in Normandy, gave its name to the entire order. This beer is not made there, but in the Schaapskooi ("Sheep Pen") brewery at Koningshoeven ("King's Gardens") Trappist monastery, near the city of Tilburg, in the Netherlands. Outside Belgium, this is the only brewery operating in a Trappist abbey, but it is no longer run by the order. In 1998–99, it was acquired by the large independent Dutch brewer Bavaria. The strongest of the La Trappe products, Quadrupel is a very long, smooth, oily, syrupy, fruity (prunes, oranges?) beer, with a dry, warming, coriander-like finish.

LAKEFRONT RIVERWEST STEIN BEER

🛡 **REGION OF ORIGIN** Midwest US

🍾 **STYLE** Vienna Lager

％ **ALCOHOL CONTENT** 4.7 abw (5.9 abv)

🍺 **IDEAL SERVING TEMPERATURE** 48° F (9° C)

The city of Milwaukee, divided by several rivers that flow into Lake Michigan, was once infamous for producing some of the world's most watery-tasting beers. Today, it has big-tasting beers from little breweries such as Lakefront, founded in 1987 in a former bakery by a beat cop and his brother. Riverwest Stein Beer has evolved over the years into a superb deep-amber lager. It has a lovely balance of bigness and drinkability, with aniselike malt flavors and a crisp finish.

LAMMSBRÄU KRISTALL WEIZEN

L

🛡 **REGION OF ORIGIN** Franconia, Bavaria, Germany

🍶 **STYLE** *Kristall Weisse/Weizen*

(%) **ALCOHOL CONTENT** 4.1 abw (5.1 abv)

🌡 **IDEAL SERVING TEMPERATURE**
48–54° F (9–12° C)

Organic beers are the speciality of this brewery, which dates from at least 1628. The brewery is in the pencil-producing town of Neumarkt, in a valley 25 miles (40 km) southeast of Nuremberg. The enterprise began as an inn, "The Golden Lamb," and is family-owned. When the present family member took over, he insisted that "pure" beer began with the farmer: no artificial fertilizers, herbicides, or fungicides. He believes that organic malt is cleaner-tasting and the hops more aromatic. A hundred farmers grow barley on a crop-rotation basis, and five cultivate hops organically to meet the brewery's needs. It took them two or three years to switch and four or five to achieve the desired quality. The brewery's wide range includes a distinctive *Kristall Weizen*, which has a very fresh hop character, a creamy malt accent, and a cherryish fruitiness.

LE COQ PORTER

🛡 **REGION OF ORIGIN** Estonia

🍺 **STYLE** Porter/Imperial Stout

% **ALCOHOL CONTENT** 5.2 abw (6.5 abv)

🍺 **IDEAL SERVING TEMPERATURE** 48–55° F (9–13° C)

An historic name revived. Albert Le Coq was a Belgian, based in London, who exported strong porter from 1807. His shipments to the Russian Empire led to the later use of the term "Imperial Stout" for this style of beer. Just before World War I, his company acquired a lager brewery within the empire – at Tartu, in what is now Estonia – and switched it to the production of porter. In 1869, a ship carrying A. Le Coq Porter sank, and the vessel was found by divers in the Baltic Sea in 1974. The brewery had ceased brewing porter about five years earlier. In 1999, under new ownership, the brewery reintroduced A. Le Coq Porter. The beer is less of a true porter than an earthy, peppery, coffeeish, strong, dark lager, but a welcome manifestation nonetheless.

LEES HARVEST ALE

🛡	**REGION OF ORIGIN**	Northwest England, UK
🍾	**STYLE**	Strong Ale
%	**ALCOHOL CONTENT**	9.2 abw (11.5 abv)
🥛	**IDEAL SERVING TEMPERATURE**	50–55° F (10–13° C)

A classic from the John Willie Lees brewery, in Middleton, Greater Manchester. This brewery, founded in 1828, produces ales with the malty dryness that is typical of the region. Its Harvest Ale is made from Maris Otter barley grown in specified farms in North Norfolk and malted in Yorkshire, spiced with Goldings hops, from East Kent. The new season's crops are used, and the strong, "vintage"-dated Harvest Ale is released in late November or early December each year. The beer is filtered and pasteurized, but its flavors still seem to meld over a period of months, or even years. When young, the beer is emphatically rich and malty, with a spicy, vanilla-stick tinge. With age, it becomes less sweet, spicier, and winier. There have been occasional releases of this beer aged in port-treated oak.

Harvest theme
Each year's label carries a different illustration relating to farming and the growing of barley and hops.

LEES MANCHESTER CHAMPION BEER

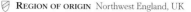

| | **REGION OF ORIGIN** Northwest England, UK |
| **STYLE** Pale Ale |
| **ALCOHOL CONTENT** 4.0 abw (5.0 abv) |
| **IDEAL SERVING TEMPERATURE** 50–55° F (10–13° C) |

Voted champion winter beer by a panel choosing seasonal brews for the British supermarket chain Tesco. This product, from the Greater Manchester brewery John Willie Lees, has a distinctly creamy, but still dryish, malt character. Its smooth texture and Brazil-nut flavor derive from the use of amber malt. There is also a minty, leafy, hop note, especially in the finish.

Cream of Manchester
Manchester is a great brewing
city which should be better
known for the products of local
breweries like Lees, Holt's,
Hyde's, and Robinson's. All have
greater character than the more
widely known Boddington's.

LEFEBVRE SAISON 1900

REGION OF ORIGIN Province of Walloon Brabant, Belgium

STYLE *Saison*

ALCOHOL CONTENT 4.2 abw (5.2 abv)

IDEAL SERVING TEMPERATURE 50° F (10° C)

The turn of the century was the peak year for the production of *saison* beer at the Lefèbvre brewery, in Quenast, just south of Brussels. This surprisingly robust but crisp, cleansing, summer style faced its toughest task there. The brewery was built in the 1870s to slake the thirst of workers at the nearby stone quarries, where ballast is now dug for the trans-European express railways. Saison 1900 has a firm, hard-toffee maltiness, developing to a spritzy, citric finish.

Arty allusion
The label typeface alludes to the Art Nouveau style for which Belgium is renowned.

LEFFE RADIEUSE

REGION OF ORIGIN Province of Namur, Belgium

STYLE Abbey

ALCOHOL CONTENT 6.6 abw (8.2 abv)

IDEAL SERVING TEMPERATURE 59–64° F (15–18° C)

Notre-Dame de Leffe is a Norbertine abbey at Dinant, near Namur, Belgium. The abbey grows herbal plants to make infusions, but has not brewed beer since the French Revolution. In the 1950s, to raise money for maintenance, the abbot licensed a local brewer to make Leffe beer. The brews are now made by Interbrew (Artois), at Leuven. Radieuse, meaning "halo," is the biggest in flavor. It has a cherrylike fruitiness, a portish texture, and a faintly roasty, cinnamon-tinged finish.

LEINENKUGEL'S AUTUMN GOLD

🛡 **REGION OF ORIGIN**	Midwest US
🍾 **STYLE**	Vienna Lager
⅏ **ALCOHOL CONTENT**	3.8 abw (4.8 abv)
🍺 **IDEAL SERVING TEMPERATURE**	48° F (9° C)

The name means "Linen Bobbin." The German Leinenkugel family established their brewery in Chippewa Falls, Wisconsin, in 1867. The family still run the brewery today, though it is now owned by the national giant Miller. There is now a second Leinenkugel brewery in Milwaukee, and a further-flung brewpub in Phoenix, Arizona. The Autumn Gold, slightly fuller in color than its name suggests, has spicy, malt-loaf aromas and flavors, and a dryish hop balance. A wide range of speciality styles is produced by Leinenkugel. The name is often affectionately abbreviated to "Leiney" by Midwestern beer lovers.

Leinenkugel's lively labels...
...stylishly and credibly evoke
the brewery's history.

LIEFMANS GLÜHKRIEK

🛡 **REGION OF ORIGIN** Province of East Flanders, Belgium

🍺 **STYLE** Spiced Cherry Beer

% **ALCOHOL CONTENT** 5.2 abw (6.5 abv)

🍺 **IDEAL SERVING TEMPERATURE** 158° F (70° C)

Anyone who has ever skiied in the Alps has been offered *glühwein*. "Glow" wine is warmed and spiced, typically with cloves and cinnamon. The familiar German prefix is used by the otherwise Flemish-speaking Belgian brewery Liefmans to promote the same notion. This beer, based on the cherry brew Liefmans Kriek (*see p.283*), contains the same two spices, but also anis. The cinnamon seems most obvious in the aroma, with ironlike, medicinal flavours giving way to sweet, sugared-almond notes, balanced by fruity acidity and a clovey finish. The aromas increase and the sweetness diminishes if the beer is mulled. It is intended to be heated as though it were hot chocolate. This is best done in a double boiler (*bain-marie*), though a simple pan, or even microwave, can be used.

Cherry Christmas
The typical Liefmans tissue comes in Christmassy colors for this brew, but Glühkriek might better be enjoyed with winter sports.

LIEFMANS GOUDENBAND

REGION OF ORIGIN	Province of East Flanders, Belgium
STYLE	Oudenaarde Brown
ALCOHOL CONTENT	6.5–7.0 abw (8.0–8.5 abv)
IDEAL SERVING TEMPERATURE	55° F (13° C)

The wineyness and slight sourness of "Gold Riband" place it as the classic brown ale in the style of its original home, the historic town of Oudenaarde, East Flanders. The brews of this town are quite different from the sweeter, more overtly malty and nutty brown ales of the English-speaking world. Liefmans Goudenband is actually brewed in Dentergem, just across the West Flanders border, but still fermented and matured in Oudenaarde. The brewery traces its history from 1625, but its kettles were retired in 1991. The beer's distinctive flavors – which are also irony, salty, and toasty – derive from a sodium bicarbonate water treatment; the use of a multistrain yeast; between four months and a year's maturation; a blending of young and old beers; and bottle-aging in the cellars at Oudenaarde.

LIEFMANS
KRIEKBIER

🛡	**REGION OF ORIGIN**	Province of East Flanders, Belgium
🍶	**STYLE**	Oudenaarde Brown, with Fruit
%	**ALCOHOL CONTENT**	5.2 abw (6.5 abv)
🌡	**IDEAL SERVING TEMPERATURE**	50° F (10° C)

This cherry beer is based on Goudenband, the classic brown ale of Oudenaarde, Belgium. In the fruit variation, the beer stays on a blend of Danish cherries and the smaller, drier, Belgian "kriek" variety for at least six months. About 30 lb (13 kg) of cherries and a small amount of juice are added per 180 pts (100 liters). For maximum contact between fruit and beer, the tanks are horizontal and very shallow. The person spreading the cherries has to crawl inside. So do the people who remove the pits and skin. The beer has an excellent fruit aroma, brandyish flavors, and a balancing, tannic dryness. There is a beer restaurant at the brewery.

Wrapped with pride
At any one time, four people are engaged in wrapping the beers, each handling between three and five thousand bottles a day. The tissue announces a triumph in a British tasting.

L

LINDEMANS CUVÉE RENÉ

🛡 **REGION OF ORIGIN** Province of Flemish Brabant, Belgium

🍾 **STYLE** *Gueuze-Lambic*

% **ALCOHOL CONTENT** 4.0 abw (5.0 abv)

🍷 **IDEAL SERVING TEMPERATURE** 55° F (13° C)

The winey-tasting *lambic* beers of Belgium, with their wild-yeast character, can be just too dry for some drinkers, so many of the more popular labels are sweetened. While this is true of the regular Lindemans products, Cuvée René is in a much drier style. Owner René Lindemans gives his name to a delicious, full-flavored beer: hugely foamy and lively, with the nuttiness of a Palo Cortado sherry; a soft, rounded sweetness; then a long, drying finish. The beer is a blend of lambics from six months to three years old. The average age of the blend is one year. The Lindemans were originally farmers, growing grain and brewing as a sideline. Commercial brewing started in 1809, and farming stopped in 1930.

LINDEMANS FRAMBOISE

🌿 **REGION OF ORIGIN** Province of Flemish Brabant, Belgium

🍾 **STYLE** *Framboise/Frambozen-Lambic*

％ **ALCOHOL CONTENT** 1.9 abw (2.5 abv)

🍺 **IDEAL SERVING TEMPERATURE** 55° F (13° C)

A raspberry beer based on the *lambic* of this Belgian farmhouse brewery. It has the typically seedlike, stemmy, woody, tobaccoish fragrance of real raspberries. The flavor begins flowery, then becomes very sweet, suggesting a heavy hand with fruit juice. In the finish, the sherryish acidity and tartness of the lambic emerges as a late, surprising balance. One of the more popular-style fruit beers, but still with some complexity.

L

LINDEMANS TEA BEER

🛡 **REGION OF ORIGIN** Province of Flemish Brabant, Belgium

🍾 **STYLE** Flavoured *Lambic*

％ **ALCOHOL CONTENT** 2.8 abw (3.5 abv)

🍺 **IDEAL SERVING TEMPERATURE** 55° F (13° C)

While pure *lambic*, and even the more Champagnelike *gueuze*, require a sophisticated palate, younger drinkers often prefer sweeter blends. Lindemans has had great success with a peach lambic, and has also produced a blackcurrant version. Both of these were launched in the late 1980s. In 1995, a tea lambic was added. The beer is matured on tea-leaves, and flavored with lemon juice. It has a sweetish, lemony aroma; a smooth, limey, marmalady taste; and a late, perfumy tea note.

LION STOUT

🛡	**REGION OF ORIGIN** Sri Lanka
🍾	**STYLE** Strong Tropical Stout
%	**ALCOHOL CONTENT** 6.6 abw (8.2 abv)
🍺	**IDEAL SERVING TEMPERATURE** 55° F (13° C)

Several tropical countries have rich, strong stouts. Perhaps the tastiest is this one, from Ceylon Breweries, of Sri Lanka. Lion Stout was for many years bottle-conditioned. It is still unfiltered, but is now pasteurized. Another change in recent years has been an increase in its alcohol content to the level shown above. It has big, pruny, mocha aromas and flavors, developing an intense bitter-chocolate finish. In Sri Lanka, it is sometimes laced with the local *arrack*, a spirit made from coconuts. The original Ceylon/Lion brewery is in the tea-planting town of Nuwara Eliya, in the mountains near the holy city of Kandy. In its traditional region, an astonishing 75 percent of the brewery's sales are for its stout, rather than its lagers. Since 1998, it has also had a brewery near Colombo, the capital. Sri Lanka is perhaps the only country in which every brewery (albeit there are only three) makes a stout.

L

LOUWAEGE HAPKIN

🛡 **REGION OF ORIGIN** Province of West Flanders, Belgium

🍺 **STYLE** Belgian-style Strong Golden Ale

% **ALCOHOL CONTENT** 6.8 abw (8.5 abv)

🍺 **IDEAL SERVING TEMPERATURE** 50° F (10° C)

Named after an ax-wielding Count of Flanders, Boudewijn Hapkin. (All beers in this style have names that are in some way diabolical.) In complexity, Hapkin perhaps comes closest to the similar but better-known Duvel *(see p.151)*. This beer has a very perfumy aroma; a soft maltiness; a clean, smooth fruitiness; a persistent bead; and a spritzy, very dry finish. Hapkin is made by the family-owned Louwaege brewery, at Kortemark, southwest of Bruges.

MACARDLES
TRADITIONAL ALE

M

REGION OF ORIGIN	Republic of Ireland
STYLE	Irish Red Ale
ALCOHOL CONTENT	3.2 abw (4.0 abv)
IDEAL SERVING TEMPERATURE	50° F (10° C)

The Macardle and Moore brewery is opposite Harp, in Dundalk, roughly equidistant between Dublin and Belfast, and close to the border that divides Ireland. The brewery was built, in handsome Victorian style, in 1863, to serve both cities, and has been owned by Guinness since the 1950s. The site had originally been settled by Huguenot weavers, and is known as Cambric Ville. Macardles Traditional Ale, one of the darker Irish examples of ale, is toasty and nutty, with a faint chocolate-cookie dryness.

McAuslan Bière
à la Framboise

🛡 **REGION OF ORIGIN** Province of Quebec, Canada

🍾 **STYLE** Raspberry Ale

⦿ **ALCOHOL CONTENT** 4.0 abw (5.0 abv)

🍺 **IDEAL SERVING TEMPERATURE**
48–50° F (9–10° C)

This Canadian fruit beer pours with a superbly rocky head that is well retained. It has a genuine raspberry color, rather than the shriller reds of some examples. The aroma is also very genuine, but the flavor is less obviously raspberryish, even though real fruit is used (in the form of purée). There is even a suggestion of blackberries (which are not used). Because it is based on an ale, it lacks the acidity and tartness of *lambic* fruit beers. The McAuslan brewery, in Montreal, is better known for its St-Ambroise Pale Ale *(see p.391)*.

ÉTÉ

5% alc./vol.
341 mL

Bière à la framboise
Raspberry Ale

McAUSLAN

McEwan's 80/-

🛡 **REGION OF ORIGIN** Southern Scotland, UK

🍾 **STYLE** Scottish Ale

％ **ALCOHOL CONTENT** 3.6 abw (4.5 abv)

▮ **IDEAL SERVING TEMPERATURE** 50–55° F (10–13° C)

Scotland's biggest beer-maker, which merged with Younger's, then acquired Newcastle Breweries and later Courage. The resultant company, Scottish Courage, is the biggest brewer in Britain. In Edinburgh, McEwan's products include this 80/−, very slightly lighter in body than its competitors, on the dry side, with a touch of burned toast. The label emphasizes the use of roasted barley, suggesting that this is a "classic" ingredient in a Scottish ale.

McGuire's Old Style Irish Ale

🛡	**REGION OF ORIGIN** Southeast US
🍶	**STYLE** Irish Red Ale
%	**ALCOHOL CONTENT** 3.6 abw (4.5 abv)
🍺	**IDEAL SERVING TEMPERATURE** 50° F (10° C)

Bill McGuire Martin, an American of Irish origin, put a tiny brewery into his pub in Pensacola, Florida, in 1988–89. In a town founded by the Spanish in the 1550s (and thus the oldest European settlement in what is now the US), the Erinophile McGuire also installed a collection of bagpipe memorabilia and a society called The Irish Politicians' Club. His Irish Red Ale was a pioneering example of the style among American microbrews. On tap the beer has a perfumy aroma; a touch of butteriness and plummy sweetness; and a firm grip of maltiness in the finish. The bottled version, called Irish Old Style Ale, is produced at a slightly bigger brewery in Louisiana. It is paler, lighter, and drier, but still very tasty. McGuire's rich, gingery, cakey Barley Wine is verbosely called "I'll Have What The Gentleman on the Floor is Having."

MACKESON STOUT

REGION OF ORIGIN	Southeast England, UK
STYLE	Sweet Stout
ALCOHOL CONTENT	2.4 abw (3.0 abv)
IDEAL SERVING TEMPERATURE	55° F (13° C)

The world's most widely known sweet stout was developed with the help of a dietician in 1907. It was originally made by the Mackeson brewery, in the small English port of Hythe, Kent. After several changes of ownership, the product came into the hands of the national brewer Whitbread. Mackeson Stout contains lactose, and a milk churn is shown on the label. The beer is light, smooth, and creamy, with hints of evaporated milk and coffee essence, and a liqueurish finish.

A hint of cream
With glitzier packaging, it could be the beer world's answer to Bailey's.

MACLAY HONEY WEIZEN

REGION OF ORIGIN Central Scotland, UK

STYLE Wheat Ale

ALCOHOL CONTENT 4.0 abw (5.0 abv)

IDEAL SERVING TEMPERATURE 50° F (10° C)

The much-loved Maclay's brewery, established in 1830 in the Scottish beer town of Alloa, closed in 1999, but its beers are still being made. Production switched to a new microbrewery in the town. This brewery is called Forth, after the stretch of water on which the town stands. Maclay's Honey Weizen borrows the German term for a wheat beer. This product, also made with Scottish heather honey, has a deliciously flowery aroma, with a touch of wheat fruitiness. Its flavor is distinctly honeyish, but quite dry. There is a firm but complex sweet-and-dry finish. It is made with a British ale yeast, not a German wheat-beer culture.

Flower of Scotland
The label emphasizes heather and a beehive, and the beer's floral, honeyed notes are more asssertive than the typical fruity tartness imparted by the wheat.

MACLAY OAT MALT STOUT

🛡 **REGION OF ORIGIN** Central Scotland, UK

🍾 **STYLE** Oatmeal Stout

％ **ALCOHOL CONTENT** 3.6 abw (4.5 abv)

🍺 **IDEAL SERVING TEMPERATURE** 55° F (13° C)

Such stouts are usually made with rolled oats, but this one was designed with the malted version of the grain. The aim was a rounder, fuller, sweeter character. This brew emerges with a malted-milk aroma, and does have a well-rounded palate, though quite a light body. It finishes with a buttery, toasty dryness. It is delicious with another Scottish oat confection: the dessert Atholl brose, which also contains cream, honey, and whiskey.

MACLAY THRAPPLE QUENCHER

REGION OF ORIGIN Central Scotland, UK

STYLE Golden Ale

ALCOHOL CONTENT 4.2 abw (5.2 abv)

IDEAL SERVING TEMPERATURE 50° F (10° C)

A thrapple is a throat in the English dialect of the Borders and Lowlands, as used by Scotland's national poet, Robert Burns, among others. This light, quenching ale from Maclay, produced at the Forth brewery, has a fresh, tempting, lemon-sherbet aroma; a light, delicate body; clean, marmaladey flavors; and a very dry, appetizing finish. A refreshing golden ale for summer or autumn.

Thirst aid
The thirsty Scot on the label has been dancing a Highland fling, from the looks of the small cartoons behind the main image. He has also been throwing the hammer.

MCMULLEN CASTLE PALE ALE

REGION OF ORIGIN Southern England, UK

STYLE Pale Ale

ALCOHOL CONTENT 4.0 abw (5.0 abv)

IDEAL SERVING TEMPERATURE 55° F (13° C)

This fine pale ale, which deserves to be better known, honors the ruins of a Norman castle in the McMullen brewery's home town, Hertford, north of London. Castle Pale Ale gains some fruity complexity in a period of warm maturation, during which it is also dry hopped with the East Kent Goldings variety. The beer starts malty, but develops a fresh, crisp, pearlike acidity as it warms, then finishes with a cedary, earthy, creamy dryness from the hop.

M

McNeill's Dead Horse India Pale Ale

🛡 **REGION OF ORIGIN** Northeast US

🍺 **STYLE** India Pale Ale

% **ALCOHOL CONTENT** 4.6 abw (5.8 abv)

🍶 **IDEAL SERVING TEMPERATURE** 50–55° F (10–13° C)

Cellists Ray and Holiday McNeill opened a bar in 1985, and added a brewery in 1991, in the somewhat arty and Bohemian town of Brattleboro, Vermont. Their 19th-century, clapboard building, with a cupola, looks like a tiny chapel but is actually a former firehouse and police station. The brewhouse is in the cells. Their beers are available cask-conditioned in the pub, but also bottled. They are made with great attention to style and, despite disconcerting names, are wonderfully appetizing. Dead Horse IPA is aromatic, with long, oily, hop flavors; a firm, malt background; and a cedary, dry finish. It is dry-hopped with East Kent Goldings. This is one of the best IPAs on the East Coast (Brooklyn's East India Pale Ale being another fine manifestation), but the US is dense with outstanding examples.

MAC QUEEN'S NESSIE

	REGION OF ORIGIN Austria
	STYLE Whisky-malt Lager
	ALCOHOL CONTENT 5.8 abw (7.3 abv)
	IDEAL SERVING TEMPERATURE 48° F (9° C)

The mythical monster Nessie is said to live in a Scottish loch, not a lake in the Alps, but its fame captures the imagination far and wide. The beer called Nessie is made by the castle brewery of Eggenberg, in lake country at Vorchdorf, between Salzburg and Linz, Austria. This incarnation of Nessie is a deep gold or bronze rather than the full "red" extravagantly promised on the label, but there is a real heftiness of malt in both the aroma and palate, with a late dryness and faint smokiness.

Monstrously royal
Just in case Nessie is not
sufficiently Scottish-sounding,
the brewery has borrowed the
name Mac Queen's from an
importer of its beers.

MAGIC HAT BLIND FAITH IPA

REGION OF ORIGIN Northeast US

STYLE India Pale Ale

ALCOHOL CONTENT 4.9 abw (6.1 abv)

IDEAL SERVING TEMPERATURE 50–55° F (10–13° C)

One of the founders said, "The idea of opening a brewery? We pulled it out of a hat." Magic Hat first fired its kettle in 1994. The brewery has a purple ceiling, with moons and stars suspended as mobiles. It is in the Vermont city of Burlington, noted over the years for Leftish politics and "alternative" philosophies. Blind Faith IPA has a light but firm, crisp body; very good, spicy, hop flavors; a smooth, toffeeish, malt background; and the hops and malt round beautifully in the finish. Blind Faith's swirly label design continues the "alternative," magical theme of the brewery. "Blessed with hops," says the small print, giving a spiritual overtone. Even the most down-to-earth brewers often refer to each addition of hops as a "gift."

MAISEL'S WEISSE DUNKEL

⬚ **REGION OF ORIGIN** Franconia, Bavaria, Germany

🍾 **STYLE** *Dunkel/Weisse/Weizen*

% **ALCOHOL CONTENT** 4.3 abw (5.4 abv)

🍺 **IDEAL SERVING TEMPERATURE** 48–54° F (9–12° C)

This Bayreuth brewery, one of several in Bavaria owned by families named Maisel, is known to some beer-lovers for an alelike speciality called *Dampfbier* ("steam beer") but has in recent years given more emphasis to its wheat beers. Even among dark wheat beers, its Weisse Dunkel has a particularly full color. There is a hint of coffee in the aroma and flavor, along with suggestions of cherry brandy and passion fruit. It has a very smooth body.

Star brewery
Traditionally, brewers displayed a star, like the one on Maisel's label, when they had a new batch of beer. This symbol of brewing is universal, but especially used in Franconia.

MAISEL'S WEISSE KRISTALLKLAR

M

🛡 **REGION OF ORIGIN** Franconia, Bavaria, Germany

🍾 **STYLE** *Kristall Weisse/Weizen*

％ **ALCOHOL CONTENT** 4.2 abw (5.2 abv)

🥛 **IDEAL SERVING TEMPERATURE** 48–54° F (9–12° C)

The filtered version of Maisel's wheat beer, Weisse Kristallklar, has a very fresh fruitiness of aroma; flavors of lemon pith or zest; and an extremely refreshing, crisp finish – like biting into an ice-cream sandwich. The original Maisel brewery, dating from 1886–87, is kept in working order and beautiful condition as a museum of beermaking and coopering, next door to the present (1970s') premises. The old bottling hall has been converted into a bar intended to evoke the "Roaring Twenties." Franconia may be a long way from New York or Chicago, but one of the owning Maisels married an American.

MALT SHOVEL JAMES SQUIRE ORIGINAL AMBER ALE

REGION OF ORIGIN New South Wales, Australia

STYLE Amber Ale

ALCOHOL CONTENT 4.0 abw (5.0 abv)

IDEAL SERVING TEMPERATURE 50–55° F (10–13° C)

James Squire, from Kingston near London, was transported as a convict to Botany Bay, Australia, in 1787, and is said to have become the first professional brewer in the then-colony. He had a pub called the Malt Shovel. The brewery now bearing this name was established in Sydney in 1988. It was founded by American brewer Chuck Hahn, who runs it as part of the Australasian group Lion Nathan. Its Amber Ale has a light but distinct hoppy aroma and a delicate balance of flavors. It is soft-bodied, with clean, creamy, malt flavors; a lightly spicy, dryish, cinnamon-like hop character; and a restrained, melony fruitiness. Very refreshing.

Shovel's progress
The Amber Ale has a series of labels with drawings and texts telling the story of James Squire's progress from thief to brewer, constable, banker, and magistrate.

MALT SHOVEL JAMES SQUIRE ORIGINAL PILSENER

REGION OF ORIGIN	New South Wales, Australia
STYLE	Pilsner
ALCOHOL CONTENT	4.0 abw (5.0 abv)
IDEAL SERVING TEMPERATURE	48° F (9° C)

Australia is best known for its golden lagers, but most are very bland, and contain large proportions of cane sugar. James Squire Original Pilsener is altogether different. Malt Shovel's principal, Chuck Hahn, is a keen exponent of Pilsner-style lagers. He produces this example from pale and Munich malts (no sugar) and the classic Saaz variety of hops. It has a lightly flowery, spicy, hop aroma; a body that seems at first slender but firm, then gradually reveals a fuller malt background; and a rounded, appetizing, hop bitterness, especially in the finish.

Hard-working brew
Barley and hops are justifiable emblems on the label. The text pays tribute to "the industrious people of Plzen" (the Czech spelling).

MANNS ORIGINAL BROWN ALE

🛡	**REGION OF ORIGIN**	Southern England, UK
🍾	**STYLE**	Brown Ale/Mild
%	**ALCOHOL CONTENT**	2.2 abw (2.8 abv)
🍺	**IDEAL SERVING TEMPERATURE**	50–55° F (10–13° C)

This style of dark, malty, sweetish, low-strength brown ale was once made by every English brewery as a bottled version of its draft mild. Few have such a product today, but this minor classic survives, at least for the moment. The Manns were a brewing family in London in the early 1800s, but were taken over by Watney's in the 1950s. In recent years, Manns Original Brown Ale has been made by Ushers, in Trowbridge, Wiltshire. Now, the future of that brewery is in question. In its most recent manifestations, the Brown Ale has been light, but smooth and creamy, with flavors of chocolate-coated raisins.

MÄRKISCHER LANDMANN SCHWARZBIER

REGION OF ORIGIN Berlin/Brandenburg, Germany

STYLE Black Beer

ALCOHOL CONTENT 4.1 abw (5.1 abv)

IDEAL SERVING TEMPERATURE 48° F (9° C)

The expression *Märkischer Landmann* refers to a citizen of the state of Brandenburg, which centers on Berlin. The Märkischer Landmann Schwarzbier was launched by the Berliner Kindl brewery in 1995, at the time when black brews were becoming fashionable. It has a licorice-like, malt aroma; a light, dry, grainy palate; and a slightly oaky, sappy finish.

An elegant glass…
…for a fashionable beer style. The extra-dark type of lager known as Schwarzbier *was rediscovered when the Berlin Wall fell.*

MARSTON'S OWD RODGER

🛡 **REGION OF ORIGIN** Trent Valley, England, UK

🍶 **STYLE** Old Ale/Barley Wine

% **ALCOHOL CONTENT** 6.1 abw (7.6 abv)

🍺 **IDEAL SERVING TEMPERATURE** 50–55° F (10–13° C)

Who was "Owd" (Old) Rodger? The renowned Marston's brewery, in Burton, England, does not know, except that his name has been used since at least the 1950s, and perhaps even before that. Several such beers are named after long-gone brewers, drinkers, cellarmen, publicans, or local characters. Owd Rodger is the stronger style of old ale and has a warming alcohol note. It pours with a dense head, leaving good lacework; has an almost purple color; a licorice aroma; a rooty palate; a lightly creamy body; and a juicy, fruity, portlike finish.

MARSTON'S OYSTER STOUT

	REGION OF ORIGIN Trent Valley, England, UK
	STYLE Dry Stout
	ALCOHOL CONTENT 3.6 abw (4.5 abv)
	IDEAL SERVING TEMPERATURE 55° F (13° C)

This does not contain oysters, but is offered by the brewery as the perfect accompaniment to the shellfish. Among dry stouts reasonably widely available in Britain, it has the fruitiest of flavors, with suggestions of onion or shallot and a firm, woody, cedary background. These complex flavors are beautifully combined. Marston's Oyster Stout was launched in January 1995, initially as part of an ever-changing range of special editions. Within six months, it had been added to the brewery's regular selection of bottled beers. Soon afterward, it won a gold medal at the International Brewing Industry Awards.

MARSTON'S PEDIGREE

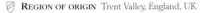 **REGION OF ORIGIN** Trent Valley, England, UK	
STYLE Pale Ale/Bottled Bitter	
ALCOHOL CONTENT 3.6 abw (4.5 abv)	
IDEAL SERVING TEMPERATURE 55° F (13° C)	

This is the most subtle and complex of all pale ales or bottled bitters, due in part to Burton's hard calcium sulfate water, and yet more significantly to the brewery's unique method of fermentation. The brew circulates through halls of huge oak barrels, linked in a "union" – a Victorian system that other breweries have long abandoned. The Burton Union system makes for a lively, cleansing fermentation, producing a beer of light, malty, nutty dryness and subtle, dessert-apple fruitiness. The 1870s brewery, which has been Marston's since 1898, added further "unions" in 1991. Marston's was acquired by Wolverhampton and Dudley Breweries in 1999, but continues to operate.

MARSTON'S SINGLE MALT

🛡 **REGION OF ORIGIN**	Trent Valley, England, UK
🍾 **STYLE**	Golden Ale
% **ALCOHOL CONTENT**	3.4 abw (4.2 abv)
🌡 **IDEAL SERVING TEMPERATURE**	50–55° F (10–13° C)

The term "single malt" belongs to whiskey, most often from Scotland, but has been cheekily borrowed by this English brewery to identify a cleanly delicious golden ale. In the world of whiskey, the term refers to a malt distillate made at a single site and not blended with any product from elsewhere. In the instance of this beer, the singularity is that only one variety of malting is used. Coincidentally, the variety is Golden Promise, favored by the famous malt whiskey Macallan for its rich, nutty flavors. Marston's Single Malt has the aroma and flavor of nutty, toasty cookies, but a surprising crunch of crisp hoppy dryness. It is to be hoped that Marston's is not punished for its impertinence. An earlier beer called Single Malt was produced during the 1990s by a Northern English brewery, Mitchell's, of Lancaster. Shortly afterward, the brewery closed.

MATER WIT BIER

🍃 **REGION OF ORIGIN**	Province of East Flanders, Belgium
🍶 **STYLE**	Belgian Wheat Beer
% **ALCOHOL CONTENT**	4.0 abw (5.0 abv)
🍺 **IDEAL SERVING TEMPERATURE**	48–50° F (9–10° C)

The ancient Romans probably established the oddly named village of Mater, near Oudenaarde, on the old route from Cologne to the sea. A family named Roman has for 14 generations run this beautifully kept brewery. Like the three neighboring breweries in the Oudenaarde area, it is best known for its brown beer. It also has this enjoyable white, with the fresh flavors of homemade lemonade, sherbet, and a balancing, dry spiciness.

Walker's **Witbier**
The area around Oudenaarde is, by the standards of Flanders, hilly. It is known as "The Flemish Ardennes." Here's a quencher for hikers.

MATILDA BAY DOGBOLTER SPECIAL DARK LAGER

M

🛡 **REGION OF ORIGIN** Western Australia

🍾 **STYLE** Munich Dark Lager

⊘ **ALCOHOL CONTENT** 4.2 abw (5.2 abv)

🍺 **IDEAL SERVING TEMPERATURE** 48° F (9° C)

The first new-generation brewpub in Australia was the Sail and Anchor, founded in Fremantle, in 1984. This enterprise gave rise to a micro, Matilda Bay, between Fremantle and Perth. That brewery is now owned by the national company Foster's. The name Dogbolter, "borrowed" from a British brewer, was first applied to an ale, but is now a dark lager, in broadly the Munich style. It has a distinctly cocoa-ish aroma, with the same character in the palate, balanced by a nutty dryness and rounded with smooth maltiness.

MATILDA BAY
REDBACK ORIGINAL

REGION OF ORIGIN	Western Australia
STYLE	South German Wheat Beer
ALCOHOL CONTENT	3.7 abw (4.7 abv)
IDEAL SERVING TEMPERATURE	48–54° F (9–12° C)

The redback is a poisonous spider indigenous to Australia. The implication of danger perhaps adds to the youthful appeal of this innocent but refreshingly tasty wheat beer, launched in the early days of Redback. The beer has undergone some changes over the years, but it remains one of the most distinctive brews in Australia. There are few wheat beers in Australia, and this was the first. It has a vanilla-like aroma; a smooth but definite, oily clove note (as in a classic South German wheat beer); and a lemony, crisp, spritzy finish.

Splashy classic
Redback's stenciled bottle offers a splash of modernism over a Bass-like diamond and the upright oval of the traditional beer label. The combination adds up to a packaging classic.

MICHELOB HEFEWEIZEN

M

REGION OF ORIGIN	Midwest US
STYLE	*Hefeweizen*
ALCOHOL CONTENT	4.0 abw (5.0 abv)
IDEAL SERVING TEMPERATURE	48–54° F (9–12° C)

The world's biggest brewing company, and producer of American Budweiser, has in recent years experimented with a wide range of specialities, including dark lagers, Bock beers, very hoppy ales, porters, and several wheat beers. In the last category, the one that seems to have become established is under the "super-premium" brand Michelob. This *Hefeweizen* is quite full in color; freshly aromatic; fruity and sherbety; with a suggestion of banana toffee.

MIKE'S MILD ALE

REGION OF ORIGIN North Island, New Zealand

STYLE Mild Ale

ALCOHOL CONTENT 3.2 abw (4.0 abv)

IDEAL SERVING TEMPERATURE 50° F (10° C)

Mike Johnson, a brewer with 12 years' experience, set up on his own in 1989. His White Cliffs brewery is on the coast at Urenui, on New Zealand's North Island. From the start, Mike Johnson's flagship product has been his Mild Ale. This has a fresh, earthy aroma; a smooth body; appetizing and pronounced cookie, milk-chocolate, and malt flavors; and a very lightly roasty dryness in the finish. It shows an outstanding balance of mild ale malt character, though it lacks somewhat in ale fruitiness.

MIKE'S MILD ALE
Naturally Brewed
330ml 4% vol
WHITE CLIFFS
BREWING
CO.

Under the volcano
The label shows North Island's Mount Taranaki (18,200 ft high/2,500 m), which is nearby.

MITCHELL'S OLD 90/- ALE

M

REGION OF ORIGIN Western Cape, South Africa

STYLE Strong Scottish Ale

ALCOHOL CONTENT 5.6 abw (7.0 abv)

IDEAL SERVING TEMPERATURE Store at 41° F (5° C); Serve at 50° F (10° C)

The spread of the Scottish people has done much to introduce their beer styles to a wider world. Alexander Angus Mitchell was from Blairgowrie, in Perthshire. He fought in a famous Highland regiment, the Black Watch, in the wars between the British and Dutch farmer (*Boer*) settlers in Southern Africa at the turn of the century. He married locally, and his grandson Lex founded the Mitchell's brewery, in Knysna, Western Cape, in 1984. The term 90/–, on his Scottish ale, refers to the old British unit of currency, the shilling. Traditionally, a "Ninety Shilling" was a strong ale. This unfiltered, unpasteurized example is spiced with cinnamon. It has an aroma reminiscent of Scotch whiskey; a malty palate; and a dry, slightly tart finish.

MITCHELL'S RAVEN STOUT

REGION OF ORIGIN	Western Cape, South Africa
STYLE	Strong Dry Stout
ALCOHOL CONTENT	4.8 abw (6.0 abv)
IDEAL SERVING TEMPERATURE	50–55° F (10–13° C)

Lex Mitchell previously worked for South African Breweries and, since founding Africa's first microbrewery in Knysna in 1984, has since opened Mitchell's pubs in Johannesburg and Cape Town. His smooth, firm, malty beers are unfiltered and unpasteurized. Raven Stout has a slatey black color; a creamy aroma; a rummy middle; and a hopsack, burlaplike dryness in the finish.

Flexible packaging
Big brewers buy a lot of glass bottles. In monopolistic markets, micros make do with plastic.

M

MOCTEZUMA NOCHE BUENA

REGION OF ORIGIN Province of Veracruz, Mexico

STYLE Munich Dark Lager/Bock

ALCOHOL CONTENT 4.8 abw (6.0 abv)

IDEAL SERVING TEMPERATURE 48° F (9° C)

The name means "Good Night," referring to Christmas Eve. This is the time when Mexicans have their Christmas dinner. Noche Buena, a strong, dark lager, is one of the tastiest beers from Mexico. It has a deep, amber-brown color, and is very smooth, with both malty sweetness and hoppy dryness in its long finish. Noche Buena is made by Moctezuma, which also produces the popular Vienna-style Dos Equis.

Scarlet leaves
The label shows a poinsettia.
Because it turns red in midwinter,
it is a symbol of Christmas.

MOHRENBRÄU SCHLUCK

REGION OF ORIGIN Rhine Valley, Austria

STYLE Vienna Lager

ALCOHOL CONTENT 4.2 abw (5.2 abv)

IDEAL SERVING TEMPERATURE 48° F (9° C)

One of the Three Wise Men who attended the birth of Jesus was said to have been a Moor – a king from what is now Morocco or Mauretania. The term Moor has its origins in Latin or Ancient Greek. The Moor's Head was once a common name for an inn, perhaps originally in an abbey. Mohrenbräu, dating from at least 1743, started as a brewpub. The brewery is in the town of Dornbirn ("prickly pear"), in Austria, not far from St. Gallen, Switzerland. It makes soft, smooth, light, well-balanced, rounded, Vienna-style beer under the name Schluck (implying a quick drink).

MOKU MOKU BISUCUIT WEIZEN

M

🛡 **REGION OF ORIGIN** Honshu, Japan

🍶 **STYLE** Belgian-German Wheat Beer

% **ALCOHOL CONTENT** 3.6 abw (4.5 abv)

🍺 **IDEAL SERVING TEMPERATURE** 48–50° F (9–10° C)

The phrase *Moku Moku* refers to smokescreens historically used by Ninja warriors, practitioners of martial arts in the local mountains. The brewery is near Ueno, east of Kyoto and Osaka, Japan. The beer's name alludes to biscuit malt, though this Belgian term sits oddly with the German *Weizen*. The beer has an orangey color; starts with a nutty maltiness; and finishes perfumy, fragrant, and slightly smoky. An interesting hybrid from Japan.

Mountain maltsters
Moku Moku imports its biscuit malt from Belgium. It does also have a small maltings of its own, as implied by the label.

Moku Moku Smoked Ale

- **REGION OF ORIGIN** Honshu, Japan
- **STYLE** Smoked Ale
- **ALCOHOL CONTENT** 4.0 abw (5.0 abv)
- **IDEAL SERVING TEMPERATURE** 50–55° F (10–13° C)

This Japanese brewery's odd name, a reference to the use of smokescreens by Ninja warriors, especially suits this ale. It is earthy, oily, and woody – with a late surge of fresh, seemingly oaky, smoke. In fact, peated malt, from Scotland, is the key ingredient. The brewery is part of a farmers' cooperative that also smokes ham and makes sausages. The smoked beer and ham can be tasted together in the cooperative's restaurant in Ayama, near Ueno.

MÖNCHSHOF KAPUZINER SCHWARZE HEFEWEIZEN

🛡 **REGION OF ORIGIN**	Franconia, Bavaria, Germany
🍾 **STYLE**	Dark Wheat Beer
🍷 **ALCOHOL CONTENT**	4.3 abw (5.4 abv)
🥛 **IDEAL SERVING TEMPERATURE**	48–54° F (9–12° C)

The "Monks' Courtyard" range of beers date from a Capuchin friary that was already brewing in the 1300s, in Kulmbach, in the north of Bavaria. Today, Kulmbach has two major breweries, Reichelbräu and EKU, under the same ownership, and the latter produces the Mönchshof beers. The Schwarze Hefeweizen is a very flavorsome beer, with vanilla aromas and flavors, and some banana notes, drying into molasses toffee and a hint of cloves. Kulmbach is known both for dark and strong brews, and makes a greater volume of beer per head of population than any other town in Germany. It has 30,000 people and produces 281,690,141 pints (1.6 million hectoliters) of beer per year, that is, 9,390 pints (5,300 liters) per person.

Black is beautiful
"Black" lagers became fashionable in Germany when examples from the East were rediscovered after the Berlin Wall tumbled. Mönchshof had long made a black lager, and now has this almost ebony wheat beer.

MORAVIA PILS

REGION OF ORIGIN	Lower Saxony, Germany
STYLE	Pilsner
ALCOHOL CONTENT	3.8 abw (4.8 abv)
IDEAL SERVING TEMPERATURE	48° F (9° C)

Although the name honors the Czech barley-growing region, it is the export of Bohemian hops down the Elbe River that seems to have inspired the especially assertive Pilsners of north Germany. Moravia Pils is one of the best-known examples. It has a flowery, minty aroma; a light, firm, clean, dry maltiness; a big hit of hop bitterness; and a gently dry finish. The Moravia brewery is modern, but its earlier buildings, in Lüneburg's step-gabled style, now accommodate a beautifully arranged museum and a restaurant serving local dishes. Moravia is owned by Holsten.

MORDUE WORKIE TICKET

REGION OF ORIGIN Northeast of England, UK

STYLE Bitter/Pale Ale

ALCOHOL CONTENT 3.6 abw (4.5 abv)

IDEAL SERVING TEMPERATURE 50–55° F (10–13° C)

A 23-year-old brewer with no formal training, Matthew Fawson won Champion Beer of Britain with this ale in 1997, only two years after he and his brother Gary had established their brewery. They named their business after a brewery that had operated in the 1800s in the building where they were living. Their brewery is in a village called New York, near the town of Wallsend and the city of Newcastle, England. In the local slang, a "workie ticket" is a troublemaker. The ale has a lively, grassy, hop aroma; a sweetish, malty palate; and an appetizing, emphatic, nutty dryness in the finish.

Moretti La Rossa

⬚ **REGION OF ORIGIN** Northern Italy

🍾 **STYLE** Vienna Lager/*Maibock*

% **ALCOHOL CONTENT** 5.8 abw (7.2 abv)

🌡 **IDEAL SERVING TEMPERATURE** 48° F (9° C)

The American love of beer with pizza is gaining global currency. Could Moretti La Rossa be the ultimate pizza beer? So long as there is enough dough to mop up the high alcohol. While pizza originates from winey southern Italy, the country's most characterful beers come from the cooler, grainier north. The Moretti brewery, established in 1859, in the handsome city of Udine, north of Venice, was for well over 100 years family-owned. In recent years, it has changed hands, been renamed Castello, and now specializes in a flowery golden lager. The Moretti beers are now among a range of 30 products made in five Italian breweries by Heineken. Under its new owners, La Rossa remains a characterful brew. It has almost the aroma of straight-from-the-oven pizza dough; a fresh, sweetish, lively, smooth malt character; finishing with a spicy dryness.

MORT SUBITE KRIEK

M

> **REGION OF ORIGIN** Province of Flemish Brabant, Belgium
>
> **STYLE** *Kriek-Lambic*
>
> **ALCOHOL CONTENT** 3.4 abw (4.3 abv)
>
> **IDEAL SERVING TEMPERATURE** 47–48° F (8–9° C)

The small, dark, dry-tasting cherry typically used in Belgian fruit beers is in Flemish called a *kriek*. Mort Subite, meaning "sudden death" is a version of a dice game that was played in a famous café in Brussels. Mort Subite eventually became the name of the café and its house beer, made in the Zenne Valley. Mort Subite contracts orchards to grow specific cherries for its beer. It is a beautifully balanced beer, with a creamy, almondy, cherry-stone note, and a lightly tart finish. Look out, also, for the drier Mort Subite Fond Gueuze, an unfiltered blend of young and old *lambics*.

Sudden death, long life
Mort Subite traces its history
to 1686. The brewery is in
Kobbegem, near Brussels. The
café is an institution in the city.

MÜHLEN KÖLSCH

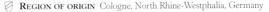

🏷 **REGION OF ORIGIN**	Cologne, North Rhine-Westphalia, Germany
🍾 **STYLE**	*Kölschbier*
% **ALCOHOL CONTENT**	3.8 abw (4.8 abv)
🍺 **IDEAL SERVING TEMPERATURE**	48° F (9° C)

The *Malzmühle* (Malt Mill) is an old-established, unpretentious brewpub making a distinctly malty, almost marshmallow-like *Kölschbier*. Mühlen Kölsch pours with a dense head, has a very fresh aroma, and a balancing spicy dryness. The brewpub is in the center of Cologne, on the square called the Haymarket (*Heumarkt*). An interesting contrast is offered at the opposite end of the square by Päffgen, a smarter bar-restaurant offering a hop-accented *Kölsch*. Päffgen has a brewpub in Friesenstrasse.

Brewing in the wind
Was the Malt Mill wind-powered?
Unlikely, as the brewery dates from
only 1858. Perhaps there were
windmills by the banks of the Rhine.

MURPHY'S IRISH STOUT

🛡	**REGION OF ORIGIN**	Republic of Ireland
🍷	**STYLE**	Dry Stout
%	**ALCOHOL CONTENT**	3.2 abw (4.0 abv)
🍺	**IDEAL SERVING TEMPERATURE**	50–55° F (10–13° C)

From what was Cork city's "Roman Catholic" brewery, named after a well consecrated to Our Lady. Murphy's brewery was established in the 1850s, and has on occasion produced an oyster stout, made by adding a broth of the shellfish to the brewkettle. Its regular stout, at 4.0 percent, is only mildly dry, with soda-bread graininess and the faintest hint of peat.

Draft in the bottle
In the British Isles, this term means that the bottle contains a nitrogen capsule to give the beer the creamy foam of a "draft" pint.

New Belgium Old Cherry Ale

Region of Origin	Southwest US
Style	American/Belgian Ale, with fruit
Alcohol Content	4.0 abw (5.0 abv)
Ideal Serving Temperature	50° F (10° C)

This pioneering Belgian-style brewery in Fort Collins, Colorado, makes an elegant fruit beer from locally grown Montmorency "sour" pie cherries. The beer has a pale, orange-pink color; a very lightly fruity, dryish aroma; a slightly oily, barley-sugar, malt background; and a very lightly acidic, balancing dryness in the finish. The brew is based on a lightly hopped amber ale, and the cherries are intended to add the tart edge.

From Paris to Fort Collins
Montmorency cherries are named after their place of origin, near Paris, France. They are known for their bright color and sourness.

NEW GLARUS WISCONSIN CHERRY BEER

REGION OF ORIGIN Midwest US

STYLE Belgian-style Cherry Beer

ALCOHOL CONTENT 4.0 abw (5.0 abv)

IDEAL SERVING TEMPERATURE 48–50° F (9–10° C)

The old Glarus is near St. Gallen, Switzerland; the new one is in Wisconsin. Deborah Carey owns this brewery with her husband Dan. He is a young veteran of the microbrewery movement. Cherries grown around Brussels, Wisconsin, are used in this award-winning brew, which also employs wheat, barley-malt, and semiwild yeasts from Belgium. The brew has almondy, cherry-stone aromas; sweet, fresh-fruit flavors; a textured maltiness; and notes of iron and tart acidity in the finish.

It's not Belgian…
…but its stylistic ancestry clearly is.
It has elements of Kriek and
reminders of a Flemish red ale.

NEWCASTLE BROWN ALE

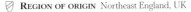

🛡 **REGION OF ORIGIN** Northeast England, UK

🍾 **STYLE** Brown Ale

% **ALCOHOL CONTENT** 3.8 abw (4.7 abv)

📖 **IDEAL SERVING TEMPERATURE** 50° F (10° C)

The most popular bottled ale in Britain, with a great student following. Its macho image has less to do with alcoholic potency than with its origin in a muscular city once known for the nearby coal mines and shipyards. This paler, drier style of brown ale was launched in 1927 by a head brewer whose not-quite appropriate name was Colonel Porter. If it is not excessively chilled, or gulped, this beer has a surprisingly nutty, flowery, winey delicacy.

What ales you?
In 2000, the marketing men at Newcastle announced that the word "ale" would be removed from the famous label, on the grounds of its being old-fashioned.

North Coast Old Rasputin Russian Imperial Stout

🛡 **Region of origin** California, US

🍾 **Style** Imperial Stout

％ **Alcohol content** 7.1 abw (8.9 abv)

🍶 **Ideal serving temperature** 55–64° F (13–18° C)

Grigori Rasputin was a monk, mystic, and drunkard who exercised great influence over the Russian royal family in the years immediately before the revolution. He was assassinated by a group of noblemen. The "mad monk" is celebrated with some irony in this rich, buttery, toffeeish, rummy imperial stout. It is produced by the North Coast brewery, in the one-time whaling port of Fort Bragg, California. Founded in 1987, the brewery began life in an old Presbyterian church and mortuary. It is a highly regarded brewery with a range of products. Among them is another stout, of more conventional strength, called Old No. 38. The name derives from a train that runs past the brewery and through the Redwood Forest.

NUSSDORFER OLD WHISKY BIER

	REGION OF ORIGIN Vienna, Austria
	STYLE Whisky-malt *Altbier*
	ALCOHOL CONTENT 4.9 abw (6.1 abv)
	IDEAL SERVING TEMPERATURE 48° F (9° C)

Having Anglicized his name for "Sir Henry's" *(see p.334)*, Baron Henrik Bachofen von Echt next turned his Vienna brewery to a Scottish theme with this satisfyingly malty brew. Among whiskey-malt beers, this example has notably lively, fruity, complex flavors. Though the smokiness is very restrained, it is just enough to provide a good, balancing dryness. This brew is based on Nussdorfer's *Altbier (see p.335)*.

NUSSDORFER SIR HENRY'S DRY STOUT

🛡 **REGION OF ORIGIN** Vienna, Austria
🍶 **STYLE** Dry Stout
📊 **ALCOHOL CONTENT** 4.5 abw (5.6 abv)
🍺 **IDEAL SERVING TEMPERATURE** 50–55° F (10–13° C)

Nussdorf is on the edge of the Vienna Woods. The name means "nut village," referring not to its inhabitants but to the local walnuts. In the wine cellars of his château at Nussdorf, Baron Henrik Bachofen von Echt makes Sir Henry's Stout. With its chocolatey flavors, this stout could be over-rich, but there is an appetizing dryness in the fruity finish. The cellars next door to the brewery have been known to contain hundreds of bottles of sparkling wine. An invitation to blend stout and Sekt into a "Black Velvet"? Regrettably, the local wine is not sufficiently dry.

NUSSDORFER ST. THOMAS BRÄU

	REGION OF ORIGIN Vienna, Austria
	STYLE *Altbier*
	ALCOHOL CONTENT 3.8 abw (4.8 abv)
	IDEAL SERVING TEMPERATURE 48° F (9° C)

Thomas, the patron saint of the village of Nussdorf, on the edge of Vienna, Austria, gives his name to this *Altbier*, produced there by Baron Bachofen von Echt. A Nussdorfer brewery established in 1819, and run by the Baron's family for five generations, closed in the 1950s, but he revived the tradition in 1984. His St. Thomas Altbier has robust malt flavors – sweet, creamy, nutty, and juicy – with a good hop balance.

Pure by law
The top line of the label makes clear that this Austrian beer is brewed according to the German Purity Law.

OASIS CAPSTONE ESB

REGION OF ORIGIN Southwest US

STYLE American Ale/Extra Special Bitter

ALCOHOL CONTENT 4.5 abw (5.6 abv)

IDEAL SERVING TEMPERATURE 50–55° F (10–13° C)

Every good watering hole is an oasis, but this pub and microbrewery pushes the point with its Egyptian-style interior. The brewpub is in the college town of Boulder, Colorado. Its bottled Capstone ESB has a full reddish-amber color and fine bead; a dense head, creamy aroma, and malt accent; and satisfying flavor development. It is silky smooth, with toast and marmalade notes, and a cedary finish.

Watchful eye
The thirst-making
Egyptian sun god peers
out from the label.

OASIS ZOSER STOUT

🛡 **REGION OF ORIGIN**	Southwest US
STYLE	Oatmeal Stout
ALCOHOL CONTENT	4.0 abw (5.0 abv)
IDEAL SERVING TEMPERATURE	55° F (13° C)

With its Ancient Egyptian theme, this respected brewery and pub in Boulder, Colorado, names its oatmeal stout after the mythical gatekeeper to heaven. The beer, which has an almost tarlike appearance and a very dense head, has a fragrant, perfumy, bitter-chocolate aroma and palate; a firm body; and a smoky finish reminiscent of a smooth Scotch malt whiskey.

Winter warmer
Perhaps the Rocky
Mountains and high plains
inspired the counter-images
of pyramids and desert.

OBERDORFER WEISSBIER

REGION OF ORIGIN Swabia, Bavaria, Germany

STYLE *Hefeweizen*

ALCOHOL CONTENT 3.9 abw (4.9 abv)

IDEAL SERVING TEMPERATURE 48–54° F (9–12° C)

One of the more widely available examples of the style in export markets. The brewery derives its name from its home town, Marktoberdorf (The Market of the Upper Village). The town is in green, rolling countryside about halfway between Munich and Lake Constance. The brewery traces its history to a tavern in the 1500s. Oberdorfer Weissbier is lively and very light, with a perfumy, bubblegum character.

The Dorf
The classic Bavarian village, a familiar
symbol on the region's beer labels, is a
clichéd image... but usually true to life.

ODELL'S 90 SHILLING

REGION OF ORIGIN	Southwest US
STYLE	Scottish Ale
ALCOHOL CONTENT	4.5 abw (5.6 abv)
IDEAL SERVING TEMPERATURE	50–55° F (10–13° C)

Doug Odell is an American of Welsh extraction who visited Scotland on vacation, enjoyed the beers, went home to Colorado, gave up his landscaping business, and in 1989 established a microbrewery in Fort Collins. One of his first beers was his 90 Shilling. It is appropriately malty in both its fresh aroma and satisfying balance of light, smooth syrupiness and nuttiness, finishing with a restrained, appetizing dryness. It is not billed as specifically a Scottish ale, but fits broadly into the style.

Beer with a rocky head
The label features the
Rocky Mountains, not
Ben Nevis or Snowdon.

O'HANLON'S WHEAT BEER

🛡 **REGION OF ORIGIN**	London, England, UK
🍾 **STYLE**	Wheat Ale
% **ALCOHOL CONTENT**	3.2 abw (4.0 abv)
🍺 **IDEAL SERVING TEMPERATURE**	48–54° F (9–12° C)

John O'Hanlon grew up in a pub in County Kerry, Ireland. In 1996, he established a pub under his name in Clerkenwell, a revived area of arts and crafts studios just to the east of Central London. At a time when imitation Irish pubs were enjoying great popularity, he introduced the real thing, with hearty food to match. It still operates, at 8 Tysoe St., London, EC1. He established a brewery in Vauxhall, London, initially to serve the pub. His most typical beer is a good, solid, chocolatey, dry stout, but more adventurous styles have also won a following. O'Hanlon's Wheat Beer has a lemon-zest aroma (perhaps from the addition of coriander); a light but oily, Martinilike body; and a cleansing, very dry, grapefruity (from Cascade hops), appetizing finish.

Winning wheat
The label announces that the brew was named British Wheat Beer of the Year in 1999. The competition was organized by the Society of Independent Brewers.

OKHOTSK MILD STOUT

⬛ **REGION OF ORIGIN** Hokkaido, Japan

🍶 **STYLE** Dry Stout

%⃝ **ALCOHOL CONTENT** 4.0 abw (5.0 abv)

🌡 **IDEAL SERVING TEMPERATURE** 50–55° F (10–13° C)

Close to the Okhotsk Sea, at the small town of Kitami near the east coast of Hokkaido, Japan, a pub and brewery make some delicious beers – flavorsome interpretations of classic styles. This mildly dry, very drinkable stout has a purply-black color; pours with a dense, rocky head; has an earthy hop aroma; roasted chestnuts in the palate; a creamy body; and a yogurty tartness in the finish.

Mild mannered
The word mild usually implies a sweetish ale. This brew is certainly mild in flavor, but a stout in style.

OKOCIM PORTER

REGION OF ORIGIN	Province of Galicia, Poland
STYLE	Strong Porter/Imperial Stout
ALCOHOL CONTENT	6.5 abw (8.1 abv)
IDEAL SERVING TEMPERATURE	55–64° F (13–18° C)

The district of Okocim is in the town of Brzesko, to the east of Cracow, Poland. The brewery there was founded in 1845 and makes a porter in the northerly, Baltic tradition. It has a soothing, almost medicinal character, with hints of cinnamon, drying in a cedary, appetizing finish. Other Polish strong porters include a notably smooth example from the town of Zywiec and a more raisiny interpretation from the Elblag brewery.

Imperial helmet?
This grandiose mug was designed to mark one of the brewery's anniversaries.

OLD DOMINION BREWING CO. OCTOBERFEST

REGION OF ORIGIN Mid-Atlantic US

STYLE *Märzen-Oktoberfest* Lager

ALCOHOL CONTENT 4.6 abw (5.8 abv)

IDEAL SERVING TEMPERATURE 48° F (9° C)

Users of Washington, D.C.'s Dulles airport may be familiar with several bars there strongly featuring the flavorsome and popular beers of Old Dominion. There is also a pub at the brewery, in the nearby Virginia suburb of Ashburn. "The Old Dominion" is a term for Virginia. One of the brewery's products is an *Oktoberfest* with an attractively subtle, ripe-apricot color and a perfect malty smoothness, firmness, and nuttiness. Among the several malts used is a Vienna type, and its contribution is very evident in a "barley sugar" sweetness and spiciness. The overall malt character is very good indeed. There is a late, herbal, fragrant hop balance. The hop varieties used are the German Hallertau, Czech Saaz, and American Liberty.

The American way?
In writings on beer style, Oktoberfest is usually spelled with a "k", the German way. In this label, the Anglo-American "c" is preferred.

OLIVER ESB

🛡 **REGION OF ORIGIN**	Mid-Atlantic US
🍾 **STYLE**	American Ale/Extra Special Bitter
﹪ **ALCOHOL CONTENT**	4.5 abw (5.6 abv)
🍺 **IDEAL SERVING TEMPERATURE**	50–55° F (10–13° C)

A family called Oliver from Kent, England, by way of Canada, brews this ESB in Baltimore, Maryland. The Olivers' brewery and Wharf Rat pub opened in 1993. The ESB is served on hand-pumps at the pub, and in half-gallon "growlers" to go. It has an attractive, reddish-amber color and fine bead; pours with a pillowy head, leaving a good lace; has a peppery hop-and-malt aroma; a nutty palate; a quenchingly tart finish; and a late, typically appetizing dryness.

Growling parrot
Where local laws allow, American brewpubs often offer to tap their draft beers into these takeout flagons.

OMMEGANG

	REGION OF ORIGIN Northeast US
	STYLE Abbey "Double"
	ALCOHOL CONTENT 6.8 abw (8.5 abv)
	IDEAL SERVING TEMPERATURE 59–64° F (15–18° C)

The name, suggesting "walkabout," refers to a Renaissance parade each July in the Grand Place of Brussels. The Ommegang brewery, making a range of Belgian-style beers, is near Cooperstown, New York. This was once a hop-growing region. The brewery was established in 1997 by Don Feinberg and Wendy Littlefield, importers of Belgian beer. Their interest in beer had originally been fired by a visit to Belgium in 1980. Their brewery is intended to have some architectural resemblance to a Belgian abbey. The beer, called simply Ommegang, is a lighter-bodied, more aromatic interpretation of a Belgian Abbey "Double." It nonetheless has the fullness imparted by candy sugar. There are also suggestions of vanilla, dark chocolate, prunes, orange peels, and aniseed. The finish is dry, medicinal, and warming.

OP-ALE

🛡️ **REGION OF ORIGIN** Province of Flemish Brabant, Belgium

🍶 **STYLE** Belgian Ale

％ **ALCOHOL CONTENT** 4.0 abw (5.0 abv)

🍺 **IDEAL SERVING TEMPERATURE** Brewery suggests 45° F (7° C), but the flavors are more evident at around 50° F (10° C)

In Flemish, *op* means "up", as in "drink up" – an apt abbreviation for Opwijk, the town where this ale is made. Op-Ale has a refreshing, sweet-apple fruitiness; a light, clean, dry, crisply malty palate; and a citric spritziness in the finish. It is made by the De Smedt brewery, which also produces beers for the abbey of Affligem.

Pride of the province
*Not only the local breweries but
also the province adopts the
Brabant horse as a symbol.*

ORKNEY SKULLSPLITTER

🏷️ **REGION OF ORIGIN**	Orkney Islands, Scotland, UK
🍾 **STYLE**	Strong Scottish Ale/Wee Heavy
🍷 **ALCOHOL CONTENT**	6.8 abw (8.5 abv)
🍺 **IDEAL SERVING TEMPERATURE**	55° F (13° C)

Many skulls were said to have been split by a Viking ruler of Orkney in the ninth century. During renovations of the island's cathedral in 1919, a split skull was found sealed into a pillar. This beer, if taken in excess, seems to promise an eternal sleep. The Orkney brewery's Skullsplitter is a wee heavy. It has a raisiny, sweet aroma; a very creamy taste, developing flavors like a fruitcake dunked in port; and a toasty finish. The brewery is in a former schoolhouse, in the windswept hamlet of Quoyloo, on the largest of the Orkney Islands. Its beers also include the chocolatey Dark Island, at a more conventional strength.

Drinking helmet
Orkney has more Scandinavian
history than Scottish or Celtic
heritage, but its beers are
matched by fine whiskies.

ORVAL

🏷️ **REGION OF ORIGIN** Province of Luxembourg, Belgium

🍾 **STYLE** Abbey (Authentic Trappist)

% **ALCOHOL CONTENT** 5.0 abw (6.2 abv)

🥃 **IDEAL SERVING TEMPERATURE** Store at around 57° F (14° C);
Serve no colder than 50° F (10° C)

The abbey's name derives from *Vallée d'Or* (Valley of Gold).
Legend has it that a countess lost a gold ring in a lake there, and
vowed that she would establish a monastery if it were ever returned.
A trout appeared from
the waters with her
gold ring in its
mouth, and she
was as good as her
word. Monks have
occupied the site,
in the Ardennes,
since 1070. Today's
1930s' abbey is an
architectural gem, and
the beer a classic. It gains
its color from its own
specification of malt, and is
dry-hopped. The hopsack aroma
is from the use of a semiwild yeast,
Brettanomyces, which adds a light,
firm body and fresh acidity of finish.

A touch of glass
The Orval glass was
designed by Henri Vaes,
the abbey's architect.

OTARU HELLES

🛡 **REGION OF ORIGIN** Hokkaido, Japan

🍾 **STYLE** *Helles* Lager

% **ALCOHOL CONTENT** 4.0 abw (5.0 abv)

🍺 **IDEAL SERVING TEMPERATURE** 48° F (9° C)

German brewer Johannes Braun created this outstanding *Helles*, albeit an especially far-flung example of the style. He developed this beer at a brewpub in Otaru, a major port on Hokkaido, the northern island of Japan. In the center of the pub is a copper-clad brewhouse built in Bamberg, Bavaria. Otaru Helles pours with a huge, rocky head, and has a bright gold color. It has the flowery aroma and flavor of German Tettnang hops, with a cookie maltiness in the middle. The brewpub also produces an orangey-brown dark lager and seasonal specialities such as a smoked beer.

Deep "growler"
Unfiltered beer is filled into litre "growlers" but the yeast sediment drops during storage to reveal a bright brew.

PALM SPECIALE

🛡	**REGION OF ORIGIN**	Province of Flemish Brabant, Belgium
🍶	**STYLE**	Belgian Ale
⅏	**ALCOHOL CONTENT**	4.0 abw (5.0 abv)
🍺	**IDEAL SERVING TEMPERATURE**	54° F (12° C)

The biggest-selling Belgian Ale. The brewery dominates the village of Steenhuffel, on the old road from the hop-growing town of Aalst to the regional capital Mechelen (also known by its French name, Malines). A farm called De Hoorn, dating from 1597, gave rise to the business. The brewery has operated since at least 1747, and is still family-run. After World War I, a low-strength dark ale was made prior to the launch of Palm. The name was suggested by a family member who was a priest. The beer has an aromatically toasty maltiness, balanced by a Goldings hop character, and a rounded, orangey finish from the house yeast.

Uncommon style
The term "Speciale" is sometimes used on labels in Belgium to indicate an ale rather than a more common lager style.

PARK SLOPE INDIA PALE ALE

	REGION OF ORIGIN Northeast US
	STYLE India Pale Ale
	ALCOHOL CONTENT 4.8 abw (6.0 abv)
	IDEAL SERVING TEMPERATURE 50–55° F (10–13° C)

Where the borough of Brooklyn, New York City, slopes toward its elegant Prospect Park, a neighborhood of imposing brownstones has become a "village" of food shops and cafés. An 1890s' bakery there was in 1994 turned into a pub and brewery. The pub still operates, but with a larger brewery on a separate site nearby. Its IPA is perfumy, with sweet apple flavors, but beautifully balanced and drinkable, with lingering hop notes and a crisp finish.

Indian mahogany?
The original Park Slope brewpub's mahogany storefront decorates the label. Contrary perhaps to popular image, Brooklyn is in parts very handsome.

PATER LIEVEN BLOND

🛡 **REGION OF ORIGIN** East Flanders, Belgium

🍶 **STYLE** Abbey Ale

% **ALCOHOL CONTENT** 5.2 abw (6.5 abv)

🍺 **IDEAL SERVING TEMPERATURE** Store at about 57° F (14° C);
Serve no colder than 50° F (10° C)

Made in the "Flemish Ardennes," at the village of St. Lievens Esse, between Oudenaarde and Ninove, and not far from Brussels. The term Pater is intended to hint at a monastic father. The brewery is near the parish church, but has no monastic connections. It began in 1897 as a farm, and looks quite agricultural inside, though the facade has a touch of Art Nouveau. It is owned by the third generation of the Van den Bossche family, and is known simply by their name. Pater Lieven Blond has a fresh, fruity, creamy aroma; a notably refreshing, crisp palate; and a dry, faintly salty finish. In the same range, the brewery makes a Bruin and a bronze Tripel, the latter called Lamoral, after a patriotic count who was beheaded during the period of Spanish rule.

PAULANER HEFE-WEIZEN

🛡 **REGION OF ORIGIN** Munich, Upper Bavaria, Germany

🍺 **STYLE** *Hefeweizen*

% **ALCOHOL CONTENT** 4.4 abw (5.5 abv)

🥤 **IDEAL SERVING TEMPERATURE** 48–54° F (9–12° C)

The famous Paulaner brewery of Munich is especially known for its lagers, most notably its Salvator Double Bock *(see p.355)*, but in recent years it has also responded to the youthful popularity of wheat beers. The most commercially minded breweries often produce relatively bland wheat beers, but the sizable Paulaner does offer a flavorsome example. It has the typical clove aroma of the style, with suggestions of honey and fruit; notes of peach, banana, perhaps even strawberry, and certainly vanilla, in the palate; and a good malt background.

PAULANER ORIGINAL MUNICH

P

> ⬙ **REGION OF ORIGIN** Munich, Upper Bavaria, Germany
>
> 🍾 **STYLE** Munich *Helles* Lager
>
> % **ALCOHOL CONTENT** 4.4 abw (5.5 abv)
>
> 🍺 **IDEAL SERVING TEMPERATURE** 48° F (9° C)

The first lagers brewed in Munich were dark brown, and this style, perfected in the late 1830s, is still associated with the city. There is also a Munich style of golden lager, with a distinct malt accent (as opposed to the hoppier brew developed in Pilsen or the drier Dortmund type). This type of lager is usually identified as a *Münchner helles* ("pale"). There is some argument as to which Munich brewery should take credit for the style, but Paulaner seems to have popularized it, in the late 1920s and 1930s. The beer shown here has the same name in its own country (but in German, of course: Münchner Urtyp). It has a spicy, flowery, camomile-like aroma; a rounded, firm attack of malt; then a surprising degree of hoppy dryness in the finish.

PAULANER SALVATOR

REGION OF ORIGIN Munich, Upper Bavaria, Germany

STYLE Double Bock

ALCOHOL CONTENT 6.0 abw (7.5 abv)

IDEAL SERVING TEMPERATURE 48° F (9° C)

Germany's most famous spring beer is made by the Paulaner. This brewery was founded in 1634 by monks in the order of St. Francis of Paula. They brewed an especially malty beer as "liquid bread" to sustain them during Lent. They called it "Salvator," Latin for "The Savior." The brewery is no longer owned by monks, but its products still include Paulaner Salvator. The new season's brew is ceremonially tapped each year before Lent. This extra-strong lager has a head like whipped cream; a rich, deep, amber-brown color; a buttery-malty aroma; and a toffeeish flavor, drying in a long, enticing finish. Before the introduction of registered trademarks, other breweries making beers in this style labeled them Salvator as though it were a description of style. Later, they simply used names ending in -ator. Today the style is technically known as Double Bock.

A suitably small serving…
…for a very strong lager, but the Germans often use steins for this style. The beer is high in malt but relatively low in hops, so it satisfies rather than makes the drinker hungry.

PAUWEL KWAK

REGION OF ORIGIN	Province of East Flanders, Belgium
STYLE	Strong Belgian Ale
ALCOHOL CONTENT	6.4 abw (8.0 abv)
IDEAL SERVING TEMPERATURE	55° F (13° C)

The spectacular glass in which this beer is traditionally served is perhaps better known than the brew itself. The vessel is modeled on a stirrup cup from the days of horse-drawn coaches. At a coaching inn, the driver could, while still in position, have a drink, then set down the glass in his stirrup. Pauwel ("Paul") is said to have been an innkeeper who made a famously sustaining beer. *Kwak* implies a bloblike fat man. Today's brew is made from three malts and a small proportion of white confectioner's sugar. It is malty, toffeeish, and nougatlike, with a fruity, brandyish, warming finish. The brewery, set round a small "château" in Buggenhout, East Flanders, dates from 1791, and has been in the Bosteels family (from which it takes its name) for seven generations.

PECONIC COUNTY RESERVE ALE

🛡 **REGION OF ORIGIN**	Northeast US
🍾 **STYLE**	Wheat Beer, with fruit
% **ALCOHOL CONTENT**	5.0 abw (6.2 abv)
🍺 **IDEAL SERVING TEMPERATURE**	50° F (10° C)

The name refers to a region that wishes to secede from Suffolk County, on Long Island, New York State. The Southampton Publick House there makes a lightly hopped wheat beer, using both raw and malted versions of the grain, and adds Chardonnay grapes grown at the nearby Sag Pond winery by native Bavarian Roman Roth. The beer is matured in white wine casks. It emerges with a raisiny, brandyish aroma; a crisp attack; a restrained fresh-apple and maple palate; and a big, woody, dry finish.

King Charles
On the label, the wine-grower meets the King of Beer, who in this rendition bears a strong resemblance to homebrew guru Charlie Papazian.

BREWED IN 1996
SPH

PECONIC COUNTY
RESERVE ALE
(ale brewed with grapes)

CONTENTS: 1 PINT 9.4 FL. OZ. (750 ml)
BREWED AND BOTTLED BY SOUTHAMPTON PUBLICK HOUSE, SOUTHAMPTON, NY

PELFORTH AMBERLEY

P

🛡 **REGION OF ORIGIN** Northern France

🍶 **STYLE** Whiskey-malt Lager

% **ALCOHOL CONTENT** 5.6 abw (7.0 abv)

🍺 **IDEAL SERVING TEMPERATURE** 48° F (9° C)

This *bière aromatisée au malt à whisky* is made by Pelforth, in Lille, France. Amberley is smooth, firm, and dry. Among European examples of the style, it has perhaps the most obvious late smokiness. Whiskey-malt beer was pioneered in Alsace, France, by the lightly grainy-peaty Adelscott. There is a companion brew of a much darker style called Adelscott Noir. These beers are produced at the Adelshoffen brewery.

Magnificent Amberleys
The brand neatly combines "amber"
with a suggestion of typical Scottish
names like Waverley.

PELFORTH GEORGE KILLIAN'S

🛡	**REGION OF ORIGIN** Northern France
🍾	**STYLE** Irish Red Ale
%️	**ALCOHOL CONTENT** 5.2 abw (6.5 abv)
🍺	**IDEAL SERVING TEMPERATURE** 50° F (10° C)

A brewery dating from a 15th-century friary in Enniscorthy, County Wexford, Ireland, inspired this beer. The brewery, which made a Ruby Ale, closed in 1956. A member of the owning family, George Killian Lett, licensed Pelforth, of France, to maintain the tradition. The French interpretation has a very malty aroma and flavor, and a faintly smoky dryness. A slightly weaker version is made with a lager yeast by Coors of Colorado. This has a fuller color, but is much lighter in flavor.

Red ale…
…is suggested by the French
words arched over the (Irish?)
horse on the label.

PENN OKTOBERFEST

P

🛡	**REGION OF ORIGIN**	Northeast US
🍾	**STYLE**	*Märzen-Oktoberfest* Lager
%	**ALCOHOL CONTENT**	4.6 abw (5.8 abv)
🍺	**IDEAL SERVING TEMPERATURE**	48° F (9° C)

Some of America's finest German-style lagers are made by the Penn brewery and pub. This was established in 1986 in the 1880s' building of the long-closed Eberhardt and Ober brewery, in the old German quarter of Pittsburgh, Pennsylvania. Its wide range of classic styles includes this *Oktoberfest*. The beer has a full gold to bronze color; a deliciously fresh malt aroma; a smooth, lightly sweet, appetizingly nutty palate; and a spicily dry hop finish. It is a very German interpretation of the style, created by a Munich-trained brewer.

Peroni Gran Riserva

🏳 **Region of origin**	Italy
🍾 **Style**	Strong Golden Lager
⅌ **Alcohol content**	5.28 abw (6.6 abv)
🍺 **Ideal serving temperature**	48° F (9° C)

Although Italy is a wine country, the north has a beer tradition. Francesco Peroni established this company near Milan, and his family still manages it, though it is now heaquartered in Rome. Peroni's Nastro Azzurro, the best-known Italian beer, is a typically light, refreshing, spritzy Italian lager, albeit higher than some in alcohol. In 1996, to mark the company's 150th anniversary, Peroni Gran Riserva was launched. This is broadly in the style of a *Maibock*, though it is a year-round product. It has a full, golden color; a smooth, firm, lightly nutty, malt character; a crisp, dry finish; and a late, warming touch of alcohol. It is a delicately balanced beer, malt-accented but dryish. It is made entirely from Pilsner malt (with a double decoction mash) and Saaz hops, and is said to have two months' lagering.

The original Peroni
The mustachioed man on this label is
Giovanni Peroni, upon whose recipe
Gran Riserva is allegedly based.

PETRUS OUD BRUIN

P

REGION OF ORIGIN	Province of West Flanders, West Flanders, Belgium
STYLE	Flemish Red/Brown
ALCOHOL CONTENT	4.4 abw (5.5 abv)
IDEAL SERVING TEMPERATURE	48–55° F (9–13° C)

In the Petrus range, this reddish-brown brew in the Flemish style is the one that at least superficially resembles the wine with the similar name. It is a complex brew, with a tannic aroma and a very smooth palate, with a clean, toffeelike maltiness, hints of chocolate, and cinnamon-dusted pears. This is from the De Brabandere brewery, of Bavikhove, West Flanders. It is in the reddish-brown, sweet-and-sour style of the region. In the classic local procedure, it is a blend of beers. The older part of the blend is matured for 20–24 months in huge horizontal casks that once held white wine and, before that, Calvados.

Vintage visitors
The name spurred a curiosity visit from the Bordeaux château, but the visiting winemakers are recalled as having been very friendly.

PETRUS SPECIALE

	REGION OF ORIGIN Province of West Flanders, Belgium
	STYLE Belgian Ale
	ALCOHOL CONTENT 4.4 abw (5.5 abv)
	IDEAL SERVING TEMPERATURE 50° F (10° C)

The name Petrus sounds like a famous Bordeaux wine but is intended simply to signify St. Peter, known as "holder of the keys to heaven." The Petrus range is made by the De Brabandere brewery, of Bavikhove, West Flanders. Its Speciale is an assertive ale, with an earthy aroma; a textured malt background; coriander in the palate (this spice is added); and a rooty, hoppy finish.

Hop happy
Hops feature on many beer labels. In this case, the illustration is justified. Petrus Speciale is one of the hoppier Belgian ales.

PETRUS TRIPLE

P

> 🛡 **REGION OF ORIGIN** Province of West Flanders, Belgium
>
> 🍾 **STYLE** Abbey Triple
>
> 🌿 **ALCOHOL CONTENT** 6.0 abw (7.5 abv)
>
> 🍺 **IDEAL SERVING TEMPERATURE** Store at around 57° F (14° C);
> Serve no colder than 50° F (10° C)

The holy name Petrus ("holder of the keys to heaven") is used by the Belgian brewery Bavik for a full range of specialities, but perfectly suits a strong, abbey-style beer like a Triple. This example has a spicy, orange-blossom aroma; a light body for the style, though it is firm and smooth; a hint of syrupy sweet lemon; and a dry finish. A very small amount of coriander is used, and Saaz is the dominant hop. Petrus Triple is a bottle-conditioned beer, and was launched in 1990 as a successor to the similar, filtered and pasteurized, slightly darker, Cuvée St. Amand.

PIKE PALE ALE

🛡 **REGION OF ORIGIN** Pacific Northwest US

🍾 **STYLE** Pale Ale

% **ALCOHOL CONTENT** 3.6 abw (4.5 abv)

🌡 **IDEAL SERVING TEMPERATURE** 50–55° F (10–13° C)

Pike Place Market is at the heart, or perhaps the stomach, of Seattle, a city that loves food almost as much as it prizes ale. The Pike brewery has its own pub but no longer operates the bookshop and museum that made it such a focus for beer-lovers. It is to be hoped that a change of ownership in recent years will not diminish the character of its beers in the long term. Its pale ale is very big indeed, with a rich, creamy, sweet malt character; an almost voluptuous body; a hint of peachy fruitiness; and a punch of earthy hop bitterness in the finish.

P

PILSNER URQUELL

REGION OF ORIGIN Pilsen, Bohemia, Czech Republic

STYLE Pilsner

ALCOHOL CONTENT 3.5 w (4.4 abv)

IDEAL SERVING TEMPERATURE 48° F (9° C)

The term *Urquell* means "original source" in German, the official language of Bohemia when it was a part of the Austrian empire. Bohemia now forms, with Moravia, the Czech Republic. In Czech, the beer is called Plzeňský Prazdroj. This is the original Pilsner, copied throughout the world, often by lesser, blander beers. Its golden color was a novelty at the time when glass vessels were replacing stoneware steins and pewter tankards, but the beer's fame was also due to its quality. The famous Bohemian Saaz hop imparted the flowery, spicy aroma and bitter finish; the equally renowned Moravian barley malt provided a soft, delicious balance. Both characteristics have diminished slightly in recent years, but Pilsner Urquell is still one of the world's great beers.

The Pilsner glass
Tall, conical glasses are often used to present Pilsner-style beers. This shape helps to sustain the sparkle.

PINK ELEPHANT MAMMOTH

	REGION OF ORIGIN South Island, New Zealand
	STYLE Strong Ale
	ALCOHOL CONTENT 5.6 abw (7.0 abv)
	IDEAL SERVING TEMPERATURE 50–55° F (10–13° C)

In the hop county of Kent, a brewery with an elephant symbol inspired Roger Pink when he was growing up in England. Now, having moved to New Zealand, he uses the brand Pink Elephant for beers he makes in an orchard near Blenheim, in the Marlborough winemaking region. Among his products is Mammoth, a strong ale, smooth and packed with satisfying flavors. It has a peppery aroma; a fruity palate, reminiscent of strawberries; and a coffeeish bitterness in the finish.

This elephant…
…was inspired by that of the Fremlins' Maidstone brewery, acquired by Whitbread in 1967, and closed in 1972.

P

PINK ELEPHANT PBA

REGION OF ORIGIN South Island, New Zealand

STYLE Bitter/Pale Ale

ALCOHOL CONTENT 4.0 abw (5.0 abv)

IDEAL SERVING TEMPERATURE 50–55° F (10–13° C)

Names comprising initials are popular among British brewers. Sometimes the original meaning has been forgotten. In other instances, it is deliberately left unspoken. British-born New Zealand brewer Roger Pink declines to elaborate on PBA. Pink's Best Ale? Pink's Bitter Ale? It is hoppy from the start, in a wonderfully fresh aroma and dry palate, and its malty background does nothing to detract from a late, lingering bitterness. Three New Zealand varieties of hop are used. There are three additions and the beer is also dry-hopped.

330 ml of
GENUINE
ALE

PINK ELEPHANT

PBA
A HOPPY ALE
OF 5% ALC.
Best Imbibed at 12°C

THE
PINK ELEPHANT

BREWERY
MARLBOROUGH · NEW ZEALAND

Other elephants…
…include Denmark's Carlsberg,
Holesovice, of the Czech
Republic, and, naturally
enough, Tusker, of Kenya.

PINKUS MÜLLER ALT

🛡 **REGION OF ORIGIN** Münster, North Rhine-Westphalia, Germany

🍺 **STYLE** Münster *Altbier*

💧 **ALCOHOL CONTENT** 4.0 abw (5.0 abv)

🥛 **IDEAL SERVING TEMPERATURE** 48° F (9° C)

Unlike the better-known *Alt* ("Old Style") beers of Düsseldorf, this is golden in color and wheat-tinged in its fruity, crisp, dry flavors – which are balanced by a buttery maltiness. This version of Altbier evolved in the university city of Münster, capital of North Rhine-Westphalia. This version is made only at a famous brewery and pub called Pinkus Müller. This establishment began in 1816 as a bakery and brewery in the Old Town, and has expanded over the years through nine houses. In summer, the beer is offered laced with soft fruits.

PINKUS MÜLLER HEFE WEIZEN

REGION OF ORIGIN Münster, North Rhine-Westphalia, Germany

STYLE *Hefeweizen*

ALCOHOL CONTENT 4.2 abw (5.2 abv)

IDEAL SERVING TEMPERATURE
48–54°F (9–12° C)

Such has been the success of south German wheat beers that many northern breweries have devised their own examples of this style. In Münster, the Pinkus Müller pub and brewery has a *Weizen* that is distinctly its own. The beer has a typical southern balance of wheat to barley malt, but a northern yeast character: flowery, dry, and slightly acidic. A smooth, delicate, and appetizing beer.

In the pink
The label's period photograph of the Pinkus Müller tavern on a busy night provides an image once familiar in any German town in the Old or New World.

PINKUS MÜLLER ORGANIC

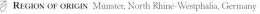 **REGION OF ORIGIN** Münster, North Rhine-Westphalia, Germany

STYLE Organic *Altbier*

ALCOHOL CONTENT 4.0 abw (5.0 abv)

IDEAL SERVING TEMPERATURE 48° F (9° C)

The term organic, when applied to beer, indicates that no fertilizers or pesticides have been used in the cultivation of the barley and hops. This is particularly difficult in respect of hops, which are very susceptible to diseases and pests. One solution is to introduce predators that will keep down any pests. Germany, with its enthusiasm for "green" issues, has several organic hop farms. Pinkus Müller has been a pioneer of organic beers. These brews are usually identified in Germany by adjectives such as Öko or Bio. Pinkus Müller Organic has a distinctly pale color; a notably clean, lightly malty-buttery aroma; a light but firm, rounded body; and a perfumy, faintly fruity dryness in the finish.

P

PITFIELD'S 1850 SHOREDITCH PORTER

🛡 **REGION OF ORIGIN** London, England, UK

🍺 **STYLE** Porter

％ **ALCOHOL CONTENT** 4.0 abw (5.0 abv)

🍺 **IDEAL SERVING TEMPERATURE** 50–55° F (10–13° C)

To many beer lovers far beyond London, the phrase "Pitfield Street" brings instantly to mind a small shop selling some of the world's best and most genuinely unusual beers. Neither the street nor the shop is very large, but the premises also manage to accommodate a small brewery. Pitfield Street runs into the London neighborhood of Shoreditch, where the first porter is said to have been made in 1722. Pitfield's 1850 Shoreditch Porter is based on a recipe from that year from Whitbread, the major brewer most strongly associated with the style. Pitfield's interpretation is light-bodied but smooth and dry, with flavors reminiscent of maple syrup and charcoal. In the year 2000, the Pitfield brewery began a switch to organic ingredients for all its products.

PITFIELD'S

1850
SHOREDITCH
ABV 5%
PORTER

LONDON'S AWARD
PITFIELD'S
WINNING BREWERS

POPERINGS HOMMEL BIER

REGION OF ORIGIN Province of West Flanders, Belgium

STYLE Strong Golden Ale

ALCOHOL CONTENT 6.0 abw (7.5 abv)

IDEAL SERVING TEMPERATURE 50° F (10° C)

Near the World War I graves around Ypres, the town of Poperinge is the center of a small hop-growing region. Although the word hop is used in Flemish, there is also a local variation, *hommel*, from the Latin *humulus*. This beer, highlighting the local hops, is made by the Van Eecke brewery, in nearby Watou. It is a bottle-conditioned ale, with a roselike floweriness, honeyish notes, orange-zest hop flavors, and a late spicy, cumin-seed dryness.

Hedging the hops
The label shows the town skyline peeking over hedges of hops. In late summer, such hedges are a landmark in all hop-growing districts.

P

PORTLAND BREWING
MACTARNAHAN'S GOLD MEDAL

REGION OF ORIGIN	Pacific Northwest US
STYLE	Scottish/Northwestern Ale
ALCOHOL CONTENT	3.4 abw (4.2 abv)
IDEAL SERVING TEMPERATURE	55° F (13° C)

Portland, Oregon, has 20-odd breweries, more than any other city in the world. The boom began in the mid-1980s, and Portland Brewing dates from that time. In 1992, the brewery won a gold medal at the Great American Beer Festival for its MacTarnahan's. The product is named after a friend of the brewery. Beyond the Scottish-sounding name, this beer does have an appropriate maltiness in the aroma. A touch of butterscotch, perhaps. It then rounds out to a fruity, hoppy dryness that speaks more of the American Northwest.

Scottish whisper
The small print on the label
describes MacTarnahan's as a
Scottish-style amber ale.

Pyramid Espresso Stout

REGION OF ORIGIN	Pacific Northwest US
STYLE	Coffee Stout
ALCOHOL CONTENT	4.5 abw (5.6 abv)
IDEAL SERVING TEMPERATURE	55° F (13° C)

In espresso-loving Seattle, the Pyramid brewery and pub produces a stout with the local flavor. The espresso character is achieved through the use of dark malts and highly roasted barley. These seem to mimic one of the fruitier varieties of coffee bean. The beer has remarkably coffeelike flavors, right through to a long, dry finish. Pyramid was founded in 1984 by a couple who had previously run a speciality food store, but was later acquired by entrepreneurs. It was originally in Kalama, Washington State, but no longer brews there. It has a further brewpub in Berkeley, California. A wide variety of styles is produced.

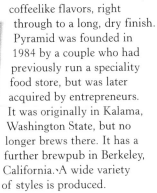

PYRAMID WHEATEN ALE

REGION OF ORIGIN Pacific Northwest US

STYLE Wheat Ale

ALCOHOL CONTENT 4.1 abw (5.1 abv)

IDEAL SERVING TEMPERATURE 50° F (10° C)

The name alludes to a pyramid-shaped peak in the Cascade Mountains. Pyramid and its brother brewery Thomas Kemper now share premises in Seattle, with an additional brewpub in Berkeley, California. The brewery began in Kalama, Washington, in 1984, and pioneered the idea of a wheat brew made with an ale yeast. This unusual approach was signaled in the odd name Wheaten Ale. The beer is perfumy, with a hint of honey; clean, grainy, and lightly refreshing; with a very slight tartness in the finish.

RADEBERGER PILSNER

	REGION OF ORIGIN Saxony, Germany
	STYLE Pilsner
	ALCOHOL CONTENT 3.8 abw (4.8 abv)
	IDEAL SERVING TEMPERATURE 48° F (9° C)

The King of Saxony was supplied with beer from this brewery in Radeberg, northeast of Dresden. The area, with its own history of hop-growing, is close to the Czech region of Bohemia. The brewery dates from 1872, and its Pilsner survived as a speciality during East Germany's 40-odd years of communism. Radeberger Pilsner is aromatic, with earthy hop flavors, a firm body, and a crisp, dry finish.

Head fit for a king
Radeberger pours with a huge
head, half-filling its elegant
flute glass.

RAUCHENFELSER STEINBIER

REGION OF ORIGIN	Upper Bavaria, Germany
STYLE	Stone Beer
ALCOHOL CONTENT	3.9 abw (4.9 abv)
IDEAL SERVING TEMPERATURE	48° F (9° C)

The first word means "smoking rocks." This wheat beer was first made in 1982 near Coburg and is now produced near Augsburg. It started the revival of the technique in which rocks rendered white-hot (in this instance, in a beechwood furnace) are craned into the brewkettle to bring it to the boil. The procedure dates from the days before metal brewkettles. A fire could not be set under a wooden kettle to boil the brew. When this old method is used, the brew caramelizes around the rock, gaining a smoky, molasses toffee flavor. The beer is light and lively, with a clean, softly burned finish.

RED HOOK DOUBLE BLACK STOUT

🛡️ **REGION OF ORIGIN** Pacific Northwest US

🍶 **STYLE** Coffee Stout

%⃝ **ALCOHOL CONTENT** 5.5–5.6 abw (6.9–7.0 abv)

🍺 **IDEAL SERVING TEMPERATURE** 55° F (13° C)

While Red Hook was popularizing micro-brewed beer, another Seattle company, Starbucks, was leading the espresso movement. Both companies were the idea of the same man – Seattle entrepreneur, Gordon Bowker. His two notions are married in this Red Hook beer flavoured with Starbucks coffee. It has a smooth, nutty middle, and a rounded expresso bitterness in the finish.

RED HOOK ESB

🛡 **REGION OF ORIGIN** Pacific Northwest US

🍾 **STYLE** American Ale/ESB

% **ALCOHOL CONTENT** 4.3 abw (5.4 abv)

🍺 **IDEAL SERVING TEMPERATURE** 50–55° F (10–13° C)

A name that suggests fishing, for a brewery in the maritime towns of Seattle, Washington, and Portsmouth, New Hampshire. Established in 1982, Red Hook was one of the first new-generation ale breweries. A winter ale was also introduced in 1987 and later dubbed ESB, pioneering that term in the US. The beer is pale for the style; hop-accented in its big bouquet and appetizing dryness; but with a firm malt balance.

Traditional brew
The small print on the label emphasizes the use of a traditional, top-fermenting ale yeast.

REISSDORF KÖLSCH

🗺 **REGION OF ORIGIN**	Cologne, North Rhine-Westphalia, Germany
🍾 **STYLE**	*Kölschbier*
% **ALCOHOL CONTENT**	3.8 abw (4.8 abv)
🌡 **IDEAL SERVING TEMPERATURE**	48° F (9° C)

Heinrich Reissdorf, from an old agricultural family, established this brewery in 1894. After World War II, it pioneered the style of *Kölsch* as universally brewed in Cologne today. The company is still privately owned, and said to be very conservative. It is in the St. Severin district, in the south part of Cologne's inner city. Its beer has a minty, hop aroma; sweet, vanilla-like, malt flavors; and a crisp, dry, cedary finish. A delicious Kölsch, which briefly inspired a very fruity beer called St. Severin's Kölsch in California.

R

RICHMODIS KÖLSCH

◇ **REGION OF ORIGIN** Cologne, North Rhine-Westphalia, Germany

▯ **STYLE** *Kölschbier*

◷ **ALCOHOL CONTENT** 3.8 abw (4.8 abv)

▮ **IDEAL SERVING TEMPERATURE** 48° F (9° C)

A spritzy, lemony, dryish *Kölsch*, with a crisp finish, from a Cologne brewery. The original brewery, built in 1888, was destroyed by Allied bombs in 1944. Richmodis is in Gremberghaven, south of the river. The beer is widely available in Cologne taverns and restaurants. A good outlet is Zum Neuen Treffpunkt (The New Meeting Point), 25 Nussbaumerstrasse.

Mother country
In Roman times, Cologne was a colonial capital, hence the name. This beer's label remembers "Colonia est Mater." Coeln and Cöln are old spellings, Köln today's German form.

RIDDER DONKER

🏷 **REGION OF ORIGIN** Province of Limburg, the Netherlands

🍶 **STYLE** Old Brown Lager

% **ALCOHOL CONTENT** 2.8 abw (3.5 abv)

🍺 **IDEAL SERVING TEMPERATURE** 46–48° F (8–9° C)

This brewery's parish church in Maastricht is St. Martin's, named after one of the Knights Templar (the order that protected pilgrims). *Ridder* means rider, or knight; *Donker* means dark. A suit of armor can be seen in the conference room of the brewery. The Ridder brewery was founded in 1857 by the van Aubel brothers. When there was no successor, in 1982, it was acquired by Heineken. Ridder Donker is a typical *oud bruin*, with its own soft, fluffy, licorice-like maltiness.

Donker blend
The back label on this beer suggests that it be used to make a sjoes, comprising half-and-half of old brown and Pilsner-style lager.

R

RIDLEYS ESX BEST

🛡 **REGION OF ORIGIN** Eastern England, UK

🍶 **STYLE** Bitter/Pale Ale

％ **ALCOHOL CONTENT** 3.4 abw (4.3 abv)

🍺 **IDEAL SERVING TEMPERATURE** 55° F (13° C)

The Ridley family trace their history to the tenth century, and have contributed a bishop martyred at the stake in 1555, a Master of Eton, and a physician to the Czar of Russia. A grain mill on the Chelmer River in the 1700s gave rise to their brewery. It is in the hamlet of Hartford End, near Great Dunmow and the town of Chelmsford, in the more rural part of Essex. The brewery's present buildings date from 1842. Ridleys' beers are typically fruity, with suggestions of blackberry and apple emerging from the house yeast. As a change from beers called ESB, Triple X, or Four X, Ridleys plays on the county's name with ESX. This beer has very lively flavors: beginning malty, developing lots of fruit, and finishing long and hoppy.

ROBINSON'S OLD TOM

  REGION OF ORIGIN Northwest England, UK

  STYLE Old Ale/Barley Wine

  ALCOHOL CONTENT 6.8 abw (8.5 abv)

  IDEAL SERVING TEMPERATURE 50–55° F (10–13° C)

Many breweries have a cat to keep mice away from the barley malt. Perhaps it was such a cat that inspired a brewer at Robinson's to draw a tom cat's face in his log when he made a batch of this malty beer in 1899. This beer has been known as Old Tom since at least that time. In those days, most breweries would have called it simply Old Ale or Barley Wine. Old Tom has a huge roundness of flavors, suggestions of cherry brandy, and a distinctive dryness in the finish. It is an all-malt beer. Pale, crystal, and chocolate malts are used, and Goldings hops. The beer is dry-hopped. The Robinson family trace their history in the Stockport area of what is now Greater Manchester to 1594. In 1838, Frederic Robinson bought a pub with its own brewery, in Stockport's town center. The present brewery, on the original site, was built in the 1920s, in the towering redbrick style favored by local textile mills.

RODENBACH

🛡 **REGION OF ORIGIN** Province of West Flanders, Belgium

🍾 **STYLE** Flemish Red/Brown

⅌ **ALCOHOL CONTENT** 4.0 abw (5.0 abv)

🍺 **IDEAL SERVING TEMPERATURE** 48–55° F (9–13° C)

During Austrian rule in Belgium, the first Rodenbach arrived from the Rhineland as a military doctor, and later married into a Flemish family. In 1820, a Rodenbach bought a brewery, and subsequently founded the present establishment in 1836. The family was involved until the late 1990s, when the brewery was acquired by Palm. With nearly 300 fixed wooden vessels, Rodenbach is one of the world's most unusual breweries. The basic Rodenbach is a blend of 75 percent "young" beer (matured in metal tanks for four to five weeks) and 25 percent aged brew (more than two years in wood). It emerges with a fruity perfume; passion fruit, iron, and oakiness in the palate; and a late, puckering tartness.

RODENBACH ALEXANDER

REGION OF ORIGIN Province of West Flanders, Belgium

STYLE Flemish Red, with fruit essence

ALCOHOL CONTENT 4.8 abw (6.0 abv)

IDEAL SERVING TEMPERATURE 53° F (12° C)

For years, Belgium's famous Rodenbach brewery fretted that some consumers, finding its regular beer just too tart, "spoiled" it by adding grenadine syrup. Finally, the brewery realized that it would be a good idea to make a sweetened version – though the addition here is cherry essence. The background of its oak-aged Grand Cru *(see p.388)* brings a "live yogurt" tartness and ironlike, passion fruit balance to the clean, sweet, lightly syrupy, cherry character. Is it sharp or sweet? A complex of both. The future of this beer was placed in doubt when Rodenbach was acquired by Palm in the late 1990s. Palm also has an involvement in Boon, which makes its own *(lambic-*based) fruit beers.

R

RODENBACH GRAND CRU

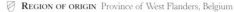

REGION OF ORIGIN Province of West Flanders, Belgium

STYLE Flemish Red Ale

ALCOHOL CONTENT 4.8 abw (6.0 abv)

IDEAL SERVING TEMPERATURE 50° F (10° C)

While the regular version of this famous Flemish "Red Ale" is a blend of old and young beers, the Grand Cru is a straight bottling of the long-matured, stronger component. It is aged in ceiling-high oak tuns for at least two years. The result is a lively (what the wrapper calls "racy") bouquet, with vanilla-like oakiness that extends into the palate; passion-fruit flavors; and a clean, sharp acidity like that found in sour cream. Rodenbach Grand Cru would feature in any connoisseur's list of the world's top ten beers. Like many highly distinctive products, it has relatively small sales. After the brewery was acquired by Palm, a rumor spread in the United States that Grand Cru was at risk of being withdrawn. Palm quickly denied this. It is to be hoped they are as good as their word.

ROGUE MAIERBOCK ALE

⬡ **REGION OF ORIGIN** Pacific Northwest US

🍾 **STYLE** May Bock (top-fermenting)

％ **ALCOHOL CONTENT** 4.8 abw (6.0 abv)

🍺 **IDEAL SERVING TEMPERATURE** 48° F (9° C)

The local Rogue River gives its name to this microbrewery, founded in 1988, in Newport, Oregon, in the beery Pacific Northwest of the US. Rogue is noted for colorful, big-tasting beers. Its brewer's family name is Maier; hence the jokey naming of this product. The beer aims for the smooth yet crisp character of a true May Bock, but is made with an ale yeast. It achieves its objective remarkably well.

Rogue brewer
Brewer John Maier features on his own label, but just for one punning beer in a big range.

SAGRES DARK

REGION OF ORIGIN Portugal

STYLE Munich Dark Lager

ALCOHOL CONTENT 3.4 abw (4.3 abv)

IDEAL SERVING TEMPERATURE 48° F (9° C)

Outside of the main beer countries, many breweries have in their ranges both golden and dark lagers. This is true in Spain and Portugal, for example. The two biggest Portuguese breweries both have dark lagers. The example shown here, Sagres, has a toffeeish, caramel character, while its rival Cristal Preta has more of a fresh-bread, malt-loaf note. On the Portuguese island of Madeira, a dark lager is blended with the local wine and chocolate in a home-made drink called a "goat's foot."

St-Ambroise Pale Ale

REGION OF ORIGIN Province of Quebec, Canada

STYLE Pale Ale

ALCOHOL CONTENT 4.0 abw (5.0 abv)

IDEAL SERVING TEMPERATURE 50° F (10° C)

A monk named Ambroise is said to have been Montreal's first brewer. He gave his name to the street where Peter McAuslan and Ellen Bounsall established their brewery in 1989. Their pale ale is very perfumy, outstandingly hoppy in aroma and flavor, dry, and appetizing. It has a light, soft body, but full, long flavors, developing lemony-orangey notes, and an elegant dryness in the finish. Other products include a remarkably smooth oatmeal stout, also labeled as Bière Noire. Under the Griffon name, there is a lightly dry extra pale ale, labeled as Blonde, and a nutty, honeyish, reddish-brown ale called Rousse.

SAINT ARNOLD KRISTALL WEIZEN

🛡 **REGION OF ORIGIN**	Southwest US
🍾 **STYLE**	Wheat Ale
⑳ **ALCOHOL CONTENT**	3.9 abw (4.9 abv)
🍺 **IDEAL SERVING TEMPERATURE**	50° F (10° C)

Two different saints called Arnold are patrons of Belgian and French beermakers, and either sits oddly with the German term *Kristall Weizen*. What the Saint Arnold brewery offers under this name is, in fact, a Wheat Ale. It is a light, perfumy beer; firm and smooth; with hints of vanilla; a very slight, sweet-orange fruitiness; and a crisp finish. Saint Arnold, a well-regarded micro, was established in 1994, in Houston, Texas. Its founders were two graduates of the local Rice University, both homebrewers who had worked as investment bankers. Both are Americans, but one is of Prussian origin and the other has family from Alsace. The brewery also makes amber and brown ales.

Saintly swallow
At least 20 saints are associated with brewing. Germans often look to St. Florian, who used beer to extinguish a fire in Nuremberg.

St. Galler Klosterbräu
Schützengarten Naturtrüb

🛡 **REGION OF ORIGIN**	Switzerland
🍾 **STYLE**	Unfiltered Lager/Export
% **ALCOHOL CONTENT**	4.2 abw (5.2 abv)
🌡 **IDEAL SERVING TEMPERATURE**	48° F (9° C)

When Irish monks reintroduced civilization to Continental Europe after the Dark Ages, they probably took beer with them. Among them was Saint Gall, who founded an abbey in Switzerland. In the 800s, the abbey had a series of brewhouses, the plans for which survive in a library in the town. These are the world's oldest brewery drawings. The abbey was reconstructed several times, most recently in the 1700s, but no longer functions. The town is said once to have had eight breweries. The last survivor is Schützengarten, from 1895. It had electricity before the town (and still makes its own), and boasted the first truck in the area. Its "naturally turbid" (unfiltered) speciality has the appropriate strength and color to be deemed an Export. It has an excellent balance of malty sweetness and flowery, herbal, peppery hop.

St Georgen Keller Bier

REGION OF ORIGIN	Franconia, Bavaria, Germany
STYLE	*Kellerbier*/Unfiltered Pilsner
ALCOHOL CONTENT	3.9 abw (4.9 abv)
IDEAL SERVING TEMPERATURE	48° F (9° C)

In Germany, Pilsner beers are normally filtered; this beer is not, and therefore it is, strictly speaking, a *Kellerbier* (taken from the cellar while still hazy). Nonetheless, it is of a typical Pilsner strength, with a superbly appetizing, fresh, flowery, hop character. The hop is balanced by a lightly nutty maltiness and a yeasty acidity in the finish. The beer is made by St. Georgen, at Buttenheim in Bavaria, near the great brewing town of Bamberg.

A seasonal saint St. George's Day sometimes marked the season's last brew.

St Peter's Spiced Ale

🛡 **REGION OF ORIGIN** Eastern England, UK

🍶 **STYLE** Spiced Dark Ale

% **ALCOHOL CONTENT** 5.2 abw (6.5 abv)

🌡 **IDEAL SERVING TEMPERATURE** 50–55° F (10–13° C)

The 13th-century St. Peter's Hall is a manor house, near Bungay, Suffolk, England. It was acquired in 1995 by an expert on marketing, with an enthusiasm for the drinks industry, and turned into a brewery, bar, and restaurant. A wide range of beers has been produced, one of the most assertive being this dark ale spiced with cinnamon and apple. It has a deep ruby color; a very aromatic, dark-chocolate bouquet; an oily, smooth body; a palate suggesting mocha, nuts, and port; and a very dry, tannic finish.

*One green bottle
The design of the St.
Peter's bottle was based
on one made for gin in the
US in the late 1700s.*

SAINT SYLVESTRE 3 MONTS

REGION OF ORIGIN Northern France

STYLE *Bière de Garde*

ALCOHOL CONTENT 6.8 abw (8.5 abv)

IDEAL SERVING TEMPERATURE 50° F (10° C)

The hamlet of St. Sylvester's Chapel is among hop gardens near Hazebrouck, in the Flemish-French countryside between Dunkirk and Lille. The St. Sylvestre farmhouse brewery produces a very lively, winey, fruity (dessert apples?), yeasty, top-fermenting, unpasteurised golden beer, with a robustly dry finish and great length, called 3 Monts. The three "mountains" are small hills in an area otherwise known for being very flat. One of the hills, Mont des Cats, has a Trappist abbey that once brewed its own beers. St. Sylvestre also produces darker beers for Christmas and spring.

Open with care
Beneath the foil is cork, held in place by a metal clasp. When this clip is removed, the cork can escape with some force.

SAISON DE PIPAIX

🏷 **REGION OF ORIGIN** Province of Hainaut, Belgium

🍶 **STYLE** *Saison*

% **ALCOHOL CONTENT** 4.8–5.2 abw (6.0–6.5 abv)

🍺 **IDEAL SERVING TEMPERATURE** 50–55° F (10–13° C)

Spiced with black pepper, anise, and a medicinal lichen, this is a dry, leafy, sourish interpretation of Belgium's robust summer style. It is brewed by a schoolteacher, Jean-Louis Dits. He revived a steam-powered brewery from the early industrial period, and operates it as a working museum. The brewery is at Pipaix, near Leuze. Another of its beers, La Cochonne, contains chicory root.

Steam brew
The label's "Brasserie à Vapeur"
("Steam Brewery") meant "state of the
art" in the early industrial period.

S

SAISON DUPONT

🛡 **REGION OF ORIGIN** Province of Hainaut, Belgium

🍾 **STYLE** *Saison*

💠 **ALCOHOL CONTENT** 5.2 abw (6.5 abv)

🍺 **IDEAL SERVING TEMPERATURE** 50° F (10° C)

The best-known *saison*. In the French-speaking part of Belgium, the word for "season" sometimes appears on beer labels. The season in question is always summer. As the Belgians like strong beers, even their summer brews are relatively potent. They are firm and dry, with a yeasty, fruity acidity like that of an orange, and usually unfiltered. Saison Dupont is a lively, hoppy classic. It is made at a farmhouse brewery at Tourpes, near Leuze, east of the town of Tournai. The brewery makes several variations on this theme, some labeled Moinette, the name of the farm. (In French, *moine* means monk, and the farm is on what is believed to have been an abbey estate.) The farm also makes breads (some using grain from the brewery) and a range of cheeses (one spiced with finely chopped hops).

SAKU HELE

🛡	**REGION OF ORIGIN** Estonia
🍾	**STYLE** *Helles* Lager
%	**ALCOHOL CONTENT** 3.9 abw (4.9 abv)
🍺	**IDEAL SERVING TEMPERATURE** 48° F (9° C)

A German landowner established a brewery on his estate at Saku, near Tallinn, the capital of Estonia, in 1820. The Saku brewery, now owned by a Baltic group, is especially known for its cedary, coffeeish, strong Christmas porter. The German *Hell* or *Helles*, describing a pale or golden lager, emerges in Estonia as *Hele*. This year-round beer pours with a dense, bubbly head and has a very pale color; a light but firm body; and a very hoppy, appetizing finish. Fairly dry for the style.

SAKU JÓULU PORTER

🛡 **REGION OF ORIGIN** Estonia

🍶 **STYLE** Porter/Imperial Stout

﹪ **ALCOHOL CONTENT** 6.4 abw (8.0 abv)

🍺 **IDEAL SERVING TEMPERATURE** 55–64° F (13–18° C)

A great survivor among the family of Imperial Stouts and Baltic Strong Porters. This example was made even during the period when Estonia was part of the Soviet Union, and is still going strong. It is available at Christmas, hence the term Jóulo ("Yule"). Saku Porter has the aroma of freshly-sawn cedar, or perhaps a log fire, with some smokiness. The palate begins with mouth-filling, toasted marshmallow notes, becoming gingery, then softening to a quick, silky finish. A sweetish interpretation, but richer and more assertive than its historically significant local rival, the recently revived Le Coq Porter *(see p.275)*.

Juniper Claus
As the gnome's tankard and spoon suggest, wooden implements (usually juniper) were traditional in Estonia.

Sam Adams Triple Bock

REGION OF ORIGIN	Northeast US
STYLE	Barley Wine
ALCOHOL CONTENT	14.0 abw (17.5 abv)
IDEAL SERVING TEMPERATURE	48° F (9° C)

Sauterne wines are said to be scented, intensely sweet, and oily, and to become Madeira-like with time. This beer has a minty aroma, chocolatey maple and vanilla flavors, and all the fatness and power of such a wine. Californian "Champagne" yeast ferments this brew, which is made in Wisconsin and aged in Tennessee and Kentucky whiskey casks in Boston. The result might better be described as a barley wine; it is not a Bock. Try it with a very rich, nutty terrine. An even stronger (about 16.0 abw; 20.0 abv), richer version, aged in oak for four or five years, was released for the millennium, at $200 a bottle. Samuel Adams makes a wide range of innovative brews and classic styles, in Cincinnati, Boston, and elsewhere. Its flagship Boston Lager has a full gold to pale bronze color and an outstanding aroma and flavor of German Hallertau Mittelfrüh hops.

S

Samuel Smith's Imperial Stout

Region of origin	Northern England, UK
Style	Imperial Stout
Alcohol content	5.6 abw (7.0 abv)
Ideal serving temperature	55–64° F (13–18° C)

This famous Yorkshire brewery, dating from 1758, is best-known in Britain for its cask-conditioned bitter and worldwide for its bottled pale ale *(see p.404)*, but it has many other specialities. Several are only available in the bottle, and some are harder to find in Britain than in export markets. Samuel Smith's Imperial Stout was launched during the 1980s. The "liquid Christmas pudding" character (raisins and burned fruit) found in traditional imperial stouts shows very well in this spicy example. It is also very rich, despite being less strong than some counterparts.

Designer brew
The label was created by Charles Finkel of Seattle, who has designed many great labels.

SAMUEL SMITH OATMEAL STOUT

REGION OF ORIGIN Northern England, UK

STYLE Oatmeal Stout

ALCOHOL CONTENT 4.0 abw (5.0 abv)

IDEAL SERVING TEMPERATURE 55° F (13° C)

The fashion for using oatmeal in stout was part of the vogue for "nutritious" beers in Britain after the rigours of World War II. The style waned in the 1960s and vanished in the 1970s, but was revived in the 1980s by Samuel Smith's, in the brewing village of Tadcaster. This Oatmeal Stout has a fresh, flowery, oloroso sherry aroma; a clean, sweet creaminess; and a silky dryness in the finish.

SAMUEL SMITH OLD BREWERY PALE ALE

REGION OF ORIGIN	Northern England, UK
STYLE	Pale Ale
ALCOHOL CONTENT	4.1 abw (5.2 abv)
IDEAL SERVING TEMPERATURE	50–55° F (10–13° C)

Why "Old" brewery? Because this one, founded to serve a coaching inn, predated family rival John Smith's in the Victorian era. In the heyday of pale ales, the town of Burton's fame for the style was rivaled by that of Tadcaster, home to both Smiths. "Tadcaster" ales were even brewed in the US, where Samuel Smith's Pale is today something of an icon. The brewery's Yorkshire stone square system of fermentation accentuates the malt accent of Samuel Smith's beers. The Pale Ale is maltier and fuller-bodied than some examples of the style, but its light nuttiness is balanced with a subtle underpinning of Fuggles and Goldings hops.

SAMUEL SMITH'S TADDY PORTER

🛡 **REGION OF ORIGIN** Northern England, UK

🍾 **STYLE** Porter

% **ALCOHOL CONTENT** 4.0 abw (5.0 abv)

🥛 **IDEAL SERVING TEMPERATURE** 50–55° F (10–13° C)

The affectionate diminutive "Taddy" has been used on labels of various Samuel Smith's beers for decades. It is a familiar abbreviation of the brewery's home village, Tadcaster. The persistence of the term is a measure of Tadcaster's long-term fame as a brewing town. Today, Taddy is applied specifically to the brewery's porter, which combines roasty, toasty dryness with the firm, rounded maltiness that is Samuel Smith's house character. This brewery also has a yet-drier Extra Stout.

The proudest county
The intensely proud county of
Yorkshire likes to brandish its
symbol, the white rose.

SAPPORO BLACK BEER

🏴 **REGION OF ORIGIN**	Hokkaido, Japan
🍶 **STYLE**	Black Beer
% **ALCOHOL CONTENT**	4.0 abw (5.0 abv)
🌡 **IDEAL SERVING TEMPERATURE**	48° F (9° C)

In Japan, sake (really a rice beer rather than a wine) was joined by locally made western-style brews in the late 1800s. These beers were a result of American, Dutch, and German influence. At that time, German lagers were dark. The brewery in Sapporo opened in 1876, before registered brands existed. This national brewer has a wide range of products, including an interesting black beer, which received its first definite mention in 1892. Today's neck label boasts "Japan's oldest brand." The beer smells like a box of chocolates; has complex, long flavors reminiscent of roasting coffee and figs; and finishes with a licorice note. Sapporo's national rivals Asahi and Kirin both have black beers, and so do many of the small, new-generation breweries in Japan.

SAPPORO YEBISU

🛡 **REGION OF ORIGIN** Hokkaido/Honshu, Japan

🍾 **STYLE** Dortmunder Lager

％ **ALCOHOL CONTENT** 4.0 abw (5.0 abv)

🍺 **IDEAL SERVING TEMPERATURE** 48° F (9° C)

Although the famous Sapporo brewery traces its origins to the northern Japanese city of the same name, this particular beer is linked with Tokyo. Yebisu (the "y" is almost silent) is the name of a Shinto god. It is also a neighborhood in central Tokyo where a famous brewery once stood. Sapporo long ago acquired the brewery, but continued to produce a highly regarded beer of this name. The beer has a malty aroma and palate; a firm, oily palate; and a very good, late balance of hop. It is broadly in the Dortmunder Export style. Sapporo now has a "Beer Station" complex of bars and restaurants at the Yebisu site.

S

SARAH HUGHES DARK RUBY

🛡 **REGION OF ORIGIN** Central England, UK

🍾 **STYLE** Old Ale

％ **ALCOHOL CONTENT** 4.8 abw (6.0 abv)

🍺 **IDEAL SERVING TEMPERATURE** 50–55° F (10–13° C)

Mrs. Hughes made this beer in the 1920s, in a tiny tower brewery and pub in Sedgeley, near Dudley, in England's West Midlands. In those days beers were stronger, and its potency might once have passed as a mild. The brewery closed in 1957, but Mrs. Hughes' grandson restored it in 1987. This bottle-conditioned beer is fruity, toasty, rich, and complex, with some winey notes. The pub, The Beacon, is a real Victorian delight.

Dudley drafts
Mrs. Hughes appears on
Dark Ruby's label. There
is a tradition of tiny
breweries around Dudley.

SCHÄFFBRAU
FEUERFEST EDEL BIER

🛡 **REGION OF ORIGIN**	Franconia, Bavaria, Germany
🍾 **STYLE**	Extra-strong Lager/Double Bock
％ **ALCOHOL CONTENT**	8.4 abw (10.5 abv)
🍺 **IDEAL SERVING TEMPERATURE**	48° F (9° C)

With its flask-shaped bottle and red "seal", this looks like a brandy, but it is a beer. The seal is stamped with a guarantee of one year's lagering, though the brewery says that the maturation is sometimes as long as 18 months. This unusually long sleep makes for a smooth, even lean, beer, despite its high alcohol content. The aroma is reminiscent of oranges in brandy; the palate pruney, figgy, coffeeish; the finish woody and sappy. The brewery is in an area of outstanding natural beauty at Treuchtlingen, south of Nuremberg, Germany.

SCHEIDMANTEL HEFE WEISSE

🍺 **STYLE** *Hefeweizen*

% **ALCOHOL CONTENT** 4.1 abw (5.1 abv)

🍺 **IDEAL SERVING TEMPERATURE** 48–54° F (9–12° C)

Founded by the Scheidmantel family in 1834, in Coburg, seat of the family that produced many of Europe's royals. The town's fortress provides a dramatic backdrop to the brewery. Today's brewery dates from the turn of the century and still has the lakes that provided ice for lagering until the 1950s. Scheidmantel Hefe Weisse is smooth, orangey, and lemony.

Château brew?
The castle of Coburg appears at the top of the label. The brewery itself is a very attractive building.

Scheidmantel Zwickel-Bier

REGION OF ORIGIN	Franconia, Bavaria, Germany
STYLE	*Zwickelbier*/Unfiltered Pilsner
ALCOHOL CONTENT	4.0 abw (5.1 abv)
IDEAL SERVING TEMPERATURE	48° F (9 °C)

This is a golden lager in broadly the Dortmunder Export style, but served unfiltered, from the Scheidmantel brewery of Coburg, Bavaria. It has the aroma of new-mown hay; a malty but firm palate; and a dry, hoppy, flowery finish. It is very appetizing and drinkable. *Zwickel* refers to a nozzle or tap – in this case, on a lagering vessel. The suggestion is that the beer was tapped direct, rather than passing through a filter. Unfiltered beers are very popular in Franconia, the northern part of Bavaria. Several terms are used to describe them, each with a slightly different implication. *Keller* ("cellar") *Bier* suggests a high hopping rate, as a protection against contamination. *Ungespundet* ("unbunged") suggests a low rate of carbonation.

SCHLOSS EGGENBERG HOPFEN KÖNIG PILS

🛡 **REGION OF ORIGIN** Austria	
🍶 **STYLE** Pilsner	
% **ALCOHOL CONTENT** 4.0 abw (5.1 abv)	
🌡 **IDEAL SERVING TEMPERATURE** 48° F (9° C)	

The castle brewery of Eggenberg, at Vorchdorf, between Salzburg and Linz, Austria, dates from the 1100s, and has sold its beer beyond its estate since 1681. Its beers include not only specialities like MacQueen's Nessie *(see p.299)* and its Urbock *(see p.413)* but also this enjoyable Pilsner. Is it a "Hop King," as its name suggests? Perhaps by Austrian standards, but certainly not in comparison with some German and American brews. The hop is evident in a good, perfumy aroma and an appetizingly lemony finish, but the middle palate is on the sweet side for the style.

Schloss Eggenberg Urbock 23°

🛡 **REGION OF ORIGIN**	Austria
🍾 **STYLE**	Double Bock
% **ALCOHOL CONTENT**	7.7 abw (9.6 abv)
🍺 **IDEAL SERVING TEMPERATURE**	48° F (9° C)

One of the best-known Austrian beers in the world at large is this hefty brew from the castle brewery of Eggenberg. The figure 23 represents its original gravity in degrees Plato, and the brewer claims to lager (mature) it for nine months. It has a bubbly, well-retained head for such a strong beer; a shimmering gold color; a surprisingly light creaminess, with suggestions of lemon, pink grapefruit, and melon rind, and perhaps a hint of cinnamon. Perfect as a dessert beer, or for after dinner. The brewery also distils a liquor from this beer.

SCHLÖSSER ALT

⬡ **REGION OF ORIGIN**	Düsseldorf, North Rhine-Westphalia, Germany
🍺 **STYLE**	*Altbier*
⑳ **ALCOHOL CONTENT**	3.8 abw (4.8 abv)
🍺 **IDEAL SERVING TEMPERATURE**	48° F (9° C)

The name derives from the word for "lock." The Schlösser family founded the enterprise as a brewpub in the Old Town in 1873. Between the two World Wars, a series of mergers and expansions began, and Schlösser is now the biggest *Altbier* brewery within Düsseldorf. It is part of the national Brau und Brunnen group. Its beer is on the light side in both body and taste. It has a syrupy start, with flavors like brown sugar, becoming nuttier, firmer, and drier in the finish.

The true tradition
Schlösser's short, cylindrical glass is the most traditional shape used for Altbier. *Some brewers have moved to taller, slimmer vessels more reminiscent of* Kölschbier.

SCHMALTZ'S ALT

REGION OF ORIGIN Midwest US

STYLE Altbier

ALCOHOL CONTENT 4.7 abw (5.9 abv)

IDEAL SERVING TEMPERATURE 48° F (9° C)

The jocular-sounding alliteration derives from a local nickname in the largely German-American town of New Ulm, Minnesota. In this instance, it applied to the late father of the brewery's principal. The August Schell brewery, founded in 1860, is one of the few old-established regional breweries left in the US. It is also the prettiest, set in woodland with its own deer park. Schmaltz's Alt is a very dark, roasty, vanilla-tinged, dry interpretation of the style.

Frontier spirit
The brewery's owning family survived a Sioux uprising in the early pioneering days – their hospitality had apparently been appreciated by the Native Americans.

SCHNEIDER AVENTINUS

REGION OF ORIGIN Upper Bavaria, Germany

STYLE Wheat Double Bock/*Weizenbock*

ALCOHOL CONTENT 6.1 abw (7.7 abv)

IDEAL SERVING TEMPERATURE 48–50° F (9–10° C)

When the famous wheat beer family Schneider was brewing in Munich, its bottling hall was on Aventine Strasse. That provided an ideal name for this "double" *Weizenbock*. Rome's Aventine Hill had a bishop, thus providing a religious allusion to match *Doppelbock* names like Salvator. With its alcoholic warmth and layers of malty complexity, balanced by clovey spiciness, figgy, raisiny fruitiness, and Champagnelike acidity and sparkle, Aventinus is a truly remarkable beer.

The beer in person
The man on the label is Johannes Thurmayr of Abensberg, a Latin scholar who called himself Aventinus. He first recorded the history of Bavaria, and mapped the region in the 1500s.

SCHNEIDER WEISSE

🛡 **REGION OF ORIGIN** Upper Bavaria, Germany

🍾 **STYLE** *Hefeweizen*

％ **ALCOHOL CONTENT** 4.4 abw (5.5 abv)

🍶 **IDEAL SERVING TEMPERATURE** 48–54° F (9–12° C)

Believed to be the oldest brewery continuously to have specialized in wheat beer. It is thought to have made the style since 1607. The present owners, the Schneider family, have been making wheat beer for six generations, originally as lessees of the Royal Court brewery in Munich, and in their own right from 1872. They had a brewery in the center of Munich, at Tal ("Dale") street, where they still operate a beer restaurant. After World War II, they moved into their current, historic brewery, north of the city, at Kelheim on the Danube. Among the widely available wheat beers, those from Schneider are the best examples of the clove-tasting, spicy, full-flavored style. The principal version, called simply Schneider Weisse, is a darkish interpretation of the *Hefeweizen* style. It is very lively, with complex, fruity flavors, maltiness, almondy nuttiness, and clove.

SCHNEIDER WEISSE KRISTALL

REGION OF ORIGIN Upper Bavaria, Germany

STYLE Kristall Weisse/Weizen

ALCOHOL CONTENT 4.25 abw (5.3 abv)

IDEAL SERVING TEMPERATURE 48–54° F (9–12° C)

After years of producing only its strong Aventinus *(see p.416)* and its tan-colored, hazy, Schneider Weisse *(see previous page)*, this renowned brewery began to add further versions in the mid-1990s. In 1994, a sedimented, golden Weizenhell was introduced. This version is less complex and spicy, more fruity and orangey. Then came the filtered Kristall shown here, which is in character somewhere between the Weizenhell and the classic Schneider Weisse. The Kristall has a lightly honeyed, apricot note. There is even a low-alcohol version, at 2.3 abw (2.9 abv).

Still foaming in Munich
The building depicted on the label is
the Munich premises that now houses
a beer restaurant. Specialities include
offal dishes like lungs.

Schultheiss Berliner Weisse

REGION OF ORIGIN	Berlin, Northern Germany
STYLE	*Berliner Weisse*
ALCOHOL CONTENT	3.0 abw (3.7 abv)
IDEAL SERVING TEMPERATURE	48–54° F (9–12° C)

A classic from one of Berlin's two big brewers. Schultheiss and its local rival Kindl are both components of national groups, with Schultheiss belonging to Brau und Brunnen. Since the reunification of Germany, Schultheiss has closed its breweries in Kreuzberg and Spandau and moved production to a brewery dating from 1902, in Hohenschönhausen, in the former East. Its *Berliner Weisse* has a secondary fermentation in the bottle, resulting in a more complex character. It is flowery, pollenlike, with hints of celery, and a lemony finish.

Rejuvinating the style
Schultheiss decorates its classic Weissbier "saucer" with contemporary depictions of Berlin and its youth. The two big brewers have both presented this very traditional style in a younger context.

SCHUMACHER ALT

🛡 **REGION OF ORIGIN** Düsseldorf, North Rhine-Westphalia, Germany

🍺 **STYLE** *Altbier*

％ **ALCOHOL CONTENT** 3.7 abw (4.6 abv)

🍺 **IDEAL SERVING TEMPERATURE** 48° F (9° C)

A family-owned brewery and pub in the modern center of the city. The Schumacher family were beermakers even before they owned their first brewery, in 1838, and the present premises date from the 1870s. This café-like brewpub and beer garden is more restful than some of the pubbier establishments in the Old Town. Its beer is one of the paler examples in color; sweetish, malt-accented, and softly, nuttily fruity; but with a good balance. The brew is a good accompaniment to Rhineland dishes like *Sauerbraten* (marinaded beef) from Schumacher's kitchen.

Symbols of brewing
The malt shovel and mashing fork on
the label are symbols of the brewer's
art. The mini-barrel is used like a
ladle. The big vessel is a mash tun.

Schwaben Bräu
Das Schwarze

🛡 **Region of origin** Baden-Württemberg, Germany

🍾 **Style** Black Beer

% **Alcohol content** 3.9 abw (4.9 abv)

🌡 **Ideal serving temperature** 48° F (9° C)

In English, Swabia refers to a medieval Duchy that stretched from the Stuttgart area to parts of modern Bavaria and Switzerland. The term Swabian is still used to describe the industrious people of this region, noted for precision engineering, from cuckoo clocks to Mercedes and Porsches. The Schwaben brewery merged in 1996 with its Stuttgart neighbor Dinkelacker, but both brewery's names are still used. *Schwarze* refers to a "black" beer. Schwaben Bräu Das Schwarze is a dryish example of the style. It has an earthy hop aroma; a toffeeish, licorice-like palate; and a rooty, woody, faintly salty finish.

SCHWABEN BRÄU FESTMÄRZEN

REGION OF ORIGIN Baden-Württemberg, Germany

STYLE *Märzen/Festbier*

ALCOHOL CONTENT 4.4 abw (5.5 abv)

IDEAL SERVING TEMPERATURE 48° F (9° C)

The September-October "People's Festival" in Stuttgart has coaxed several similar beers from the merged Schwaben and Dinkelacker breweries. While Dinkelacker's Volksfestbier *(see p.143)* seems quite hoppy for the style, Schwaben's Festmärzen is perhaps slightly more malty. It has a fragrant aroma (hops from nearby Tettnang?) but a more dominant syrupy sweetness. A further, very similar product called Schwaben Bräu Das Echte Märzen seems accented toward a slightly more dry maltiness.

Schwarzer Steiger

> **REGION OF ORIGIN** Dresden, Saxony, Germany
>
> **STYLE** Black Beer
>
> **ALCOHOL CONTENT** 3.8 abw (4.8 abv)
>
> **IDEAL SERVING TEMPERATURE** 48° F (9° C)

A *Steiger* is someone who walks in the hills or, in this instance, patrols underground, in a mine. The excavation of silver was once important in the area of Dresden, where Steiger is an old local beer brand. Today's Schwarzer Steiger is produced by Feldschlösschen (Castle in the Fields), one of several breweries with that name. The modern brewery is on the edge of the city, but part of the original survives in the center. This beer has an aroma of violets and dark chocolate; a firm, slightly cedary palate; and a big, Vienna-coffee finish.

SESTER KÖLSCH

🏷 **REGION OF ORIGIN** Cologne, North Rhine-Westphalia, Germany

🍾 **STYLE** *Kölschbier*

％ **ALCOHOL CONTENT** 3.8 abw (4.8 abv)

🍺 **IDEAL SERVING TEMPERATURE** 48° F (9° C)

A very fragrant, firm-bodied *Kölsch*, smooth and slightly oily, with an orangey fruitiness. The beer's long-time slogan, *Trink Sester mein Bester*, means "Drink Sester, my friend." The firm of Sester was founded in 1896, but in recent years the beer has been made by the Bergische Löwen brewery. Sester's symbol is a team of dray horses, called Max and Moritz, after characters in a book by German poet, painter, caricaturist, and satirist Wilhelm Busch (1832–1908). The characters inspired an American comic strip, the Katzenjammer Kids.

SHEPHERD NEAME
BISHOPS FINGER

🛡 **REGION OF ORIGIN**	Southeast England, UK
🍾 **STYLE**	Bitter/Pale Ale
⑳ **ALCOHOL CONTENT**	In bottle: 4.2 abw (5.2 abv); On draft: 4.0 abw (5.0 abv)
▮ **IDEAL SERVING TEMPERATURE**	50–55° F (10–13° C)

In the heart of East Kent hop country is the Shepherd Neame brewery. Its home town of Faversham is believed to have had an abbey brewery in the 1100s. Shepherd Neame itself dates from 1698, and is Britain's oldest brewing company. The name Bishop's Finger, the subject of salacious jokes, refers to an old style of signpost once typical in the area. This ale has a hoppy aroma (East Kent Goldings), but is very well-balanced, with a malty palate hinting at vanilla, licorice root, and raisins, and a touch of tart fruitiness in the finish. The Shepherd Neame brewery's recipe book offers a soup made with Bishop's Finger, beef stock, potatoes, and cinnamon-spiced apples.

SHEPHERD NEAME ORIGINAL PORTER

REGION OF ORIGIN	Southeast England, UK
STYLE	Porter/Stout
ALCOHOL CONTENT	4.2 abw (5.2 abv)
IDEAL SERVING TEMPERATURE	50–55° F (10–13° C)

This brewery, in the county of Kent, is not far from London, the traditional home of porter. In its publicity, it often reproduces a particularly beautiful poster, from the

late 1800s or early 1900s, announcing: "Stock and Mild Ales, London Stout and Porter." Shepherd Neame reintroduced porter in the early 1990s. Its soothing and very tasty example has hoppy and oaky, sherryish notes in its aroma; a hint of dry, rooty licorice (an ingredient); and a good malt background reminiscent of barley-sugar sweets. The brewery's recipe book offers a porter and chocolate truffle ice cream.

SHEPHERD NEAME SPITFIRE

🛡 **REGION OF ORIGIN** Southeast England, UK

🍾 **STYLE** Bitter Ale

％ **ALCOHOL CONTENT** In bottle: 3.8 abw (4.7 abv); On draft: 4.5 abv (3.6 abw)

🌡 **IDEAL SERVING TEMPERATURE** 50–55° F (10–13° C)

Named after the famous World War II fighter plane, Spitfire was launched in 1990 to mark the 50th anniversary of the Battle of Britain. It was launched as a special edition to raise money for the Royal Air Force Benevolent Fund, but is now a regular brew. Spitfire is a pale, hop-accented ale. It has a fresh hop aroma; a light, firm body; a lively, dry palate; and a lingering, enticing bitterness. Lovers of aromatic, dry, hoppy beers will also enjoy single-variety specials such as Goldings Summer Ale, Early Bird, and Late Red from Shepherd Neame.

SIERRA NEVADA CELEBRATION ALE

🛡 **REGION OF ORIGIN** California, US

🍾 **STYLE** Ale/IPA

% **ALCOHOL CONTENT** 4.8 abw (6.0 abv). May vary

🍺 **IDEAL SERVING TEMPERATURE** 50–55° F (10–13° C)

Perhaps the most famous new-generation brewery in the US is near the Sierra Nevada mountains, in Chico, California. The brewery is known for beers full of character and complexity. Its winter holiday Celebration Ale is typically aromatic and lively in flavor, with hints of oily dark chocolate and lots of lemony hop bitterness. The variety of hops varies each year, and experimental growths are sometimes used. The beer is broadly in the style of an India Pale Ale. Sierra Nevada's other classics include its year-round Pale Ale, blossoming with hops yet beautifully balanced; its outstanding example of a "plain" porter; and its huge Bigfoot Barley Wine. The brewery was established in 1981, initially using converted dairying vessels. Today, it has a handsome copper brewhouse.

SILLAMÄE MÜNCHEN

	REGION OF ORIGIN Estonia
	STYLE Munich Dark Lager/Bock
	ALCOHOL CONTENT 5.2 abw (6.5 abv)
	IDEAL SERVING TEMPERATURE 48° F (9° C)

The second word is simply "Munich" in German. This remarkable dark lager is so assertive and strong that it could equally be regarded as a Bock. It has a rich, malty aroma; a surprisingly light and smooth drinkability; and a clean, toasted-nut dryness; developing to a juicy, warming finish. It is made in Estonia, in a microbrewery established in 1993, in Sillamäe, a Russian-speaking town that was formerly a center for the defense industry. The brewery's founder is a Kazak, its workers are from Belarus and the Ukraine, and the beer was created by a German.

SINEBRYCHOFF PORTER

🛡 **REGION OF ORIGIN**	Finland
🍾 **STYLE**	Baltic Porter/Imperial Stout
% **ALCOHOL CONTENT**	5.8 abw (7.2 abv)
🍺 **IDEAL SERVING TEMPERATURE**	55–64° F (13–18° C)

When Nikolai Sinebrychoff founded this brewery (also known as "Koff") in Helsinki, in 1819, the city was under Russian rule. Koff has brewed porter from the start, apart from a period of prohibition in Finland in the early part of the 20th century. The porter was reintroduced for the 1952 Olympics. The yeast is said to have been propagated from a bottle-conditioned Guinness (see p.204). The Finnish brew is lively and flavorsome: dry, smooth, oily, coffeeish, and flowery, with fresh wood notes. Its rich, warming finish is an antidote to the Baltic cold.

SINGHA

◈ **REGION OF ORIGIN** Thailand

🍶 **STYLE** Strong Pilsner

% **ALCOHOL CONTENT** 4.8 abw (6.0 abv)

🍺 **IDEAL SERVING TEMPERATURE** 48° F (9° C)

Named after a mythical creature resembling a lion, this famous Thai lager has much more character than is usual in brews from countries too hot to grow malting barley or hops. When the brewery was established in the 1930s, its practices were laid down by a German brewmaster. Singha might best be described as a strong Pilsner, though it does not seem to punch at its proclaimed 6.0 percent. Its body is lightened with the use of some sugar, but this is not evident in the flavor. It has a hint of firmly chewy maltiness, but its dominant feature is a robust late dryness, with spearminty hoppiness. Some Saaz hops are employed.

SISSONS WISE GUY WEISSBIER

🛡 **REGION OF ORIGIN** Mid-Atlantic US

🍾 **STYLE** *Hefeweizen*

% **ALCOHOL CONTENT** 3.3 abw (4.1 abv)

🌡 **IDEAL SERVING TEMPERATURE** 48–54° F (9–12° C)

R esting actors are often found tending the bar; Hugh Sisson was able to do so in his family's tavern in Baltimore, Maryland. In 1989 a brewery was added, initially making ales and more recently this punning ("Wise") *Weisse*. The beer has a lemony fruitiness. It begins with hints of lemon curd; moves to a pithlike character; and finishes with a suggestion of cloves, nuts, smokiness, and a more grainy note. A Weihenstephan yeast is used.

SLOEBER

🛡 **REGION OF ORIGIN** Province of East Flanders, Belgium

🍶 **STYLE** Strong Belgian Ale

% **ALCOHOL CONTENT** 6.0 abw (7.5 abv)

🍺 **IDEAL SERVING TEMPERATURE** 50° F (10° C)

A darker, amber competitor to Belgium's famous golden Duvel *(see p.151)*. Another variation on "Devil" is "Joker" (*Sloeber*, in Flemish). This beer is made by the Roman brewery, at Mater, near Oudenaarde, Belgium. The brewery's odd name is that of the family who have run it for 14 generations. How did they come to be called Roman? Perhaps because their birthplace, Mater, is on the old Roman road from Dunkirk to Cologne. The complex, appetizing beer is very aromatic; smooth, firm, and malty; with a very dry, orange-zest finish, at least in part deriving from Styrian hops. Big enough in flavor to accompany a robust Roman antipasto.

S

SOUTHAMPTON SAISON

	REGION OF ORIGIN	Northeast US
	STYLE	*Saison*
	ALCOHOL CONTENT	4.4 abw (5.5 abv)
	IDEAL SERVING TEMPERATURE	50° F (10° C)

New York weekenders heading for Long Island can find some extraordinary Belgian-style beers at the Southampton Publick House (40 Bowden Sq.). This rare American *saison* is aged in wine casks, to which Curaçao orange peels and grains of paradise are added. It emerges with the color of old gold; a big, creamy head; a light but soft body; and a bone-dry palate more reminiscent of a Belgian *lambic* beer.

Publick pints
The antique spelling "Publick"
is forgivable from a brewery
that has striven to make some
very traditional beers.

SOUTHAMPTON
SECRET

⬡ **REGION OF ORIGIN** Northeast US

🍶 **STYLE** Altbier

🌀 **ALCOHOL CONTENT** 4.2 abw (5.2 abv)

🍺 **IDEAL SERVING TEMPERATURE** 48° F (9° C)

Modeled on a *Sticke*. Made with imported German ingredients: no fewer than five malts (pale, Vienna, Munich, black, and wheat) and three varieties of hops (Northern Brewer, Hallertau Tradition, and Spalt) and an *Altbier* yeast. Very fresh in aroma and palate, with a sweetish, slightly chocolatey, smoothly malty start but a good balance of late dryness.

First resort
The seaside pavilions and sailboarding of Southampton seem a far cry from the cosiness of Old Town taverns by the Rhine in Düsseldorf.

SPATEN MÜNCHNER HELL

REGION OF ORIGIN Munich, Upper Bavaria, Germany

STYLE Munich *Hell* ("Pale") Lager

ALCOHOL CONTENT 4.2 abw (5.2 abv)

IDEAL SERVING TEMPERATURE 48° F (9° C)

From the viewpoint of stylistic variety, lager-brewing owes more to Spaten, of Munich, than to any other brewery. The enterprise dates from 1397, several decades beyond the possible first references to the lager method. *Lagering* had its beginnings as a modern technique at the Spaten brewery around the end of the 1830s. Spaten's first lager was dark brown in color, and is still made, with the label Dunkel. Yeast from Spaten was used to make the first Carlsberg beers, and in 1894 the Munich brewery made its first golden lager. Today's "Munich Pale" is notably aromatic; with a clean, quite sweet, malty palate; and a late, light, nutty dryness.

SPATEN OKTOBERFESTBIER

REGION OF ORIGIN Munich, Upper Bavaria, Germany

STYLE *Märzen/Oktoberfest*

ALCOHOL CONTENT 4.7 abw (5.9 abv)

IDEAL SERVING TEMPERATURE 48° F (9° C)

The classic *Märzen-Oktoberfest* lager, as introduced in 1871–72, was a strongish version of the very malty, amber-red, Vienna style. In recent years, the Munich brewers have reduced the color of their Oktoberfest beers, while maintaining a gentle malt accent. Spaten's once-definitive example is now a conventional gold. It has a creamy aroma and a clean, firm, smooth, light-malt accent. It is traditionally the first beer to be tapped at the Oktoberfest. Fuller-colored, more traditional examples are easier to find in the United States.

S

STAROPRAMEN DARK

REGION OF ORIGIN Bohemia, Czech Republic

STYLE Dark Lager

ALCOHOL CONTENT 3.7 abw (4.6 abv)

IDEAL SERVING TEMPERATURE 48° F (9° C)

This Czech brewery, the name of which means "Old Spring," is close to the centre of Prague and by the Moldau River. Set around a courtyard, it is a classic brewery from the 1870s. Staropramen is more widely known for its golden lager, but it also produces a dark (in Czech, *Tmavé*) version. This is light-bodied, but soft and smooth, with malty licorice or aniseed notes and an underlying flowery hop. Try it with fennel sausages. In Prague, a yet tastier dark lager can be found at the famous brewpub U Fleku.

STAUDER PREMIUM PILS

🏷️ **REGION OF ORIGIN**	North Rhine-Westphalia, Germany
🍾 **STYLE**	Pilsner
% **ALCOHOL CONTENT**	3.7 abw (4.6 abv)
🍺 **IDEAL SERVING TEMPERATURE**	48° F (9° C)

The term "premium" is often used on beer labels, but has no specific meaning with regard to quality. In the US, it was originally used simply to indicate a beer that was nationally marketed, as opposed to being local. In Britain, where many beers are in the range of 2.8–3.6 abw (3.5–4.5 abv), "premium" suggests something close to 4.0 (5.0). In Germany, the term is popular among brewers who specialize in just one style. Stauder specializes in Pilsner-style lager. Its Premium Pils is seen especially in restaurants and luxury hotel bars. It has a slightly fruity, grassy, new-mown hay aroma and flavor; a firm, attenuated body; and a good hop bitterness. The brewery is in Essen.

STEENDONK
BRABANTS WITBIER

🛡 **REGION OF ORIGIN** Province of Flemish Brabant, Belgium

🍾 **STYLE** Belgian Wheat Beer

% **ALCOHOL CONTENT** 3.6 abw (4.5 abv)

🍺 **IDEAL SERVING TEMPERATURE** 48–50° F (9–10° C)

A Belgian white made by the renowned Palm brewery, in Steenhuffel, to the northwest of Brussels, and marketed jointly by the people who produce the famous, strong, golden Duvel *(see p.151)*, in nearby Breendonk. The use of cinnamon is an unusual feature of this beer. The name is a marriage of the two villages. The beer is pale and milky, spicy and dry, with a melony fruit character.

STEINER MÄRZEN

🗺	**REGION OF ORIGIN**	Upper Bavaria, Germany
🍾	**STYLE**	*Märzen/Oktoberfest*
%	**ALCOHOL CONTENT**	4.4 abw (5.5 abv)
🍺	**IDEAL SERVING TEMPERATURE**	48° F (9° C)

S tein is a hamlet where a rocky cliff on the Traun River once formed the frontier between Bavaria and Austria. Caves in the cliff-face are still used for the *lagering* of beer, and contain the lagering vessels of the Schlossbrauerei ("Castle Brewery") Stein. Its Märzen (March) beer, brewed to be consumed in September, is a good example of the style.

It has the reddish bronze color that was traditional in *Märzen-Oktoberfest* lagers; a richly malty aroma (also with some spicy hop balance); and juicy, almost chewy, barley-sugar flavors.

A stein…
…might seem a more appropriate
vessel, but glass better shows the
attractive subtlety of this brew's color.

STEINER UR-DUNKEL

🛡️	**REGION OF ORIGIN** Upper Bavaria, Germany
🍾	**STYLE** Munich Dark Lager
%	**ALCOHOL CONTENT** 3.9 abw (4.9 abv)
🍺	**IDEAL SERVING TEMPERATURE** 48° F (9° C)

The "rocky cellar" maturation that rounds out such a fine *Märzenbier* at Steiner imparts a similar character to the brewery's several other lagers. Its *Ur-* ("original") *Dunkel* ("dark") lager was not the first example of the style, but is very traditional in character. Its malt flavors are light and fresh but complex, with nuttiness and fruitiness developing as the palate moves to a slightly tart balancing dryness.

STOUDT'S ABBEY DOUBLE

REGION OF ORIGIN Northeast US

STYLE Abbey Double

ALCOHOL CONTENT 5.6 abw (7.0 abv)

IDEAL SERVING TEMPERATURE Store at around 57° F (14° C);
Serve no colder than 50° F (10° C)

This is not a stout brewery – the family name is spelled with a "d", and is originally German. Mrs. Carol Stoudt runs this brewery, in Adamstown, Pennsylvania, and has won awards for many styles of beer. Her Abbey-style Double has a syrupy richness, with suggestions of vanilla, and a medicinal, phenolic finish. Five malts and one sugar are used, along with four varieties of hop and a Belgian yeast. The brewery also has a paler, fruitier, winier, stronger Tripel. The figure on the label is Michel Notredame, not a monk (despite his astonishingly appropriate surname), but a Philadelphia restaurateur.

S

STOUDT'S EXPORT GOLD

🛡 **REGION OF ORIGIN** Northeast US

🍾 **STYLE** Munich *Hell* ("Pale") Lager

% **ALCOHOL CONTENT** 4.0 abw (5.0 abv)

🍺 **IDEAL SERVING TEMPERATURE** 48° F (9° C)

This persistent award-winner from the Stoudt brewery, of Adamstown, Pennsylvania, was originally launched as an example of the Dortmunder style (hence the term Export). More recently, it has been billed as a Munich-style *Helles* ("pale") lager. Either way, it is a creamily smooth brew, with a succulent sweetness of malt character and a flowery (orange blossom?) hop balance. A Munich-style malt seems to make a big contribution to flavor; Tettnang, Hallertau, and Saaz hops are used.

Hoppy weekend
The towered building on the label is the brewery, founded in 1987. Also on the site is a steak restaurant and an antiques market. Adamstown is a popular weekend destination for Philadelphians.

STOUDT'S PILS

🛡 **REGION OF ORIGIN** Northeast US

🍾 **STYLE** Pilsner

% **ALCOHOL CONTENT** 3.6 abw (4.5 abv)

🥃 **IDEAL SERVING TEMPERATURE** 48° F (9° C)

Outside the Czech Republic and Germany, the term Pilsner is widely misused internationally, not least in the US. It does not mean simply a golden lager: a true Pilsner-style lager has a distinct hop character, in both a flowery aroma and a dry finish. Stoudt's Pils is a fine example of the real thing. The hop is quite gentle in the aroma, but comes through beautifully in the palate and in an appetizingly dry finish. Saaz hops are heavily featured.

Brewster's bouquet
The stylized image on the label bears a passing resemblance to the maker of the beer. Carol Stoudt is a lively and active spokesperson for American microbreweries. Being a woman, she is a brewster, not a brewer.

S

SÜNNER HEFEWEIZEN

🛡 **REGION OF ORIGIN** Cologne, North Rhine-Westphalia, Germany

🍶 **STYLE** *Hefeweizen*

％ **ALCOHOL CONTENT** 3.9 abw (4.9 abv)

🥤 **IDEAL SERVING TEMPERATURE** 48–54° F (9–12° C)

The northern brewery Sünner is better known for the *Kölschbier* it makes in its home town of Cologne, but it also has a *Hefeweizen*. This brew has a flowery, perfumy aroma; a smooth, soft, melony body; a light bubblegum character; and a leafy finish. The label shows the handsome brewery with its battlemented gables. In the central window, the brewkettle is clearly visible.

SÜNNER KÖLSCH

🛡 **REGION OF ORIGIN** Cologne, North Rhine-Westphalia, Germany

🍾 **STYLE** *Kölschbier*

% **ALCOHOL CONTENT** 3.8 abw (4.8 abv)

🥃 **IDEAL SERVING TEMPERATURE** 48° F (9° C)

After five generations, Sünner is the oldest family concern still making its own beer in Cologne. Christian Sünner founded the brewery in 1830 and it has been on the same site since 1859. It is across the river from the city centre, in the high street of the Kalk neighborhood. There is a beer garden at the brewery. Sünner Kölsch has a fresh, creamy aroma; a peachy fruitiness; and a dry, spicy, almost salty, hop tang in its crisp finish. The brewery also makes a rye whiskey.

Winning over wine
This brew can be enjoyed in the city
center at Im Walfisch, a typical
Cologne beer tavern on a site that was
a brewery in the 1400s. Until recently,
it was a wine restaurant.

SWALE WHITSTABLE OYSTER STOUT

⬡	**REGION OF ORIGIN**	Southeast England, UK
♦	**STYLE**	Dry Stout
⊘	**ALCOHOL CONTENT**	3.6 abw (4.5 abv)
▮	**IDEAL SERVING TEMPERATURE**	50–55° F (10–13° C)

Intended to be served with oysters, but containing none. Its tarlike aroma and flavors do evoke fishing harbors, and boats caulked with pitch. Its body is smooth enough to help a Whitstable Native slip down the hungry throat. The famous oyster town is in Kent near Sittingbourne, home of the Swale microbrewery. The name of the brewery derives from that of the borough.

The Swale Brewery Co.

Whitstable Oyster Stout
A perfect accompaniment to Whitstable Oysters

Alc 4.5% vol   500ml ℮

Good enough to swallow
In case the appetite needs
tempting, the watercolor-style
label shows baskets of oysters
being fetched ashore.

TABERNASH MUNICH

	REGION OF ORIGIN	Southwest US
	STYLE	Munich Dark Lager
	ALCOHOL CONTENT	3.9 abw (4.9 abv)
	IDEAL SERVING TEMPERATURE	48° F (9° C)

There is a town of Tabernash, west of Denver, Colorado, named after a Native American Ute chief. This mystical name also attaches to a range of microbrews produced not far away in Longmont. The Tabernash beers are in classic German styles. One of their creators studied brewing at Weihenstephan, near Munich. The Tabernash beer called simply Munich, and subtitled Dark Lager, is very smooth, with some fruity maltiness and toastiness. It has a well-rounded finish, with a hint of hoppy dryness.

TABERNASH WEISS

🛡	**REGION OF ORIGIN** Southwest US
🍶	**STYLE** *Hefeweizen*
⑨	**ALCOHOL CONTENT** 4.4 abw (5.5 abv)
🍺	**IDEAL SERVING TEMPERATURE** 8–54° F (9–12° C)

Founding partner Eric Warner, who studied brewing at Weihenstephan, near Munich *(see pp.487–89)*, has a special interest in German wheat beers. He even wrote a book on the subject. The wheat beer he created for Tabernash has a good nutmeg, clovey spiciness in the aroma; is quite sweet; and develops very good fruit flavors, especially banana. The brewery began in 1993, in Denver, Colorado. Shortly afterward, it entered the Great American Beer Festival for the first time, and won a gold medal for its Weiss and bronzes for its Golden Spike and Denargo lagers. Tabernash later moved to nearby Longmont.

White mountains
The snow-capped mountains on the label of this "white" beer are the Rockies. They dominate this part of Colorado, which is dense with small breweries.

THEAKSTON OLD PECULIER

REGION OF ORIGIN Northern England, UK

STYLE Old Ale

ALCOHOL CONTENT 4.5 abw (5.6 abv)

IDEAL SERVING TEMPERATURE 55° F (13° C)

The best-known example of an old ale as a dark brown, full-bodied, sweet, malty brew, medium-to-strong, and widely available on draft, is Old Peculier from Theakston. The tiny 1870s brewery, in Masham, North Yorkshire, England, is now owned by Scottish Courage. Old Peculier (reviving a medieval spelling) has a soft and oily body; flavors reminiscent of milk chocolate; and a raisiny, blackcurrant dryness in the finish. It is a soothing and sustaining brew. The town of Masham is in the Yorkshire Dales, where the grazing of sheep once made for a profitable wool trade. It was so economically powerful in medieval times that it had a "peculier" status, independent of the local archdeacon.

THOMAS KEMPER OKTOBERFEST

T

REGION OF ORIGIN
Pacific Northwest US

STYLE *Märzen-Oktoberfest* Lager

ALCOHOL CONTENT 4.5 abw (5.6 abv)

IDEAL SERVING TEMPERATURE
(48° F) 9° C

Among the new generation of American breweries, and especially in the ale-loving Seattle area, Thomas Kemper was an early lager producer, in 1984. Kemper has since changed location twice, and now shares a brewery and pub in Seattle with Pyramid. Its *Oktoberfest* forms a rocky head; has a full reddish color; a peachy aroma; a nutty malt character, becoming grainy and then creamy; and a late balance of flowery hop dryness.

12 FL. OZ. (355 ML)

THREE TUNS CLERICS CURE

REGION OF ORIGIN	Midlands of England, UK
STYLE	Bitter Ale
ALCOHOL CONTENT	4.0 abw (5.0 abv)
IDEAL SERVING TEMPERATURE	50–55° F (10–13° C)

A tun is a large wooden vessel used in the fermentation or maturation of alcoholic drinks. Why three? Perhaps because three additions of water to the same grain bed typically made strong, medium, and "small" beers. Near the border separating Wales from England, the Shropshire town of Bishop's Castle probably had a brewery even earlier than 1642, the date usually cited. A malt store from that period stands next to the present (1880s) brewery and inn. This was one of a handful of brewpubs left in Britain before the revival that came with the Campaign for Real Ale. There is no Bishops Brew; the name Clerics Cure was inspired by a letter in 1899, in which a local reverend suggested the brewery's beer as a remedy for agricultural depression. It is a straw-colored beer, with a tangerinelike aroma; a light but firm malt background; and a late hop dryness. Crisply refreshing and appetizing.

THURN UND TAXIS ROGGEN

🛡 **REGION OF ORIGIN** Bavaria, Germany
🍶 **STYLE** Rye Beer
📊 **ALCOHOL CONTENT** 4.0 abw (5.0 abv)
🌡 **IDEAL SERVING TEMPERATURE** 48–54° F (9–12° C)

The oddly-named royal family Thurn und Taxis for many years owned a well-known brewery in Regensburg, Bavaria, and a smaller one not far away in the town of Schierling. The latter, which had its origins in a 13th-century convent, became known in the late-1980s for a beer made with a blend of 60 percent rye (*Roggen*, in German) and wheat. This brew, intended as a more distinctive variation on a dark wheat beer, is grainy, slightly smoky, fruity, and spicy, with a bittersweet rye character. In the late 1990s, the Thurn und Taxis brewing interests were acquired by Paulaner, of Munich. The Roggenbier is now made in Regensburg.

TIMMERMANS KRIEK

REGION OF ORIGIN Province of Flemish Brabant, Belgium

STYLE *Kriek-Lambic*

ALCOHOL CONTENT 4.0 abw (5.0 abv)

IDEAL SERVING TEMPERATURE 47–48° F (8–9° C)

The Timmermans brewery dates from 1888, though there may have been a brewery on the site, in Itterbeek, since 1650. The founding family still has a share in the company, though control is in the hands of John Martin's, better known for pale ale. Among the widely available examples of *kriek*, Timmermans' has a more obvious *lambic* character than its competitors – a delicate, fino sherry acidity – before the cherry flavors emerge. An unfiltered *gueuze* called Caveau is yet drier.

TIMOTHY TAYLOR'S LANDLORD

REGION OF ORIGIN Northern England, UK

STYLE Pale Ale/Bitter

ALCOHOL CONTENT 3.3 abw (4.1 abv)

IDEAL SERVING TEMPERATURE 52–58° F (11–14° C)

Renowned brewery on the edge of the moorlands in Yorkshire's Brontë country. Timothy Taylor's is in the small wool town of Keighley. Its Landlord Strong Pale Ale was allegedly designed especially to cleanse the throats of Yorkshire coalminers. It is a very drinkable beer, with a heathery hop aroma (Styrian Goldings); a firm, grainy palate; some juicy maltiness (the variety is Golden Promise); and a touch of refreshing acidity in the finish. The brewery recommends only a gentle chilling.

Smile of success
Yorkshiremen famously ration
their smiles, but Timothy Taylor
is a persistent award-winner.

TOMINTOUL NESSIE'S MONSTER MASH

REGION OF ORIGIN Highlands of Scotland, UK

STYLE Scottish Ale

ALCOHOL CONTENT 3.5 abw (4.4 abv)

IDEAL SERVING TEMPERATURE 50–55° F (10–13° C)

Snow-melt from the Grampian Mountains fills fast-flowing burns (streams) around the village of Tomintoul. Half a mile away, a grain mill dating from the early 1700s was converted into a brewery in 1993. Its beer Nessie's Monster Mash has only a modest strength but is surprisingly rich in its texture and malty flavors. It is faintly rummy and chocolatey, with a balance of lightly nutty dryness. Below the town are whiskey distilleries and to the west is Loch Ness, where deep waters allegedly accommodate a famous monster.

The monster…
…on the label is based on photographs
from different "witnesses." Stories of a
creature date from at least the 7th century.

TOMINTOUL STAG

🛡 **REGION OF ORIGIN**	Highlands of Scotland, UK
🍾 **STYLE**	Scottish Ale
% **ALCOHOL CONTENT**	3.3 abw (4.1 abv)
🍺 **IDEAL SERVING TEMPERATURE**	50–55° F (10–13° C)

Deer are very common in the Highlands of Scotland, and the stag is a widely used emblem in the region. This ale is by no means strong in alcohol but has, in both aroma and palate, remarkable balance of typically Scottish maltiness and more leafy, lively, hop character. When this beer was first brewed, it was more heavily hopped, but the taste was seen as too "English." In the current version, the flavor develops beautifully, with the maltiness gradually emerging. This characteristic is heightened by the softness of the brewery's water, which filters through fissures in the granite. It may even pick up some peatiness as it flows over moorland to the brewery.

The monarch…
…of the glen also provides sustenance for some of Scotland's better dinner tables.

TOOHEYS OLD BLACK ALE

🛡	**REGION OF ORIGIN**	New South Wales, Australia
🍾	**STYLE**	Old Ale
%	**ALCOHOL CONTENT**	3.5 abw (4.4 abv)
🌡	**IDEAL SERVING TEMPERATURE**	50° F (10° C)

Irish-Australian brothers founded the Tooheys brewery, in Sydney, in the mid-1800s. It became known as the city's "Catholic" brewery and is now part of the national group Lion Nathan. Tooheys has maintained the tradition of an old ale, which was once brewed north of Sydney in the city of Newcastle. Toohey's Old has a modest alcohol content and a light but smooth body. The flavors are very gentle, but there are touches of bitter-chocolate, cream, and oloroso sherry spiciness, nuttiness, and fruitiness. It finishes toasty and dry and has more complexity than its local rival, from the Tooth's brewery.

Ale halo
Tooheys Old emphasizes its ale status by declaring, on the neck label, that it is made with top-fermenting yeast.

TRAQUAIR HOUSE ALE

REGION OF ORIGIN Scottish Borders, UK

STYLE Strong Scottish Ale

ALCOHOL CONTENT 5.8 abw (7.2 abv)

IDEAL SERVING TEMPERATURE 50–55° F (10–13° C)

B eer from the castle at Traquair was first mentioned in
1566. The brewery was revived in 1965, by the 20th
Laird ("Lord") of Traquair, Peter Maxwell Stuart. It is now
managed by his daughter, Lady Catherine. The brewery's
principal product has a lightly oaky aroma; touches of fresh
earthiness, pepperiness, and nutty maltiness in the palate;
and some woody, rooty tartness in the finish.

Label lore
The back label reveals that
Traquair's main gates will
remain closed until a Stuart
returns to the British throne.

TRAQUAIR JACOBITE ALE

REGION OF ORIGIN Scottish Borders, UK

STYLE Spiced Scottish Ale

ALCOHOL CONTENT 6.4 abw (8.0 abv)

IDEAL SERVING TEMPERATURE 55° F (13° C)

Traquair House is a castle on the Scottish side of the border with England, owned by a branch of the Scottish royal family, the Stuarts. Bonnie Prince Charlie is said to have visited the house during his campaign in the autumn of 1745. Jacobite Ale, produced in the house's own brewery, was launched in 1995. It is a purple-to-black ale, rich, with a sweetish, spicy, soft, rooty flavor. The brew is spiced with coriander.

Loyalty to royalty
Jacobite, after King James II,
means a supporter of the royal
Stuart succession.

TRIPEL KARMELIET

⬦ **REGION OF ORIGIN**	Province of East Flanders, Belgium
🍶 **STYLE**	Abbey Triple
% **ALCOHOL CONTENT**	6.4 abw (8.0 abv)
⬚ **IDEAL SERVING TEMPERATURE**	Store at around 57° F (14° C); Serve no colder than 50° F (10° C)

A Belgian Carmelite abbey reputedly made a three-grain beer at Dendermonde in the 1600s. This inspired the Bosteels brewery in nearby Buggenhout to create, in 1997, a *tripel* made from barley, wheat, and oats. Each is used both raw and malted, and the beer is also heavily spiced. Tripel Karmeliet is a brew of some finesse and complexity: with a wheaty lightness, sweet lemons, an oaty creaminess, and a spicy, medicinal dryness.

Lily livery
The heraldic lily on the glass does not represent the French royal symbol, but is merely decorative. The brewery's owners enjoy decorative arts. One of them, Antoine Bosteels, designed the glass.

TSINGTAO

REGION OF ORIGIN Shandong, China

STYLE Lager/Pilsner

ALCOHOL CONTENT 3.4 abw (4.25 abv)

IDEAL SERVING TEMPERATURE 48° F (9° C)

Tsingtao is the only Chinese beer widely known outside its home country. The company has about 20 breweries in China, but the original is in the old quarter of Tsingtao, today known as Qingdao, in the province of Shandong (Shantung). The coastal town includes a small island – Quingdao means "green island." At the beginning of the 1900s, Tsingtao was a German port in much the way that Hong Kong was British and Macao Portuguese. Germans founded the brewery, though it is now Chinese. The brew called simply Tsingtao Beer is relatively mild, but has notably more hop aroma and bitterness than most other golden lagers from China (every city has at least one brewing company, some with huge capacities). Tsingtao also produces an excellent, oily, coffeeish, dark lager that is very hard to find outside China.

TUCHER HELLES HEFE WEIZEN

REGION OF ORIGIN Franconia, Bavaria, Germany

STYLE *Hefeweizen*

ALCOHOL CONTENT 4.2 abw (5.3 abv)

IDEAL SERVING TEMPERATURE 48–54° F (9–12° C)

Founded as a wheat-beer brewery in 1672, and for a time owned by Bavaria's royal family. The Tucher family took over in 1855, and the brewery has had several owners since. This Nuremberg brewery again became a family business in 1994, when a member of the Bavarian brewing dynasty Inselkammer took an interest. Its *Hefeweizen* has a firm background with sweet apple flavors, moving to a spicy, dry, crisp finish.

Flag of pride
The words on the label are shown against a background of the pale blue and white diamond pattern of the Bavarian flag. This motif is widely used by brewers from this state – and some implying that they are Bavarian.

TUPPERS' HOP POCKET ALE

🛡 **REGION OF ORIGIN** Mid-Atlantic US

🍾 **STYLE** American Ale

% **ALCOHOL CONTENT** 4.8 abw (6.0 abv)

🍺 **IDEAL SERVING TEMPERATURE** 50° F (10° C)

Bob Tupper is a history teacher who gives lectures on beer at a famous bar, The Brickskeller, in Washington, D.C.. He and his wife Ellie, an editor, designed this beer, which is produced by the local Old Dominion brewery. It has a flowery aroma; a crisp, cedary, malt background; and wood-bark bitterness in its big, lingering finish. A hop "pocket" is the long sack in which pressed hops are packed. It looks like a boxer's punchbag: this beer hops and hits with the best. The more recent Hop Pocket Pils has a dizzyingly heady character.

UERIGE ALT

REGION OF ORIGIN Düsseldorf, North Rhine-Westphalia, Germany

STYLE *Altbier*

ALCOHOL CONTENT 3.6 abw (4.5 abv)

IDEAL SERVING TEMPERATURE 48° F (9° C)

Fashion icons, rock stars, punks, men in suits, old ladies with big hats… everyone in Düsseldorf drinks at Zum Uerige by the river in the Old Town (the Altstadt). Zum Uerige has its own sausage butchery, and its specialities are head cheese and a smelly Mainzer cheese marinated in beer. The beer at this rambling old brewpub, the classic example of *Alt*, is also bottled for general sale. It has a fresh hop aroma; a firm, smooth, almost slippery, clean maltiness; and a robust punch of bitterness. The name Uerige refers to a past cranky proprietor. A slightly stronger, "secret" version, given extra aroma with a hop tea, is brewed once or twice a year under the name *Sticke Bier*, a Düsseldorf tradition. Uerige Alt inspired the excellent Ur Alt of the Widmer brewery, in Portland, Oregon.

A tasty drop…
…is the meaning of "dat leckere Dröppke."
"Obergärige" is "top-fermenting." Germans
are expected to understand the significance.

UERIGES WEIZEN

- 🛡 **REGION OF ORIGIN** Düsseldorf, North Rhine-Westphalia, Germany

- **STYLE** *Hefeweizen*

- 🅐 **ALCOHOL CONTENT** 3.6 abw (4.5 abv)

- **IDEAL SERVING TEMPERATURE** 48–54° F (9–12° C)

Most Düsseldorf *Altbier* breweries have long specialized in their home-town style, some to the exclusion of any other. The classic old-town brewpub Zum Uerige remains the bedrock of Altbier, but has in recent years made a concession to the fashion for wheat beers with its Ueriges Weizen. Made with the Altbier yeast, and thus rather northern in style, it has a good, clean, malt background, and is light, flowery, gingery, and very crisp, with a minerally dryness in the finish. In Zum Uerige's pub, it has performed well with the homemade blood sausage.

UNERTL WEISSBIER

🛡 **REGION OF ORIGIN** Upper Bavaria, Germany

🍾 **STYLE** *Hefeweizen*

📊 **ALCOHOL CONTENT** 3.8 abw (4.8 abv)

🥛 **IDEAL SERVING TEMPERATURE** 48–54° F (9–12° C)

A flavorsome, traditionally made range of wheat beers is produced by the brewery of the Unertl family, in the town of Haag, about 30 miles (40 km) southeast of Munich. The principal beer is in the *Hefeweizen* style, turbid and full in color, but not identified as being dark. It has a juicy, toffee-apple character and a smoky, appetizing dryness. It is offered at the brewery's beer garden with bread and pork dripping *(Griebenschmalz)*.

Independent brew
The tower in the center of the label is a surviving part of the castle of Haag. The town was in medieval times seat of an independent Protestant state in Roman Catholic Bavaria.

UNIBROUE BLANCHE DE CHAMBLY

🛡 **REGION OF ORIGIN** Province of Quebec, Canada

🍾 **STYLE** Belgian-Style Wheat Beer

％ **ALCOHOL CONTENT** 4.0 abw (5.0 abv)

🍺 **IDEAL SERVING TEMPERATURE** 48–50° F (9–10° C)

The French language is in this instance not from Belgium but from Canada. In the Montreal suburb of Chambly, the Unibroue microbrewery produces Belgian-style beers of great character. The brewery's founders include Canadian rock singer Robert Charlebois. It received some initial consultancy from the Belgian brewery Riva. Blanche de Chambly is mouth-fillingly spritzy, with big, perfumy, orange and lemon notes. In 2000, Unibroue added a wheat beer at the strength of a Triple. This is named Don De Dieu, after a vessel that the French king sent to explore Canada in 1608. The beer has a superbly perfumy spiciness.

UNIBROUE MAUDITE

🛡 **REGION OF ORIGIN**	Province of Quebec, Canada
🍶 **STYLE**	Strong, spiced Belgian-style Ale
% **ALCOHOL CONTENT**	6.4 abw (8.0 abv)
🍺 **IDEAL SERVING TEMPERATURE**	50–55° F (10–13° C)

Inspired by the Belgian strong golden ale Duvel *(see p.151)* and its many imitators, this bottle-conditioned brew has a name meaning "damned" in French. The beer is made by Unibroue, of Chambly, near Montreal. An 1890s Quebecois story by Honoré Beaugrand – a Faustian variation on voyages of the damned – is illustrated on the label. Maudite is a darkish interpretation of the style; fruity, spiced (orange peels, coriander, pepper?), and dry. It is a hugely flavorsome beer to accompany crudités or roasted peppers.

UNIBROUE QUELQUE CHOSE

🛡 **REGION OF ORIGIN** Province of Quebec, Canada

🍾 **STYLE** Spiced Cherry Beer

％ **ALCOHOL CONTENT** 6.4 abw (8.0 abv)

🍶 **IDEAL SERVING TEMPERATURE** 158° F (70° C)

The Belgian company that owns Liefmans was originally a consultant to this very adventurous Quebecois brewery. Unibroue has some truly remarkable beers, and this is one of them. Liefmans Glühkriek and Quelque Chose have much the same base beer, but the latter is blended with a paler, stronger brew, with a complex malt specification including some whiskey malt. The resultant beer is therefore stronger, but it also seems lighter-bodied, fruitier, and tarter.

Something else…
"Is it a wine or a beer, or something else?" people asked. "It's something else! Really something!!" replied the brewer.

UNIONS BRÄU HELL

🛡️ **REGION OF ORIGIN** Munich, Upper Bavaria, Germany

🍾 **STYLE** *Helles* Lager

％ **ALCOHOL CONTENT** 3.8 abw (4.7 abv)

🌡️ **IDEAL SERVING TEMPERATURE** 48° F (9° C)

One of the smallest and most interesting breweries in Munich is Unions, on Einstein Strasse, in the stylish neighborhood of Haidenhausen. Once it was larger, formed by the union of four breweries. That incarnation ended in the 1920s, in a merger with Löwenbräu. The Unions premises reopened in 1991, as a brewpub. Its principal product is its *Helles*: sweet, malty, smooth, and slightly oily; and served from pitch-lined oak barrels. Organically grown barley and hops are used. The brewpub also offers Löwenbräu beers.

Virgin brew?
Pure beer is visualized in a perhaps triumphalist but curiously androgynous figure on the label.

USHERS AUTUMN FRENZY

	REGION OF ORIGIN West of England, UK
	STYLE Rye Ale
	ALCOHOL CONTENT 3.2 abw (4.0 abv)
	IDEAL SERVING TEMPERATURE 50–55° F (10–13° C)

One of the first English brewers to launch an autumn beer was Ushers, which has a speciality for each of the four seasons. When the leaves begin to fall, look out for the autumnal hue of this gently sustaining, dryish brew. Both the color and the smooth, nutty, spicy palate owe something to the use of rye, a grain once found only in some Baltic and Russian speciality brews. It is to be hoped that this excellent range survives recent uncertainty over the future of Ushers.

USHERS VINTAGE TAWNY ALE

🛡 **REGION OF ORIGIN**	West of England, UK
🍾 **STYLE**	Ale
% **ALCOHOL CONTENT**	5.0 abw (6.2 abv)
🌡 **IDEAL SERVING TEMPERATURE**	50–55° F (10–13° C)

Dated with the year in which the barley and hops were harvested, and bearing a back label indicating the varieties used and the styles of malting, this Tawny Ale is one of a series intended to be served with food. The handsome, embossed bottle, the dignified typography of the label, and descriptions such as "Tawny," "Ruby," and "White," emphasize that beer can grace the dinner table as wine more often does. The Tawny has a fruity, slightly smoky aroma; a lightly creamy texture; nutty, earthy, malt flavors; and an oily, perfumy dryness (from Fuggles hops) in the finish. The Ruby is slightly sweeter and fruitier (Vienna malt and Styrian hops). The White is a crisp, dry, very pale, golden ale, notably flowery and geranium-like.

Waiter... the beer list
The back labels suggest the White with poultry, the Ruby with red meat, and the Tawny with English cheeses.

VELTINS

REGION OF ORIGIN North Rhine-Westphalia, Germany

STYLE Pilsner

ALCOHOL CONTENT 3.8 abw (4.8 abv)

IDEAL SERVING TEMPERATURE 48° F (9° C)

People living in the big cities of the Rhine and Ruhr like to go walking, cycling, and sailing about 100 miles (160 km) east, in the hill-and-lake district called the Sauerland (not to be confused with the state of Saarland, further south). In a nation where environmentalism is a powerful cause, the clean air and fresh water of Sauerland inspire the thirst. Some local beers have in consequence won a widespread following. The family brewery Veltins, in Meschede-Grevenstein, is among these success stories. Its Veltins Pilsner has the grassy, new-mown hay character of a traditional German lager, and is a sweetish, robust beer, with an elegant hop bitterness in the finish.

VERHAEGHE
DUCHESSE DE BOURGOGNE

REGION OF ORIGIN West Flanders, Belgium

STYLE Flemish Red/Brown

ALCOHOL CONTENT 5.0 abw (6.2 abv)

IDEAL SERVING TEMPERATURE 48–55° F (9–13° C)

The Verhaege family, of Vichte, near Kortrijk (in French, Courtrai), Belgium, has been brewing since the 1500s, originally in a château farmhouse brewery. The present site dates from 1880, and about a dozen oak vessels from that time are still in use to mature a range of three beers in the reddish "old brown," sweet-and-sour style of the region. The strongest and richest of this group, called Duchesse de Bourgogne, has an interesting interplay of chocolate and cream notes with a long, dry, passionfruit acidity. The beer is said to have an average age of 12 months. Its name recalls the days when Flanders was ruled by the Duke of Burgundy. The beer honors the Duchess Mary of Burgundy (1457–82), famously an ally of the Flemish people.

VERHAEGHE ECHTE KRIEK

🛡 **REGION OF ORIGIN** West Flanders, Belgium

🍾 **STYLE** *Kriek*

% **ALCOHOL CONTENT** 5.4 abw (6.8 abv)

🌡 **IDEAL SERVING TEMPERATURE** 48–55° F (9–13° C)

The Dutch word for "real" is *echte*. Verhaeghe's Echte Kriek uses real cherries, rather than juice or essence. The fruit comes from St. Truiden, in Belgian Limburg. This is one of several *kriek* beers not made from a *lambic* brew. The base beer is Vichtenaar *(see p.478)*. Echte Kriek has the aroma of a Kirsch cherry brandy; a smooth, vanilla-like, oaky palate; and a late surge of ironlike, passionfruit flavors, with some acidity.

VERHAEGHE VICHTENAAR

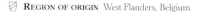

🛡 **REGION OF ORIGIN**	West Flanders, Belgium
🍾 **STYLE**	Flemish Red/Brown
% **ALCOHOL CONTENT**	4.0 abw (5.1 abv)
🍺 **IDEAL SERVING TEMPERATURE**	48–55° F (9–13° C)

The brewing family Verhaeghe honor the people of their town with this beer. The town is called Vichte and a person from there is a Vichtenaar. Although it is a very small town, the Verhaeghes are quick to point out that it adjoins Tiegem, birthplace of St. Arnold, patron of Belgian brewers. In the local style, their basic reddish "Oud Bruin" is one of the sweeter examples, but lively and layered, with notes of Madeira, vanilla, oak, and iron, and the acidity of a fresh apple.

Aged for a century?
The neck label shows a sole wooden cask. The brewery has upright tuns, ranging from 6,605 to 158,520 gallons (250 to 6,000 hectolitres). They are in buildings more than 100 years old.

VICTORY PRIMA PILS

🏷️	**REGION OF ORIGIN**	Northeast US
🍺	**STYLE**	Pilsner
⁒	**ALCOHOL CONTENT**	4.3 abw (5.4 abv)
🌡️	**IDEAL SERVING TEMPERATURE**	48° F (9° C)

The stylized hop on the label is appropriate. This is a very hoppy Pilsner. It has the "fresh sea air," gorse-like aroma of Saaz hops; almost gritty hop flavors; a lean malt background; and a firm, bitter finish. The beer is hopped twice with Saaz and once with Northern Brewer, from Germany. It is produced by the Victory brewery and pub, established in 1995–96 in Downingtown, Pennsylvania. The town, once an inland resort, is now a suburban community for Philadelphia. The brewery is in a former Pepperidge Farm bakery. One inspiration for this alliterative Pils was the famously hoppy example at the Vogelbräu brewery and pub, in Karlsruhe, Germany.

Pennsylvania prime
The state founded by William Penn was once the heartland of German-American brewing. Now, with microbreweries making some of the best lagers in the United States, it bids to be once more.

VICTORY ST. VICTORIOUS

🛡 **REGION OF ORIGIN** Northeast US

🍾 **STYLE** Double Bock

⦿ **ALCOHOL CONTENT** 5.9 abw (7.4 abv)

🥛 **IDEAL SERVING TEMPERATURE** 48° F (9° C)

No fewer than seven German malts and four varieties of hop are used in this aromatic, creamy, complex Double Bock, which has a finish like a nutty Port. It is made by the Victory brewery and pub, in Downingtown, Pennsylvania. The brewery's founders met on a school bus when they were ten years old. Why Victory? "Being near Philadelphia, we wanted to call our brewery Liberty, but that name was already taken. Then another brewery beat us to the name Independence. We decided that getting a small brewery under way was a victory in itself."

Whimsical labels...
...are often used on very strong beers, but this brew offers more than mindless muscle. It has a complexity and sophistication that makes it one of America's best Bocks.

Vieux Temps

REGION OF ORIGIN Provinces of French/Flemish Brabant, Belgium

STYLE Belgian Ale

ALCOHOL CONTENT 4.0 abw (5.0 abv)

IDEAL SERVING TEMPERATURE 50–55° F (10–13° C)

The name, meaning "old times," recalls a long-gone, but much-loved, bottle-conditioned ale from the French-speaking part of Brabant, Belgium. The original was simply an ale bearing the name of the Mont St. Guibert brewery, in the town of the same name. When the brewery started to filter its ale, in 1935, the name Vieux Temps was introduced in an attempt to sustain a sense of tradition. After the brewery closed in the 1990s, production was switched to nearby Leuven, in Flemish Brabant. Despite its new home, Vieux Temps remains Belgium's best-known "French-speaking" ale. It has a distinctly fruity, plummy, sherbety character, with a hint of fragrant smokiness, though its flavors have become softer in recent years.

WÄDI BRÄU LADY HANF

REGION OF ORIGIN Switzerland

STYLE *Weisse/Weizen* with hemp

ALCOHOL CONTENT 3.8 abw (4.8 abv)

IDEAL SERVING TEMPERATURE 48–54° F (9–12° C)

The German word for "hemp" is *Hanf*. The fashion for using hemp in beers was pioneered in 1996 by a brewpub in Wädenswil, near Zurich, Switzerland. Beers like Cannabía and Turn, both from Germany, Greenleaf from Britain, and Hempen Ale from the US, are further examples. Several methods of using non-narcotic hemp seeds, buds, or leaves have been employed. While this ingredient can be a headline-catching novelty, the brewers are quick to point out that hemp and hops are members of the same botanical family. Wädi Bräu Lady Hanf has an orange-flower aroma; a clean, sweetish, malty, nutty palate; and a lightly cedary note from the hemp leaves. The version shown here is based on a wheat beer. It is lighter in both body and alcohol content, and more flowery in palate. The notion that it is therefore more suitable for ladies might be deemed sexist in some countries.

WADWORTH 6X

🛡 **REGION OF ORIGIN** West of England, UK

🍾 **STYLE** Bitter Ale

％ **ALCOHOL CONTENT** 3.4 abw (4.3 abv)

🍺 **IDEAL SERVING TEMPERATURE** 50–55° F (10–13° C)

An open copper kettle is still used, and wooden casks are supplied to local pubs, by the traditionally-minded Wadworth brewery in the market town of Devizes, Wiltshire. The classic tower brewery was built in 1885, though earlier premises from at least the 1830s still stand. Wadworth's 6X is modest in alcohol but big in flavor and texture: an oaky aroma, with hints of Cognac; a toasted-nut maltiness; and a sappy, slightly tart dryness in the finish. Wadworth's other products include Old Timer *(see p.484)* and Farmer's Glory. In mid-September, green hops, straight from the harvest, are used to make a brief seasonal brew.

Six of the best?
*In the days when the letter "x", or perhaps
a cross, was used to indicate strength, this
must have been a more potent brew.*

WADWORTH OLD TIMER

REGION OF ORIGIN West of England, UK

STYLE Old Ale

ALCOHOL CONTENT 4.8 abw (6.0 abv)

IDEAL SERVING TEMPERATURE 50–55° F (10–13° C)

This classic English country brewery, in Devizes, Wiltshire, makes two beers broadly in the old ale style. One, called Farmer's Glory, is in the mode of a mild with extra alcohol (3.6 abw; 4.5 abv), and is intended as a compensation when summer fails to be sunny. It is malty and sweetish, but with a touch of dry hop. Old Timer is creamier, with a fresh, vanilla-pod, nutty maltiness that is both appetizing and satisfying in winter.

Old time brewing
Old Timer is traditional in
almost every painstaking
detail of production.

WALNUT
BIG HORN BITTER

REGION OF ORIGIN Southwest US

STYLE English Bitter

ALCOHOL CONTENT 4.2 abw (5.2 abv)

IDEAL SERVING TEMPERATURE
50–55° F (10–13° C)

When the Woodstock generation wanted to mellow out, they went to the college town of Boulder, in the mountains of Colorado. In the 1960s, there had been other preoccupations, but in the late 1970s President Carter repealed the federal prohibition on homebrewing. In 1981, the American Homebrewers' Association was established in Boulder. In 1990, the town gained its first brewpub, on Walnut Street. The pub is in an early 1900s post-and-beam building that was originally a plumbing warehouse. Its beers are also bottled. The Western-sounding Big Horn is, true to its designation, a very English-tasting bitter. It is refreshingly drinkable, with a lightly textured maltiness; restrained, clean fruitiness; rounded with a really appetizing hop-bitterness in the finish.

WARTECK ALT

🛡	**REGION OF ORIGIN**	Switzerland
🍾	**STYLE**	*Altbier*
%	**ALCOHOL CONTENT**	3.8 abw (4.7 abv)
🍺	**IDEAL SERVING TEMPERATURE**	48° F (9° C)

A director of the Warteck brewery developed a love of *Altbier* from his wife, who came from the Lower Rhine. From such chance origins, this brewery in Basel, Switzerland, gained its own Altbier in the late 1970s. The beer has a malty aroma; a lightly toffeeish start, developing to cinnamon spiciness and perfumy fruitiness; and a balancing touch of hoppy dryness. Warteck was acquired by a local rival, and the beer is now produced in the cathedral-like brewhouse of Feldschlösschen.

WEIHENSTEPHANER HEFE WEISSBIER

🛡 **REGION OF ORIGIN** Upper Bavaria, Germany

🍶 **STYLE** *Hefe Weisse/Weizen*

📊 **ALCOHOL CONTENT** 4.3 abw (5.4 abv)

🌡 **IDEAL SERVING TEMPERATURE** 48–54° F (9–12° C)

The world's oldest brewery is widely regarded to be that at Weihenstephan ("Sacred Stephen"), on a hillside near Freising, north of Munich. Benedictine monks established a community on the hill in at least 725 and were growing hops by 768. The first reference specifically to brewing on the site is from 1040. The monastery was destroyed in wars in the 900s and 1600s, closed by Napoleon, then acquired by the royal family of Bavaria. It is now owned by the state. Today's modern commercial brewery and beer restaurant occupies in part former monastery buildings. The site is shared with the world's best-known university faculty of brewing and a yeast library. The brewery makes about ten lagers and wheat beers, but is especially known for the latter. The Hefe Weissbier is the spiciest in the range, though all are accented more towards fruitiness.

WEIHENSTEPHANER HEFEWEISSBIER DUNKEL

REGION OF ORIGIN	Upper Bavaria, Germany
STYLE	Dark Wheat Beer
ALCOHOL CONTENT	4.25 abw (5.3 abv)
IDEAL SERVING TEMPERATURE	48–54° F (9–12° C)

This dark version of Weihenstephan's Hefe Weissbier *(see previous page)* tastes less obviously yeasty than its paler brother brew. The yeast notes are rounded by the assertive character of the dark malts. The aromas and flavors of malt are dominant, and reminiscent of maple syrup. This element melds beautifully with the fruitiness that is typical of the Weihenstephan beers. In this instance, the fruit character resembles banana, with some suggestions of apple (all of these flavors derive from water, malt, hops, and yeast – no syrups or fruits are added). A delicious beer with sweet pancakes. The brewery's dark products also include a light-bodied but creamy, dryish lager called Export Dunkel.

WEIHENSTEPHANER KRISTALL WEISSBIER

REGION OF ORIGIN Upper Bavaria, Germany

STYLE *Kristall Weisse/Weizen*

ALCOHOL CONTENT 4.4 abw (5.4 abv)

IDEAL SERVING TEMPERATURE 48–54° F (9–12° C)

The fruity notes typical of all wheat beers, but especially characteristic of the Weihenstephan range, are at their clearest and least cluttered in this bright, filtered version. Although it is quite light in body, it has rich, fresh aromas and juicy flavors. Here, the banana-like notes found in many wheat beers are given a tropical intensity by a suggestion of mango, and sharpened by a tinge of blackcurrant. These flavors are predominantly owed to the house yeast. This is a spritzy, refreshing beer. Other golden beers include a Pilsner-type and a flowery golden lager somewhere between an Export and a Bavarian Hell. That is called Weihenstephan Original.

The white vase
The vase-shaped glass is traditional for the style. The terms Weissbier *(white beer) and* Weizenbier *(wheat beer) are used interchangeably. There is no difference.*

WELTENBURGER KLOSTER BAROCK-DUNKEL

REGION OF ORIGIN Upper Bavaria, Germany

STYLE Munich Dark Lager

ALCOHOL CONTENT 3.6 abw (4.5 abv)

IDEAL SERVING TEMPERATURE 48° F (9° C)

The oldest "cloister" (monastery) in the world to have an active brewery. The monastery dates from the 600s, but definite evidence of brewing does not emerge until 1050, slightly later than Weihenstephan (see p.487–89). Weltenburg is farther north of Munich, on the Danube, near Kelheim. In the 1700s, extravagant Baroque buildings were constructed, and they have won the praise of such distant critics as present-day artist Jeff Koons. The Barock Dunkel ("dark") beer is light-bodied and smooth, with a very good malt character suggesting cookies or crackers. It has a toasty, smoky, roast-malt finish. The monastery has a tavern and beer garden (closed in January and February).

WELTENBURGER KLOSTER HEFE-WEISSBIER DUNKEL

REGION OF ORIGIN Upper Bavaria, Germany

STYLE Dark Wheat Beer

ALCOHOL CONTENT 4.0 abw (5.1 abv)

IDEAL SERVING TEMPERATURE 48–54° F (9–12° C)

A superb example of a dark wheat beer, from its zabaglione-like creamy head and spicy-chocolate aroma to its nutty (almonds?), spicy (aniseed?) palate, and the earthy dryness of its finish. There is no guarantee that a "cloister" brewery will make good beer, but perhaps monasticism goes with conservatism, usually a good thing in brewing. In the south of Bavaria, there are famous *Kloster* breweries at Andechs (near Munich) and Ettal (near Garmisch-Patenkirchen) and lesser-known examples run by nuns at Mallersdorf (near Munich) and Ursberg (near Augsburg). In the north of the state, Klosterbrauerei Kreuzberg is near Bischofsheim. Augustine monks own the Münnerstadt brewery, but lease it to a family. Some former monastery breweries also use the term Kloster. One example making outstanding beers is the Kloster brewery of Bamberg.

WERNESGRÜNER
PILS LEGENDE

🛡 **REGION OF ORIGIN** Saxony, Germany
🍾 **STYLE** Pilsner
% **ALCOHOL CONTENT** 3.9 abw (4.9 abv)
🍺 **IDEAL SERVING TEMPERATURE** 48° F (9° C)

This beer is a legend because it remained an intensely bitter speciality during the communist period. It is made at Wernesgrün, south of Zwickau and nearer to Auerbach. It has a bubbly head; an almost quinine-like, tonic-water dryness in the bouquet; a cleansing palate; and a peppery punch of arousal in the finish. As the label says, it is "fresh and spritzy," and as appetizing as a gin and tonic.

Longer than legend
The brewery traces its history
to 1436, four centuries before
the Pilsner style emerged.

WESTMALLE DUBBEL

> **REGION OF ORIGIN** Province of Antwerp, Belgium
>
> **STYLE** Abbey (Authentic Trappist) Double
>
> **ALCOHOL CONTENT** 5.2 abw (6.5 abv)
>
> **IDEAL SERVING TEMPERATURE** 59–64° F (15–18° C)

The village of West Malle, north of Antwerp, Belgium, is home to a Trappist abbey known in full as Our Lady of the Sacred Heart. The monastery was founded in 1794, and is said to have been brewing beer for the brothers' own consumption since 1836, though the product was not sold until the 1870s, and then only in the village. Brewing became a commercial business in about 1920. The brewery produces a "Single" beer for the brothers, and this is occasionally available to the outside world. The village's name is rendered as one word, and "Double" in Flemish on the label of the renowned Westmalle Dubbel, shown here. This is a deliciously malty, chocolatey beer, with hints of banana and passionfruit towards a dry finish.

W

WESTMALLE TRIPEL

> 🛡 **REGION OF ORIGIN** Province of Antwerp, Belgium

> 🍾 **STYLE** Abbey (Authentic Trappist) Triple

> % **ALCOHOL CONTENT** 7.2 abw (9.0 abv)

> 🍺 **IDEAL SERVING TEMPERATURE** Store at around 57° F (14° C);
> Serve no colder than 50° F (10° C)

The abbey of the village of West Malle had been producing darker brews for over 100 years before this pale beer was added, in the period after World War II. At the time, golden lagers were becoming more popular in Belgium, and several brewers of strong, dark ales were responding by experimenting with paler malts. High-strength, ale-yeast fruitiness, and the types of malt and hop typically used in Pilsner lagers, combined to make a whole new style. Westmalle Tripel has become a classic example, much imitated for its orangey-gold color; its combination of power and drinkability; and its complex of appetizing aromas and flavors. A freshness in the nose, from Saaz hops, herbal, sagelike notes, and an orange-skin fruitiness, are just some of the elements.

Westvleteren 8° (Blue Cap)

REGION OF ORIGIN Province of West Flanders, Belgium

STYLE Abbey (Authentic Trappist)

ALCOHOL CONTENT 6.4 abw (8.0 abv)

IDEAL SERVING TEMPERATURE 59–64° F (15–18° C)

The smallest of Belgium's five Trappist monasteries is St. Sixtus, at West Vleteren, near the hop town of Poperinge and the war graves around Ypres. Its bottles have no labels, but are identified on the crown. The 8°, with a blue cap, is the fruitiest, with suggestions of plum wine or brandy and an almondy dryness in the finish. Try it with one of the sweeter soft cheeses. The brewery has a stronger (9.6 abw; 12 abv) (yellow cap) so sweet and toffeeish as to suit the dessert course.

WESTVLETEREN BLOND

W

🏵 **REGION OF ORIGIN**	Province of West Flanders, Belgium.
🍾 **STYLE**	Abbey (Authentic Trappist) Triple
🍺 **ALCOHOL CONTENT**	4.6 abw (5.8 abv)
🍺 **IDEAL SERVING TEMPERATURE**	Store at 57° F (14° C); Serve no colder than 50° F (10° C)

In the late 1990s, a new fashion for golden beers developed in Belgium. In the French-speaking world, a golden brew is sometimes described as being "blond." The new blonds were mainly Abbey-style golden ales at around 5.2–5.6 abw (6.5–7.0 abv), though some were Triples, typically at 7.2 abw (9.0 abv). In 1999, Westvleteren introduced its first golden beer, at the lower end of this range in alcohol content. The custom of having no label was retained. The crown-top is green, and printed with the word blond. The beer has a powerful, herbal hop aroma; a soft, smooth, light body; and an intensely appetizing, perfumy dryness. A wonderful aperitif. The brewery sells its products only at the monastery shop (more of a serving hatch) and the café De Vrede opposite. A recorded message tells callers which "color" is available.

Whitbread Gold Label

🛡 **REGION OF ORIGIN**	Northern England, UK
🍶 **STYLE**	Barley Wine
% **ALCOHOL CONTENT**	8.7 abw (10.9 abv))
🍺 **IDEAL SERVING TEMPERATURE**	50–55° F (10–13° C)

Traditionally, barley wines were full in color, with the rich, syrupy flavors that come from dark malts. Gold Label was the first pale one, launched in 1951, by a brewer that later became part of the national group Whitbread. It has an amber or bronze color, but its flavors speak of pale malts. Gold Label has a firm creaminess, with shortbread flavors, developing to a fruity, spicy dryness with hints of apricot and aniseed. Originally made in Sheffield, Yorkshire, this beer now comes from a brewery near Blackburn, Lancashire.

GOLD
LABEL

VERY STRONG
SPECIAL BEER

THE
Nº1
Barley Wine

180ml
WHITBREAD PLC
LONDON EC1Y 4SD ENGLAND
ALCOHOL 10.9% VOL.
BEST BEFORE END SEE BACK LABEL

WOODFORDE'S NORFOLK WHERRY

🛡 **REGION OF ORIGIN** Eastern England, UK

🍺 **STYLE** Bitter Ale

🍷 **ALCOHOL CONTENT** 3.0 abw (3.8 abv)

🍺 **IDEAL SERVING TEMPERATURE** 50–55° F (10–13° C)

New-generation farmhouse brewery near Norwich. Some of the buildings are thatched with reeds from the nearby system of waterways known as the Norfolk Broads. A wherry

is a type of shallow boat typically used in the area. The beer named after the boat is hoppy, with a leafy, sharp, fresh-lime aroma and flavor; a crisp, cookielike, malt background; and a dry, candied-peel finish. Other excellent beers from Woodforde include Norfolk Nog, an old ale with a distinctive "Oloroso sherry" nuttiness and a touch of burnt-toast sharpness. A "Very Strong Pale Ale" (or barley wine?) called Headcracker is medicinal and peppery.

WORTHINGTON WHITE SHIELD

	REGION OF ORIGIN Formerly Trent Valley, now Southern England, UK
	STYLE Pale Ale/Bottled Bitter
	ALCOHOL CONTENT 4.5 abw (5.6 abv)
	IDEAL SERVING TEMPERATURE 50–55° F (10–13° C)

The Worthington brewery, founded in the 1700s, was acquired by Bass in 1927. The Worthington name has continued to survive on several products, notably the renowned White Shield, a pale ale which has been a bottle-conditioned counterpart to the filtered and pasteurized version under the Bass label. In 1997, Bass decided to discontinue the product but faced protests from lovers of the beer. Its production was moved to Horsham, Sussex, to the independent brewer King and Barnes. The beer has a firm maltiness; a herbal, sappy, briar-like, hop bitterness; and an underlying apple fruitiness.

WÜRZBURGER HOFBRÄU
JULIUS ECHTER HEFE-WEISSBIER

🛡 **REGION OF ORIGIN** Franconia, Bavaria, Germany

🍾 **STYLE** *Hefeweizen*

🥃 **ALCOHOL CONTENT** 4.0 abw (5.1 abv)

🍺 **IDEAL SERVING TEMPERATURE** 48–54° F (9–12° C)

The wine-growing town of Würzburg banned brewing "for ever" in 1434, but to no avail. In the 1600s, the vineyards could not quench the thirsts of the military in the 30 Years War. The local Prince Bishop decreed that the town should have a brewery, which was sited in the royal armory. The brewery later became a private business, and its present buildings date from 1882. In the 1980s, a plan to move out of the town center was defeated. A famous bishop of Würzburg is celebrated by Julius Echter Hefe-Weissbier. This beer has a hint of mint-toffee in the aroma; a lightly fruity palate, with suggestions of bananas, ripe plums, and cherries; and a refreshing acidity of finish. A *dunkel* ("dark") version has a much more pronounced toffee character and more overt plumminess.

WÜRZBURGER HOFBRÄU SCHWARZBIER

REGION OF ORIGIN Franconia, Bavaria, Germany

STYLE Black Beer

ALCOHOL CONTENT 3.8 abw (4.8 abv)

IDEAL SERVING TEMPERATURE 48° F (9° C)

The Würzburger brewery's foundation date is marked in a newish beer called 1643 Original Hell, which has a good hop aroma and a toastily malty palate, but this is just one of many lagers in its range. The brewery's history credits such "modern" beers to the work of "an Englishman," Theodor Böttinger, in 1874. As his name suggests, Böttinger was actually a German, but he first achieved prominence in England, brewing pale ales in Burton. The tendency toward innovation persists at Würzburg. One of the brewery's recent products is its Schwarzbier. This has the aroma of creamy coffee, a toffeeish palate, and a lightly nutty finish.

Würzburger Hofbräu Sympator

🛡️ **REGION OF ORIGIN** Franconia, Bavaria, Germany

🍾 **STYLE** Double Bock *(Doppelbock)*

% **ALCOHOL CONTENT** 6.3 abw (7.9 abv)

🥛 **IDEAL SERVING TEMPERATURE** 48° F (9° C)

There is nothing more sympathetic than a strong beer with friends. Perhaps the name was inspired by the famously "sympathetic" Bishop of Würzburg, Julius Echter, noted for his acts of philanthropy in the development of the city's university. The brewery having also been founded by a Prince Bishop, and being the seat of an important diocese, its portfolio should obviously include a pre-Lenten *Doppelbock*. Sympator has a creamy, well-retained head; a brandyish aroma; very clean, complex, malty flavors, and fudgy notes in the finish.

WYCHWOOD HOBGOBLIN

🏞 **REGION OF ORIGIN**	South/Midlands of England, UK
🍺 **STYLE**	Pale/Brown Ale
% **ALCOHOL CONTENT**	4.4 abw (5.5 abv)
🌡 **IDEAL SERVING TEMPERATURE**	50–55° F (10–13° C)

The forest of Wychwood, once a royal hunting ground, is on the Oxfordshire side of the gentle Cotswold Hills. In the maltings of the long-gone Clinch's brewery in Witney, a micro was established in 1983, using water from the Windrush River and yeast from the now-defunct Morlands brewery. The micro has since moved to a bigger site in the town, and its beers enjoy a considerable following. Principal Chris Moss likes beers with robust, individualistic aromas and flavors, and gives them names to match. Hobgoblin is inspired by such creatures as may haunt the forest. The beer is malty, with suggestions of chocolate-coated toffee and brown sugar, a balance of lemon-rind hoppiness, and a hint of warming alcohol in the finish.

Supernatural imagery
The wicked-looking goblin of the label is also embossed on the stylish bottle, and a witch rides the neck label.

YOUNGER OF ALLOA SWEETHEART STOUT

REGION OF ORIGIN	Scotland, UK
STYLE	Sweet Stout
ALCOHOL CONTENT	1.6 abw (2.0 abv)
IDEAL SERVING TEMPERATURE	55° F (13° C)

A famous old name in Scottish brewing, George Younger, is kept alive in this product. Branches of the family Younger have owned several breweries in Scotland over the years. George Younger's brewery in Alloa was acquired and then closed by Tennent, of Glasgow, in the 1960s. Tennent, in turn, is owned by Bass. Aptly, Sweetheart Stout is the most sugary example of the style: with vanilla, caramel, and medicinal notes. In a style that is typically low in alcohol, this example is especially modest.

Brews brothers
The sweetheart on the can is modelled on Hollywood starlet Venetia Stevenson, who married singer Don Everly.

YOUNG'S DOUBLE CHOCOLATE STOUT

🛡 **REGION OF ORIGIN**	London, England, UK
🍶 **STYLE**	Chocolate Stout
⌖ **ALCOHOL CONTENT**	4.0 abw (5.0 abv)
🌡 **IDEAL SERVING TEMPERATURE**	55° F (13° C)

The first stout to be made with added chocolate – both as bars and essence – was introduced by the London brewer Young's in 1997. It is remarkably silky-smooth and textured, with a lively complexity. The aromas and flavors begin with faint suggestions of ginger, becoming fudgy and creamy, then balancing this sweetness with a round, bitter-chocolate, finish. It is a big beer with a relatively modest five percent alcohol content. The use of chocolate surprised many drinkers, but makes perfect sense. Malts with chocolate-like flavors are often employed in stouts. This had already led to some of the richer stouts being offered with desserts at beer dinners.

The label...
...resembles that of a well-known British milk chocolate, but the beer has more character than the bar.

YOUNG'S OLD NICK

REGION OF ORIGIN London, England, UK

STYLE Barley Wine

ALCOHOL CONTENT 7.2 abw (6.8 abv)

IDEAL SERVING TEMPERATURE 55° F (13° C)

Once, every regional brewery in England had its own barley wine. Many have since dropped this traditional style on the grounds that it is a minor specialty, but the London brewery Young's – a famously stubborn enterprise – has remained loyal to the style. This example is a rich, toffeeish brew, with a banana-liqueur finish. As the label suggests, this is one to enjoy in front of the fire before retiring for the night. Although Young's is very much a local brewery in southwest London, its devilish Old Nick is sometimes easier to find in the United States.

The old devil
An "old" ale in name, Old Nick
is strong enough to be labeled as
barley wine.

YOUNG'S SPECIAL LONDON ALE

🛡 **REGION OF ORIGIN**	London, England, UK
🍺 **STYLE**	English Ale/Strong Pale Ale
% **ALCOHOL CONTENT**	5.1 abw (6.4 abv)
🍺 **IDEAL SERVING TEMPERATURE**	50° F (10° C)

London beermaker John Young is married to a Belgian, and once made a superbly hoppy English ale for her local brewery near Liège. The product survives in Britain as Young's Special London Ale. The drily aniseedy, spicy English hop is extremely powerful, but cushioned by a malty creaminess and a lively, fruity, yeast character, with suggestions of banana and orange zest. The fruitiness softens the final, peppery punch of hop bitterness. In the late 1990s, the brewery began to release bottle-conditioned batches, which have an even greater complexity. The beer is less easy to find in Young's own pubs than in supermarkets. It has won several awards in Britain and is also greatly respected in the United States.

Y

YOUNG'S WAGGLE DANCE

REGION OF ORIGIN	London, England, UK
STYLE	Honey Ale
ALCOHOL CONTENT	4.0 abw (5.0 abv)
IDEAL SERVING TEMPERATURE	50–55° F (10–13° C)

The term "Waggle Dance" refers to how bees inform each other of nectar sources, and derives from the work of Viennese sensory physiologist Karl von Frisch (1886–1982). The beer was developed by the Vaux brewery, of Sunderland, in 1995, and produced by its subsidiary Ward's, of Sheffield. When these two northern English breweries closed four or five years later, this popular product was taken up by Young's, of London. A hefty addition of honey is used, and that is evident in the beer's flavor, which seems to have become even sweeter in its new home. A delicious dessert beer.

ZIRNDORFER LANDBIER HELL

REGION OF ORIGIN Franconia, Bavaria, Germany

STYLE *Hell/Helles* (Pale Lager)

ALCOHOL CONTENT 3.9 abw (4.9 abv)

IDEAL SERVING TEMPERATURE 48° F (9° C))

Among German brewers, *Landbier* is a popular term. It implies a good, basic, country brew, but has technical definition. *Dorf* means village. Zirndorf was once a village, with its own brewery (founded in 1674), but is now a suburb of Nuremberg. Zirndorfer Landbier Hell is produced by the Nuremberg brewery Tucher. It has a perfumy, talclike aroma; an assertively malty start; a smooth, firm, toffeeish palate, rounding into a quick, dry finish. Tucher also produces beers under the names Patrizier, Lederer, Hürner, and Humbser-Grüner.

GREAT BEERS
A USER'S
GUIDE

POURING BEER

Debate rages over the way in which beer should be poured, but there is considerably less disagreement about the end result. Whether the head should be modest, creamy, blossomy, or towering depends partly upon local custom, but also upon the aroma and flavor desired from the beer.

POURING AN ALE

A gentle, steady pour down the side of the tilted glass will stop the beer from foaming excessively.

Steepen the angle and pour more directly to avoid the beer being too flat. Aim for one "finger" of foam.

Too much creaminess will rob the beer of its appetizingly bitter character. The hop oils will migrate from the beer itself and hide in the head.

POURING A STOUT

Pour stout slowly, to allow the head to develop. If it grows too quickly, stop for a moment.

A two-stage pour will make for a denser, creamier, more solid head, which will suit the coffeeish flavors of the stout.

A bottled stout will have a rockier, less rich head and a more natural flavor than the "draft" versions containing a "widget" (nitrogen capsule).

POURING A PILSNER

Bottles may take less than the seven minutes prescribed for a draft, but a real Pilsner must have a blossoming head.

A soft, sustained carbonation further enlivens the golden color with a consistent rise of small bubbles (known as the "bead").

The head should rise, almost like a soft ice cream, above the rim of the glass. This brings forward the hop aroma and holds back bitterness to the finish.

POURING A WHEAT BEER

Beers containing yeast have a high carbonation, so an especially gentle pour is required. The Belgians wet the glass to control the head.

In Bavaria, wheat beer is typically served with a huge head, especially if it is a bottle-conditioned example. Some yeast is included in the pour.

If the beer is deemed insufficiently cloudy, the last few drops may be rolled in the bottle to loosen the remaining yeast sediment. This is then added to the glass.

TASTING BEER

All good beer tastes of malted grains and hops, and a truly clean lager of little else. Good ales have both of those elements but also some fruitiness from the use of top-fermenting yeasts. Good porters and stouts have chocolatey or espresso-like flavors from the roasted malts used. Good wheat beers are tart and refreshing. But whatever the profile of the beer, if a brew is offered as a lager or ale, porter, stout, or wheat beer, it should live up to the style. If it is a good beer, the flavors will not only be appropriate but also in an interesting balance and combination. This is the meaning of "complexity." A beer with this quality seems to offer further aromas and flavors every time the glass is raised.

JUDGING BEERS

Enjoyment of great beer does not demand some special tasting talent. All it requires is an open mind, an interest in beer, and an eagerness to find aromas and flavors without fear of mockery.

Tasting conditions: Choose a naturally lit room for better evaluation of color. Music can be a distraction. Avoid cigarette smoke, cooking smells, or perfumes. For judging purposes, the beers should all be sampled in the same type of glass. A large, clear wine-glass is ideal, with some curvature to showcase the aroma.

Beer temperature: The serving temperatures indicated for each beer in this book are those at which each may be most enjoyable. They are merely suggestions, and do not always accord with the brewers' own guidelines. If, rather than being enjoyed as a drink, the beer is being judged, the aromas and flavors will express themselves most fully at room temperature.

Order of beers: Start with the beers expected to be lightest in intensity of flavor, and work upward, especially if they are in several styles.

How many beers?: Even five or six beers can confuse the palate, and 10 or a dozen are more than enough. In order fully to taste the beer, the bitterness must be sensed at the back of the mouth. Beer tasters therefore tend to swallow at least some of the fluid, and are less exhaustive in spitting than wine judges. As alcohol is ingested, the faculties become less acute.

Scoresheets: In a formal tasting, for a beer or wine club, or class, a scoresheet is a handy aide-mémoire. A simple system is to have scores for: fidelity to style (if it is labeled as a Pilsner, wheat beer, or ale, is it a good example?); appearance (head formation, color, and perhaps clarity); aroma (pleasant, appetizing, complex, true to style?); palate (the same criteria); and finish (does it develop late flavor, or simply vanish without saying "goodbye"?).

Between beers: Plain bread, crackers, or matzos will clear the palate. Avoid anything with its own flavors, such as salty pretzels, and butter or cheese, because their greasiness will flatten the beer. A neutral-tasting, noncarbonated bottled water, generously provided, is the best option.

1. THE LOOK
The pleasures of all food and drink are experienced with the eyes as well as the nose and palate. Clarity is an issue in most, but not all, types of beer. Color certainly is, and the greatest beers often have colours that are distinctive, subtle, complex, and appetizingly attractive.

2. THE SWIRL
A gentle swirl disturbs the beer enough to help release its aromatic compounds. This level of study might best be pursued at home, as serious swirling might easily be thought pretentious when conducted in a bar or restaurant.

3. THE SNIFF
Whether the drinker sniffs or not, much of what we think we taste is actually experienced through our potent and evocative sense of smell. In the finest beers, the appetizing aromas are a hugely significant element of the pleasure they impart.

4. THE SIP
Let the beer lap over the tongue. Sweet flavors (malt, for example) may be more obvious at the front of the tongue; salt (as in the water) at the front sides, fruity acidity farther back at the sides; while hop bitterness is best detected at the back.

LEXICON OF FLAVORS & AROMAS

Many aromas and flavors in beer have more than one origin. Explanations of some typical flavors are given below. Tasters often express flavors in terms of "aroma metaphors" that refer to other drinks and foods.

Acidity: An appetizing acidity, sometimes lemony, comes from hops. A fruity acidity derives from the yeast in fermentation, especially in ales and even more so in *Berliner Weisse*, Belgian *lambic* styles, and Flemish brown and red ales.

Apples: A fresh, delicate, pleasant, dessert-apple character arises from the fermentation process in some English ales, famously Marston's. A more astringent, green-apple taste can arise from insufficient maturation.

Bananas: Very appropriate in some South German wheat beers.

Bitterness: Sounds negative, but it is positive. "Good" bitterness comes from the hop. It is present to varying degrees in all beers, and especially appropriate in a British bitter. Robust bitterness, as in Anchor Liberty Ale, is appetizing. Astringency is not.

Body: Not actually a taste, but a sensation of texture or "mouthfeel," ranging from thin to firm to syrupy. Thinness may mean a beer has been very fully fermented, perhaps to create a light, quenching character. Firm, textured, or grainy beers may have been mashed at high temperatures to create some unfermentable sugars. Syrupy ones have been made from a high density of malts, possibly with some holding back of fermentation.

Bubblegum: Very appropriate in some South German wheat beers. Arises from compounds called guaiacols created in fermentation.

Burned: Pleasant burned flavors arise from highly-kilned barley or malt in some stouts. Burned plastic, deriving from excessive phenol, is a defect caused by yeast problems.

Butterscotch: Very appropriate in certain British ales, especially some from the north of England and Scotland. Unpleasant in lagers. This flavor derives from a compound called diacetyl created in fermentation.

Caramel: Most often a malt characteristic, though brewers do sometimes also add caramel itself. A malty caramel character is positive in restrained form in many types of beer. Too much can be overwhelming.

Cedary: A hop character.

Chocolatey: A malt character in some brown ales, porters, and stouts. Typically arising from chocolate malt.

Cloves: Very appropriate in some South German wheat beers. Arises from phenols created in fermentation.

Coffeeish: A malt character in some dark lagers, brown ales, porters, and stouts.

Cookielike: Typical character of pale malt. Suggests a fresh beer with a good malt character.

Earthy: Typical character of traditional English hops. Positive characteristic in British ales.

Fresh bread: *See* cookielike.

Grapefruit: Typical character of American hops, especially the Cascade variety.

Grass, hay: Can be a hop characteristic. Fresh, new-mown hay is typical in some classic European lagers. It arises from a compound called dimethyl sulfide, caused by fermentation with traditional lager yeasts.

Herbal: Hop characteristic. Examples of herbal flavors are bay leaves, mint, and spearmint.

Hoppy: Herbal, zesty, earthy, cedary, piney, appetizingly bitter.

Licorice: A characteristic of some dark malts, in German *Schwarzbier*, English old ales, porters, and stouts. In the English-speaking world, licorice itself is sometimes used as an additive.

Madeira: Caused by oxidation. In very strong, bottle-conditioned beers that have been aged many years, this will be in a pleasant balance. In another type of beer, it is likely to be unpleasant.

Malty: *See* cookielike, fresh bread, nuts, tea, toast, and toffee.

Minty: Hop characteristic, especially spearmint.

Nuts: Typical malt characteristic in many types of beer, especially northern English brown ales. Arises from crystal malt.

Orangey: Typical of several hop varieties. Can also arise from some ale yeasts. Positive if not overwhelming.

Pears: Yeast characteristic in some ales. If overwhelming, suggests that the beer has lost some balancing hop due to age.

Pepper: The flavor of alcohol. Suggests a strong beer.

Piney: Characteristic of some hops, especially American varieties.

Plums: Yeast character, found in South German wheat beers.

Raisiny: Typical in beers made with very dark malts and to a high alcohol content, for example, imperial stouts. This flavor develops in fermentation.

Resiny: Typical hop characteristic.

Roses: Can arise from hops. Also from yeast development during bottle-conditioning, especially in some Belgian beers.

Sherry: Dry, fino sherry flavors are typical in Belgian *lambic* beers. Sweet sherry can arise in strong, bottle-conditioned beers that have been aged. *See also* Madeira.

Smoky: Appropriate in "malt whisky beer," smoked beer, and some dry stouts.

Sour: Appropriate in *Berliner Weisse, lambic,* or Flemish brown or red specialities, but not in other styles of beer.

Strawberries: In extremely restrained form, and in balance with malt and hop, an appropriate fermentation characteristic in some British ales.

Tea: A strongish tea, of the type made in England (Indian, especially Darjeeling, with milk) is a good aroma metaphor for malt.

Toast: Malt characteristic in some dark ales, porters, and stouts.

Tobacco: Fragrant tobacco smoke can be evoked by the Tettnang hop, grown near Lake Constance in Germany and used in many lagers.

Toffee: Malt characteristic, especially in Vienna-style, *Märzen*, and *Oktoberfest* amber lagers. Very appetizing if not overwhelming.

Vinegary: *See* acidity.

Winey: Typical of *lambic* and some other Belgian styles aged in wood.

Yeast: The aroma of fresh yeast, like bread rising, is typical of some ales. Can appear as a "bite" in some from Yorkshire, England.

MOMENTS FOR A BEER

Not all beers are intended to be consumed by the pint in the pub or from the can with football on television. Nor are all beers simply thirst-quenchers.

Light-tasting lagers will quench the thirst, but wheat beers do the job much better, whether the Belgian style like Hoegaarden *(see p.229)* or the German *Weisse/Weizen* types. The most refreshing beers of all, after the first shock of their sour tinge, are Belgian "red" ales such as Rodenbach *(see p.386)*. In the same mood, a fruit beer can be an attractive drink with which to greet guests at a barbecue or party.

If people went to the pub simply to quench their thirsts, they would probably have one pint, then leave refreshed. Most beer-lovers prefer to stay longer than that. One pint of cold, fizzy lager might be quenching, but more can become bloating. The colder the beer, the more its carbonation is released in the warmth of the stomach, with uncomfortable effects. An hour or two in a good pub offers sociability. The most sociable of beers are less cold and gassy, softer, and appetizing, like English bitter, an ale from Belgium, or a German *Altbier* or *Kölsch*. It has been argued that all beers are sociable, but

Sociable pint
English bitter

Party greeting
Fruit beer

Thirst quencher
Wheat beer

that is not true. Apart from easy drinkability and moreishness, a sociable beer must be modest in alcohol. It is excessively modest to fall asleep, or worse, in the pub, and immodest to be roused by alcohol to aggression.

The more bitter a beer, the more appetizing it is. Anyone who has enjoyed an American pale ale knows how quickly it begins to demand a flight of chicken wings or a bowl of chilli. Lovers of the British pint in the pub, especially an India Pale Ale, are familiar with the sudden urge for a curry. The uses of particular beer styles before food, with various dishes, or afterward, are discussed on page 520.

Sweet stouts were traditionally regarded as an energy drink, and are due for rediscovery. The same is true of sweetish beers like English milds and Dutch "old brown" lagers. Although they are less sweet, the chocolatey black beers of Germany might also be regarded as restoratives. They are credited with having restored the health of Goethe, the country's greatest poet.

Some British breweries and pubs actually specify that their strong old ales or barley wines should not be served by the pint, though in Germany a potent Double Bock is sometimes offered in a mighty liter stein. These beers are intended as winter warmers. In something closer to an oversized brandy snifter, they can also make a fine accompaniment to a late-night movie on television. Or a book at bedtime.

Nightcap
Barley wine

With food
Bière de garde

After dinner
Château breu

SERVING BEER WITH FOOD

A really hoppy Pilsner lager (Jever, *see p.251*, or Christoffel Blond, *see p.121*, are just two examples) has the bitterness to arouse the appetite. Other great aperitifs are Trappist beers like Orval *(see p.348)*, or the Cinq Cents version of Chimay *(see p.118)*; strong golden ales such as Duvel *(see p.151)*; an IPA; or a hoppy ale like Young's Special London *(see p.507)* or Anchor Liberty Ale *(see p.22)*.

With soups or appetizers, try the sherryish flavors of Belgian *gueuze*. Shellfish, especially oysters or clams, like the earthy, stinging flavors of dry stouts like Guinness *(see p.204)*. Or look out for the various oyster stouts. The drier type of brown ale makes a surprisingly good match for crunchy salads. Sour-and-sweet beers like Rodenbach Grand Cru *(see p.388)* or Greene King Strong Suffolk *(see p.198)* will stand up to vinegary or pickled dishes. Strong lagers like EKU 28 *(see p.155)* have the Sauternes-like richness to accompany pâtés.

There is much more to beer-and-food pairings than lager with German sausages, but even this combination can be rendered far more interesting by the right brew. Dark lagers can be hard to find, but have a natural spiciness to match well-flavored sausages. Smoked lagers can also be elusive, but make a perfect accompaniment to smoked ham.

White wine with fish? Try a beer counterpart, a golden lager like the Czech Budweiser Budvar, for example *(see p.89)*. At the Munich Oktoberfest, hungry drinkers enjoy chicken on the spit. It's a good combination at home if you can find an *Oktoberfest* beer. A lightly malty alternative might be an Irish ale from

Kilkenny *(see p.257)*, though that style really demands corned beef and cabbage.

Red wine with red meat? Full-colored ales should have the fruitiness and complexity to do the same job. Perhaps a French *bière de garde* such as La Choulette Ambrée *(see p.269)* with lamb or an English ale like Marston's Pedigree *(see p.309)* with roast beef.

Pizza originates from Naples, but the most characterful beers in Italy are from the north. The classic pizza beer is probably Moretti La Rossa *(see p.325)*. The notion of pizza with beer is more typical in the United States. A Great Lakes Eliot Ness lager *(see p.196)* has enough malty richness to match the herby, spicy elements of a pizza.

Some Belgian Trappist monasteries make both beer and cheese. Chimay is an example. Its Grande Réserve *(see p.119)* goes well with the abbey's Trappist cheese, but is even happier with a Roquefort.

For those who prefer desserts, the range of beers may be surprising. The "toffee apple" flavors of German wheat beers, the orangey notes of their Belgian counterparts, and the same country's fruit beers all have their place. They work best, of course, with fruit desserts. Oatmeal stouts are perfect with creamy desserts like Atholl brose or tiramisu. Chocolate and coffee desserts have their natural partners in beers using those ingredients. Young's Double Chocolate Stout *(see p.505)* and Red Hook Double Black Stout *(see p.379)* are examples. Brooklyn Black Chocolate Stout *(see p.83)* and Pyramid Espresso Stout *(see p.375)* achieve excellent results with dark malts.

A dinner with beer can be a luxurious affair. A final flourish would be a cigar with a glass of rich Kasteel, from Belgium *(see p.256)*; an English barley wine or Scottish Wee Heavy *(see p.46)*, or Hair of the Dog Adam, from the United States *(see p.209)*.

COOKING WITH BEER

Beers that accompany foods well are often a useful addition to the dish itself. There are several quite different ways of using beer in the kitchen.

Vinegar originated from sour wine, but is now more often brewed from malt, like a sour beer. Before refrigerators, beer that had gone sour at the brewery was sometimes sold as malt vinegar. Some breweries today deliberately make such a product, or offer beer-flavored condiments. There is, therefore, every logic in using sour styles of beer as an alternative or complement to vinegar. Sour-tasting beers such as the *Berliner Weisse* style, Belgium *lambic* and *gueuze* brews, or Flemish "red" specialities such as Rodenbach *(see pp.387–388)* add a surprising dimension of flavor to salad dressings and vinaigrettes. Within the *lambic* family, the raspberry style *framboise* can work especially well.

In Belgium, *gueuze* is often used in the poaching of mussels. An alternative might be a lightly acidic ale. Similar beers, or fruity English-style ales, work well as a marinade to tenderize meats, and can be used to make sauces or gravies. Ales such as Bateman's XXXB *(see p.41)*, Marston's Pedigree *(see p.309)*, Timothy Taylor's Landlord *(see p.456)*, and McMullen's Castle Pale Ale *(see p.297)*, from England, all have enough acidity to work as a marinade. So do St. Ambroise

Pale Ale *(see p.391)*, from Canada, and US ales such as Oliver's *(see p.344)* or BridgePort ESB *(see p.80)*. Be careful with extremely hoppy examples, as the bitterness can sometimes become too intense during reduction.

The combination of malty sweetness and texture with grassy, herbal hop flavors, and sometimes yeasty tastes, makes beer an excellent base for soups. Malty, sweetish lagers are employed in soups based on barley or other grains, such as sweetcorn, or on shellfish such as crab, clams, or oysters. Lactic-tasting beers such as a *Berliner Weisse* or a *lambic* can even be employed in chilled fruit soups. The richer, darker, type of ale can add flavor and texture to soups featuring beef, onions, or cheese.

Beer can add piquancy to stews. This even works in relatively light dishes such as stewed mussels. A dry, hoppy beer like an IPA, if used with a light touch, also performs well with stews based on oily fish such as eel or salmon.

Meat stews need something richer, like an Irish ale, French *bière de garde*, *Märzenbier*, or *Bockbier* for pork or chicken, or a French, English, Scottish, or Belgian ale for lamb or beef. There are many recipes for the famous beef-in-beer stew Carbonade Flamande, some using Belgian *lambic* beers, others going to the opposite extreme with a stout such as Guinness *(see p.204)*. Between the two, and better than either, is a very slightly sour Flemish brown ale such as Liefmans Goudenband *(see p.282)*. The same beer is excellent in braising.

Basting moistens, tenderizes, and adds flavor to meat. If a dark, rich, and malty beer is used in the basting liquid, the malt sugars will caramelize, leaving a hint of toffeeish crustiness and sweet flavors. Perhaps because pork and ham are often served with sweet or fruity accompaniments, these meats lend themselves especially well to being basted with a sweetish beer.

One of the best-established uses of beer is in batters, bread, and cakes. In the US, beer batters are commonly used on vegetables served as finger food or in the style of tempura, or on oysters or cod. Use a yeasty German-style wheat beer or a bottle-conditioned English ale. If the beer is added to the mixture at the last minute, before it goes into the oven, the carbonation will make the batter airier and help it rise. This works very well with Yorkshire pudding. Richer, darker beers will give moisture to puddings and cakes.

In fruit-cake mixtures, an imperial stout will add moisture and enhance the raisiny, burned-currant character. A Guinness, perhaps with a touch of rum, could be used in a fruit cake that is intended to be moist in texture but dry in flavor. A spiced dark brew like Liefmans Glühkriek *(see p.281)* can also be effective. In chocolate dishes, the flavors will be enhanced by the use of a strong stout.

GLOSSARY

Abbey (Abbaye, Abdij) beer Belgian family of strong, fruity-tasting ales. Some Benedictine and Norbertine abbeys license commercial brewers to produce these beers for them. Such products are inspired by those of the authentic Trappist monastery brewers.

abv Alcohol by volume, as a percentage. The simplest and most widely used measure. Alcohol by weight (**w**) is sometimes used in the US. Because alcohol is lighter than water, this produces a lower figure.

Ale English-language term for a beer made by warm fermentation, traditionally with a "top" yeast. For example, mild, bitter, pale, brown ales.

Altbier German style of beer similar to British bitter or pale ale. Especially associated with Düsseldorf.

Amber Very unspecific term, widely used in the US. Tends to indicate an amber-red ale in broadly the Irish style, but sometimes a Vienna lager.

Barley wine English-language term for extra-strong ale.

Bavaria Former kingdom and republic, now the biggest state in Germany (and the one with the most breweries by far). Bavaria's capital is Munich.

Beer A fermented drink made from grain, most often barley-malt, and usually flavored with hops. Includes ales, lagers, wheat beers, and all styles reviewed in this book.

Bière de garde Strong, ale-like style, originally brewed to be kept in storage. Typical in the northwest of France.

Bitter Implies a well-hopped ale.

Bo(c)k Germanic term for an extra-strong beer. Often, but not always, dark. Usually a lager, but can also be a strong wheat beer. Usually 6.0abv (4.8w) or more.

Bohemia Former kingdom of Wenceslas, later a province of Austria and component of Czechoslovakia. Now,

with Moravia, comprises the Czech Republic. Bohemia's capital is Prague. Other main cities include Pilsen and Budweis.

Bottle-conditioned With living yeast in the bottle.

Brabant Former duchy, centered on the city of Brussels. Now three provinces: Walloon and Flemish Brabant (including the brewing city of Leuven), both in Belgium; and North Brabant, across the border in the Netherlands.

Brewpub Pub or restaurant making its own beer, sometimes also for sale elsewhere.

Doppelbock "Double" Bock. Usually around 6.0 abw (7.5 abv) or more.

Dortmunder Export Golden lager with a mineral-ish dryness and slightly above-average strength. (*See* Export.)

Dunkel/Dunkle/Dunkles German words for dark.

ESB Extra Special Bitter. In Britain, a specific beer

from the Fuller's brewery. Has inspired many similar beers in North America.

Export In the German tradition, a beer of slightly above-average strength, typically 4.2–4.4 abw/5.25–5.5 abv, most often in the Dortmunder style.

Flanders One of two nations (the other being French-speaking Wallonia) that form the Kingdom of Belgium. Provinces include East and West Flanders, Flemish Brabant, Antwerp, and Belgian Limburg. The Flemish language is a version of Dutch.

Framboise/Frambozen French and Flemish words used in Belgium to indicate raspberry beers.

Franconia Regional name for the three northernmost counties of Bavaria, including the cities of Nuremberg and Bamberg.

Gueuze/Geuze Young and old *lambics*, blended to achieve a sparkling, champagnelike beer.

Hefe German for yeast.

Hell/Helles German for "pale." Indicates a golden beer, often a malt-accented lager. Typical in Bavaria.

Imperial stout Extra-strong stout, originally popular in Imperial Russia.

IPA India Pale Ale. Type of ale originally made for the Indian Empire. Should be above average in both hop bitterness and alcohol content.

Irish ale Typically has a reddish color and a malt accent. It sometimes has a suggestion of butterscotch.

Kellerbier "Cellar beer" in German. It is usually an unfiltered lager, high in hop and low in carbonation.

Kloster German term for a beer that is, or once was, made in a monastery. May be any style.

Kölsch Means "from Cologne" in German. Applied to the style of top-fermenting golden ale made in and around that city.

Kriek Flemish term for a type of cherry used in beer.

Lager Beer fermented and matured at low temperatures. Can be any color or strength.

Lambic Belgian term for beer fermented with wild yeasts.

Limburg Brewing province in the Netherlands, centered on the city of Maastricht. The name Limburg is shared with an adjoining province of Belgium and a city in Germany.

Maibock Bock released in late spring (March, April, or May). Often relatively pale, hoppy, and spritzy.

Märzenbier Traditionally, a beer brewed in March and matured until September or October. In Germany and the US, usually implies a reddish-bronze, aromatically malty, medium-strong (around 4.4 abw/5.5 abv or more) lager.

Microbrewery One of the new generation of small breweries that have sprung up since the mid- to late-1970s.

Mild Ale that is only lightly hopped, and thus mild-tasting. Usually modest in alcohol. Sometimes dark. The word mild also exists in

Germany, and appears on some (relatively) gently hopped Pilsners.

Münchner, Munchener, Munich-style Typically a malt-accented lager of conventional strength, whether pale (*Helles*) or dark (*Dunkel*).

Oktoberfest Traditionally a *Märzenbier*, but today often paler.

Old ale Usually dark and classically medium-strong (around 4.8 abw/6.0 abv). Some are much stronger.

Oud bruin In the Netherlands, a very sweet dark lager. In Belgium, a sourish brown ale in the Oudenaarde style, but at a conventional strength.

Pale ale Originally a British style. Classically ranges from bronze to a full copper color. "Pale" as opposed to a brown ale or porter.

Pils/Pilsner/Pilsener Widely misused term. A Pilsner is more than just a standard golden lager of around 3.4–4.2 abw/4.25–5.25 abv. It should be an all-malt brew, with a pronounced, flowery hop aroma and dryness,

typically using the Saaz variety. The original is Pilsner Urquell.

Porter Dark brown or black. Made with highly-kilned malts, with a good hop balance, and traditionally top-fermenting. Traditionally associated with London.

Rauchbier German term for beer (usually lager) made with smoked malts. Especially associated with Bamberg, Franconia.

Red ale *See* Irish ale.

Saison Style of dry, sometimes slightly sour, refreshing, but strongish (4.0–6.4 abw/5.0–8.0 abv) summer ale, often bottle-conditioned. Typical in the province of Hainaut, Belgium.

Schwarzbier "Black" beer. Usually a very dark lager with a bitter-chocolate character. Especially associated with Thuringia and the former East Germany.

Scotch ale Smooth, malty style classically made in Scotland. Often dark, sometimes strong.

Stout Dark brown to black. Made with highly roasted grains and traditionally top-

fermenting. Sweet stouts historically associated with London, hoppier dry examples with Dublin and Cork.

Trappist Strict order of monks making strong ales of great character in several monasteries in Belgium. Labels include a logo saying "Authentic Trappist."

*Tripel/*Triple Usually an extra-strong, golden, aromatic, hoppy golden ale, modeled on Westmalle Tripel.

Vienna-style lager Bronze-to-red lager with a sweetish malt aroma and flavor. No longer readily available in its city of origin, but increasingly made in the US. The *Märzen-Oktoberfest* type is a stronger version.

Weisse/Weissbier "White" beer. German term for a wheat beer. Implies a pale head and often a cloudy brew.

Weizen "Wheat." Also used to describe the above.

White/Wit English-language and Flemish terms for Belgian-style spiced wheat beer.

UNITED STATES

NATIONAL ORGANIZATIONS

ASSOCIATION OF BREWERS
For information on US brewers, especially micros and brewpubs, and the annual Great American Beer Festival. 736 Pearl Street, PO Box 1679, Boulder, CO 80306-1679, USA.
Tel: 303-447-0816
Fax: 303-447-2825
Internet: www.beertown.org

NATIONAL PUBLICATIONS

ALL ABOUT BEER
National magazine for beer-lovers.
Tel: 919-490-0589
Fax: 919-490-0865
Email: AllAboutBeer@mindspring.com
Internet: www.allaboutbeer.com

MALT ADVOCATE
National magazine for lovers of beer and malt whiskey
Tel: 610-967-1083
Fax: 610-965-2995
Email: maltman999@aol.com
Internet: www.whiskeypages.com

FESTIVALS

The world's largest/most interesting beer festival is held each October in Colorado. It is organized by the Association of Brewers.

NORTHEAST

PUBLICATIONS

ALE STREET NEWS
Newspaper published for beer-lovers throughout the region. Based in New York/Jersey area.
Tel: 800-351-ALES
Fax: 201-368-9100
Email: tony@alestreetnews.com
Internet: www.alestreetnews.com

YANKEE BREW NEWS
Newspaper for beer-lovers in New England.
Tel: 800-423-3712
Internet: realbeer.com:80/ybn/

RETAILERS

MASSACHUSETTS
KAPPY'S
175–177 Andover Street
Peabody
MA 01960
Tel/fax: 978-532-2330
Internet: www.kappys.com

NEW JERSEY
GRAND OPENING LIQUORS
1058 High Mountain Road
N. Haledon
NJ 07508
Tel: 973-427-4477
Fax: 973-423-3471

NEW YORK
BIG Z BEVERAGE
1675 E. Jericho Turnpike
Long Island
Huntington
NY 11473
Tel: 516-499-3479
Fax: 516-499-3672

PENNSYLVANIA
SHANGY'S, THE BEER AUTHORITY
40 East Main Street
Emmaus
PA 18049
Tel: 610-967-1701
Fax: 610-967-6913
Email: shangys@aol.com
Internet: www.shangys.com

MID-ATLANTIC

PUBLICATIONS

MID-ATLANTIC BREWING NEWS
Box 20268
Alexandria
VA 22320-1268
Email: greg@brewingnews.com
Internet: www.brewingnews.com

RETAILERS

DISTRICT OF COLUMBIA
CHEVY CHASE WINE & SPIRITS
5544 Connecticut Ave. NW
DC 20015
Tel: 202-363-4000
Fax: 202-537-6067
Email: corkscrew@aol.com

DELAWARE
STATE LINE LIQUORS
1610 Elkton Road
Elkton, MD 21921
Tel: 1-800-446-9463/
410-398-3838
Fax: 410-398-1303
Email: stateline@eclipsetel.com
Internet: statelineliquors.com

MARYLAND
BUN PENNY
1080 Columbia Mall
Columbia, MD 21044
Tel: 410-730-4100
Fax: 410-730-1703
Email: jpditter@yahoo

VIRGINIA
CORKS & KEGS
7110 Patterson Avenue,
Suite A
Richmond
VA 23229
Tel: 804-288-0816
Fax: 804-285-3679

SOUTHEAST
RETAILERS
FLORIDA
WORLD OF BEER
2809 Gulf to Bay Blvd
Clearwater
FL 33759
Tel: 727-797-6905
Fax: 727-796-7623

GEORGIA
MAC'S BEER & WINE
929 Spring Street
Altanta
GA 30309
Tel: 404-872-4897
Fax: 404-872-6569

MIDWEST
PUBLICATIONS
GREAT LAKES BREWING NEWS
Based in upstate New York,
but excellent coverage of
region to west.
Tel: 716-689-5841
Fax: 716-689-5789
Email: glbrewing@aol.com

MIDWEST BEER NOTES
Based in Minnesota/
Wisconsin region
PO Box 237
Ridgeland
WI 54763-0237
Tel: 715-837-1120
Email: beernote@realbeer.com
Internet:
www.realbeer.com/beernotes

RETAILERS
ILLINOIS
SAM'S WINES & SPIRITS
1720 N. Marcey St.
Chicago
IL 60614
Tel: 312-664-4394/
800-777-9137
Fax: 312-664-8666
Email: sams@samswines.com
Internet: www.samswine.com

TOTAL BEVERAGE
1163 East Ogden Avenue
Naperville (Chicago)
IL 60563
Tel: 630-428-1122
Fax: 630-428-9660

KENTUCKY
PARTY SOURCE
95 Riviera Drive
Bellevue
Cincinnati
KY 41073
Tel: 606-291-4007
Fax: 606-291-4147

MINNESOTA
BLUE MAX LIQUORS
14640 10th Avenue South
Burnsville
MN 55337
Tel: 612-432-3350
Fax: 612-432-2048

SURDYK'S LIQUORS
303 E. Hennepin Avenue
Minneapolis, MN 55414
Tel: 612-379-3232

NORTH DAKOTA
HAPPY HARRY'S BOTTLE SHOP
2051 32nd Avenue S.
Grand Forks, ND 58201
Tel: 701-780-0902
Fax: 701-780-0905
Email:
happyharrys@corpcomm.net
Internet: www.happy-
harrys.com

OHIO
WAREHOUSE BEVERAGE
4364 Mayfield Road
South Euclid
Cleveland
OH 44121
Tel: 216-382-2400

SOUTHWEST
PUBLICATIONS
ROCKY MOUNTAIN BEER
NOTES
Based in Colorado.
Tel: 715-837-1120
Email: beernote@realbeer.com
www.realbeer.com/beernotes

SOUTHWEST BREWING NEWS
Based in Texas.
Tel: 1-800-474-7291/
512-443-3607
Fax: 512-443-3607
Email: swbrewing@aol.com

RETAILERS
COLORADO
LIQUOR MART INC.
1750 15th Street
Boulder
CO 80302
Tel: 303-449-3374
Fax: 303-938-9463
Internet: www.liquormart.com

TEXAS
WHIP-IN
1950 So. IH-35
Austin, TX 78704
Tel 512-442-5337
Fax: 512-442-1443
Email: whipin@swbell.com

MR. G'S
1453 Coit & 15th
Plano
Dallas
TX 75075
Tel: 972-867-2821
Fax: 972-867-2821 ext 8

SPEC'S
2410 Smith Street
Houston

TX 77006
Tel: 713-526-8787
Fax: 713-526-6129
Internet: www.specsonline.com

CENTRAL MARKET
4821 Broadway
San Antonio
TX 78209
Tel: 210-368-8600
Fax: 210-826-3253
Internet:
www.centralmarket.com

CALIFORNIA

PUBLICATIONS
CELEBRATOR
Based in the San Francisco
Bay area. Covers the whole
of the west, but also with
national news.
Tel: 510-670-0121
Fax: 510-670-0639
Email:
tdalldorf@celebrator.com
Internet: www.celebrator.com

RETAILERS
HI TIME CELLARS
250 Ogle Street
Costa Mesa
CA 92627
Tel: 949-650-8463
Fax: 949-631-6863
Email: hitimeclrs@aol.com
Internet: www.hitimewine.com

BEVERAGES, & MORE!
201 Baysore Boulevard
San Francisco
CA 94124
Tel: 415-648-1233
Fax: 415-641-7812

CANNERY WINE CELLAR
2801 Leavenworth Street
San Francisco
CA 94133
Tel: 415-673-0400
Fax: 415-673-0461

Internet:
www.cannerywine.com

WINE EXCHANGE OF SONOMA
452 First Avenue
Sonoma, CA 95476
Tel: 707-938-1794
Fax: 707-938-0969

HAWAII

PUBLICATIONS
GUSTO MAGAZINE
Tel: 808-259-6884
Fax: 808-259-6755
Email: editor@getgus.to
Internet: www.getgus.to

RETAILERS
KAMUELA LIQUORS
Hawaii Island
HI 96743
Tel: 808-885-4674

KONA WINE MARKET
75-5626 Kuakini Hwy
Kailua-Kona
Hawaii Island
HI 9674

KIHEI WINE & SPIRIT
Maui Island
HI 96744
Tel: 808-879-0555

THE LIQUOR COLLECTION
Ward Warehouse
Honolulu
Oahu Island
HI 96814
Tel: 808-524-8808

TAMURA'S FINE WINES &
LIQUORS
851 Pohukaina Street #C-7
Honolulu
Oahu Island
HI 96814
Tel: 808-589-1677
(Additional locations in
Wahiawa and Kailua.)

NORTHWEST

PUBLICATIONS
NORTHWEST BEER NOTES
Tel: 715-837-1120
Email: beernote@realbeer.com
Internet:
www.realbeer.com/beernotes

RETAILERS
OREGON
BELMONT STATION
4520 SE Belmont
Portland
OR 97215
Tel: 503-232-8538/
1-888-892-2337
Fax: 503-234-9107
Internet:
www.horsebrass.com/belmont
_station

BURLINGAME GROCERY
8502 SW Terwilliger
Portland
OR 97219
Tel: 503-246-0711
Fax: 503-246-0723
Internet:
www.burlingamemarket.com

WASHINGTON
LARRY'S MARKET
Totem Lake – Store #6
12321 – 120th Pl. NE
Kirkland
WA 98034
Tel: 425-820-2300
Fax: 425-820-8176
Internet:
www.larrysmarkets.com

CANADA

PUBLICATIONS
BIÉRE MAG
Tel: 514-658-8133
Fax: 514-447-0426
Internet: www.bieremag.ca

RETAILERS

The retailers below are listed by state in alphabetical order.

ALBERTA

BEERLAND AT CECIL HOTEL
415 – 4th Avenue S.E.
Calgary, Alberta,
T2G 0C8
Tel: 403-266-3344
Fax: 403-234-9756

CHATEAU LOUIS
11727 Kingsway Avenue
Edmonton, Alberta
T5G 3A1
Tel: 780-452-7770
Fax: 403-454-3436
Email: chateau
@planet.eon.net
Internet:
www.chateaulouis.com

BRITISH COLUMBIA

CAMBIE STREET LIQUOR
5555 Cambie Street
Vancouver, B.C.
V5Z 3A3
Tel: 604-266-1321
Fax: 604-264-9071
Internet:
www.bcliquorstores.com

FORT STREET LIQUOR
1960 Foul Bay Road
Victoria, B.C.,V8R 5A7
Tel: 250-952-4220
Fax: 250-595-0768
Internet:
www.bcliquorstores.com

MANITOBA

MANITOBA LIQUOR MART
(store 45)
Grant Park Shopping Centre
1120 Grant Avenue
Winnipeg, Manitoba
R3M 2A6
Tel: 204-987-4045
Fax: 204-475-7666
Internet: www.mlcc.mb.ca
(1 of around 25 stores in
Manitoba; see website.)

QUEBEC

L'EPICIER DU MARCHÉ
128 Atwater
Atwater Market
Montreal, Quebec
H4C 2G3
Tel: 514-637-3224
Fax: 514-932-7753

EPICIER DES HALLES
145 St Joseph
St Jean, Quebec
J3B 1W5
Tel: 450-348-6100
Fax: 450-348-0936

SASKATCHEWAN

8TH STREET LIQUOR
STORE #505
3120 8th Street East
Saskatoon, SK
S7H 0W2
Tel: 306-933-5318
Fax: 306-933-5219
Email:
store505@slga.gov.sk.ca

ALBERT SOUTH #557
4034 Albert Street
Regina, SK
S4S 3RS
Tel: 306-787-4251
Fax: 306-787-8075
Email:
store557@slga.gov.sk.ca

AUSTRALIA

PUBLICATIONS

NATIONAL LIQUOR NEWS
97 Victoria Street
Potts Point, NSW 2011
Tel: 02-9357-7277

LIQUOR WATCH
9 Carisbrook Street
Linley Point, NSW 2066
Tel: 02-9428-3147

Australian beer writer Willie
Simpson writes a beer column
every Tuesday in the Good
Living section of the *Sydney
Morning Herald*. Across town,
Peter Lalor writes a weekly
beer column every Wednesday
for the Food & Wine section
of rival newspaper, *The
Daily Telegraph*.

WEBSITES

BEER LOVERS AUSTRALIA
www.beerlovers.com.au
A beer club based in Victoria.

www.vintagecellars.com.au
On-line ordering site for
Vintage Cellars.

RETAILERS

The following retail chains
offer a growing range of
Australian and imported beers.
Generally, the chains have
outlets in most large towns.
Please check local listings.

LIQUORLAND
PORTERS
MAC'S
SAFEWAY (Victoria only)
DAN MURPHY'S (Victoria only)

AUSTRIA

WEBSITES

www.breworld.com/austria/
Definitive and comprehensive
information on the current
Austrian beer scene by
renowned Austrian beer expert
Conrad Seidl.

www.austrianbeer.com/beer/
An independent website
operated by beer-lovers. Beer
reviews and ratings with pub
information. Very useful for
tourists.Text in English.

bier.oesterreich.com
The official website of
"Verband der Brauereien," the
Austrian brewing industry's
professional organization.

Accurate information and statistics about Austrian breweries. Text in German.

RETAILERS

The popular supermarket chain "Interspar" carries a wide selection of Austrian and imported beer.

GETRAENKEKISTL
R.Ammersin GesmbH
Speisinger Strasse 31
1130 Wien
Tel: +43-1-804-55-08
Fax: +43-1-804-14-444
Email: ammersin@magnet.at

BELGIUM

ORGANIZATIONS

DE OBJECTIEVE BIERPROEVERS (Belgian consumer organization)
Postbus 32
2600 Berchem 5, Belgium
Tel: +32-3-323-4538
Fax: +32-3-226-8532
Email: obp@www.dma.be
Internet: www.dma.be/p/obp

CONFÉDÉRATION DES BRASSERIES DE BELGIQUE/ CONFEDERATIE DER BROUWERIJEN VAN BELGIË
The professional organization of the Belgian brewing industry. Their historic headquarters building in Brussels contains an interesting brewing museum. Consumer-oriented website with extensive links.
Maison des Brasseurs
Grand' Place 10
1000 Bruxelles, Belgium
Tel: +32-2-511 49-87
Fax: +32-2-511-32-59
Email: cbb@beerparadise.be
Internet: www.beerparadise.be

PUBLICATIONS

STEPHEN D'ARCY OF THE CAMPAIGN FOR REAL ALE (Brussels) produces a highly informative and regularly updated newsletter *A Selective Guide to Belgian Bars.*
67, Rue des Atrébates,
B-1040, Brussels, Belgium.
Tel: +32-2-736-72-18
Email:
Stephen.D'Arcy@cec.eu.int

RETAILERS

BELGIUM BEERS
2 Reyndersstraat
Antwerp
Tel: +32-3-226-6853

BIER TEMPEL
56 Rue Marché aux Herbes
Brussels
Tel/Fax: +32-2-502-19-06
Internet: www.biertemple.com

BIÈRES ARTISANALES
174 Chaussée de Ware
Brussels
Tel: +32-2-512-17-88

DRINK MARKET DELÉPINE
13 Rue Eugène Cattoir
Brussels
Tel: +32-2-640-45-64
Fax: +32-2-640-36-23

HOPDUVEL
625 Coupure Links
Ghent
Tel: +32-9-225-2068

YVES STREEKBIEREN
1 O.L. Vrouwmarkt
Roeselare
Tel: +32-53-62-67-30

DENMARK

ORGANIZATIONS

DANISH BEER ENTHUSIASTS
The national beer lovers' association. It produces the magazine *The Beer Enthusiast* and an email newsletter, and

holds regional and national meetings, beer tastings, and brewery visits.
Anders Evald
Andedammen 14
DK-3460 Birkerød
Denmark

FESTIVALS

The first national beer festival will take place in Copenhagen in autumn 2000, with the participation of most Danish breweries as well as import companies and breweries'from neighboring countries. The festival will take place every second year.

WEBSITES

www.ale.dk
A comprehensive website by THE BEER ENTHUSIASTS, including a good beer guide, and pub and retail listings for the whole of Denmark. Also information on the national beer festival.

RETAILERS

GL. STRANDS ØL & VINLAGER
Naboløs 6
DK-1206 København K
Tel: +45-33-93-93-44
Fax: +45-33-93-96-44

AMAGER ØLHUS
Italiensvej 36A
DK-2300 København S
Tel: +45-32-59-45-45
Fax: +45-32-59-45-45
Email
amager.olhus@post.cybercity.dk

MALT & HUMLE
Låsbygade 6
DK-6000 Kolding
Tel: +45-75-54-07-55
Fax: +45-75-54-07-55

CHAS E VINHANDEL
Ryesgade 5
DK-8000 Århus C
Tel: +45-86-12-14-11
Fax: +45-86-12-13-34

H.J. HANSEN VINHANDEL A/S
Vingårdsgade 13
DK-9000 Aalborg
Tel: +45-98-12-52-90

FINLAND

ORGANIZATIONS

THE FINNISH LEAGUE OF
INDEPENDENT BEER SOCIETIES
(FINNLIBS)
An umbrella organization for
Finnish beer societies,
FINNLIBS is primarily
concerned with consumer
issues. Full information at the
FINNLIBS website:
www.olut.org

WEBSITES

www.helsinginsanomat.fi/olut
helsinki
Information on the Helsinki
Beer Festival (text in English).

PUBLICATIONS

JUOMANLASKIJA MAGAZINE
www.kolumbus.fi/juomanlaskija

FESTIVALS

Finland has two main beer
festivals: the annual DARK BEER
FESTIVAL in Tampere (January)
and the HELSINKI BEER
FESTIVAL in Helsinki (April).
Information on these can be
found at the above websites.

RETAILERS

In Finland, the state-owned
retailer ALKO has the
monopoly of beers with more
than 4.7 percent alcohol.
Around 30 of its 250 outlets
keep a wide selection of beers.

ALKO OY
Heidehofintie 2,
FIN-01300 Vantaa
Tel: +358-9-576576
Fax: +358-9-57655350
Email: palaute@alko.fi
Internet: www.alko.fi

Supermarket chains including
CITYMARKET, PRISMA, and
SESTO have a good selection of
beers under 4.7 percent.

FRANCE

ORGANIZATIONS

LES AMIS DE LA BIÈRE
5 Route de Mametz
60220 Aire sur la Lys
Tel: +33-321-39-14-52
Internet: amis.biere.org

RETAILERS

BOOTLEGGER
82 Rue de l'Ouest
75014 Paris
Tel: +33-1-43-27-94-02

BRASSERIE VANUXEEM
(Consumers in northern
France visit this retailer just
over the border in Belgium)
150 Rue d'Armentières
B-7782 Ploegsteert
Belgium
Tel: +32-56-58-89-23
Fax: +32-56-58-75-59

LES CHOPES
(covered market of Wazemmes)
Place de la Nouvelle Aventure
F-59000 Lille
Tel: +33-320-13-95-25
Fax: +33-320-90-17-37

BOISSONS CASH DUBUS
27 Place République
F-59650 Villeneuve d'Ascq
Tel: +33-320-02-41-23
Fax: +33-320-05-04-08

DICKELY SELESTAT
DISTRIBUTION
Route de Muttersholtz
67600 Selestat
Tel: +33-388-92-09-30

BIÈRE ET PAIX
22 Rue des Frères
67000 Strasbourg
Tel: +33-388-36-90-04

HO' BIÈRE INTERNATIONALE
9 Avenue de la Gare
67140 BARR
Tel: +33-388-08-88-18

AUCHAN
RN1
Route de Boulogne
62100 Calais
Tel: +33-321-46-92-92
Fax: +33-321-96-81-50

GERMANY

WEBSITES

www.bier.de
Consumer-oriented site in
English and German. Contains
information about retailers.

www.brauer-bund.de
German-language site
produced by the German
brewing industry's
professional organization.

RETAILERS

HAUS DER 131 BIERE
Karlshöhe 27
D-22175 Hamburg
Tel: +49-40-640-72-99
Fax: +49-40-640-20-71
Email: 131biere@bier.de
Internet: www.biershop.de
(International mail order
service available)

BIER-SPEZIALITÄTEN-LADEN
Karl Marx Alle 56
10243 Berlin
Tel: +49-30-249-21-46
Fax: +49-30-242-71-47

AMBROSETTI
Schiller Str. 103
D-10625 Berlin
Tel: +49-30-312-47-26
Fax: +49-30-315-033-43
Email: info@ambrosetti.de
Internet: www.ambrosetti.de

BRUNO MARUHN
Pfungstädter Straße 174-176
D-64297 Darmstadt-Eberstadt
Tel: +49-61-51-5-72-79
Fax: +49-61-51-59-54-95
(Mail order service available)

COUP DE LOUP
Koellstr. 22
D-76189 Karlsruhe
Tel: +49-721-961-32-45
Fax: +49-721-961-32-43
Email:
coup-de-loup@coup-de-loup.de
Internet: www.coup-de-loup.de
(Mail order service available)

ITALY
PUBLICATIONS
IL MONDO DELLA BIRRA
In Italian, with an occasional
English edition.
Via Cagliero 21
20125 Milano
Italy
Tel: +39-2-668-2834
Fax: +39-2-607-2185
Email: monbirit@tin.it

RETAILERS
A TUTTA BIRRA
Via L. Palazzi, 15 (lat. Corso
Buenos Aires)
I-20124 Milan
Tel: +39-2-20-11-65

OASI DELLA BIRRA
Piazza Testaccio, 38/41
I-00153 Rome
Tel: +39-6-57-46-122

JAPAN
RETAILERS
MOMOYA SHOTEN
Minami 5, Nishi 5
Chuo-ku, Sapporo
Tel: +81-11-521-0646

SAKE CLUB TOKI
Daiei Hirosaki B1
2-1 Oh-machi 2-chome
Hirosaki City
Aomori Prefecture
Tel: +81-172-38-2233

TOBU DEPARTMENT STORE
Ikebukuro branch
1-1-25 Nishi Ikebukuro
Toshima-ku, Tokyo
Tel: +81-3981-2211
One of the most well-managed
beer selections in Japan. About
200 beers from 34 countries.

ISETAN DEPARTMENT STORE
Shinjuku branch
3-14-1 Shinjuku
Shinjuku-ku, Tokyo
Tel: +81-3-3352-1111
Good display of nearly 100
imported and Japanese craft
beers, with frequent new
arrivals.

BEER SPOT CHITASHIGE
3-50 Sakurayama-cho
Showa-ku, Nagoya
Tel: +81-52-841-1150

ASAO SAKATEN
6 Tanaka Nogami-cho
Sakyo-ku, Kyoto
Tel: +81-75-781-3210

KIOKA BELGIAN BEER
SPECIALTY SHOP
9-288-3 Nakamachi
Ohtori, Sakai City
Osaka
Tel: +81-722-62-1341
Over 120 varieties of Belgian
beer, along with a few other
European beers.

IYOTETSU SOGO DEPARTMENT
STORE
5-1-1- Minato-cho
Matsuyama City,
Ehime Prefecture
Tel: +81-899-48-2111

SAZAN BEFU-TEN
2-9-1 Befu
Johnan-ku, Fukuoka City
Tel: +81-92-821-2207

NETHERLANDS
ORGANIZATIONS
PINT
(PROMOTIE INFORMATIE
TRADITIONAL BIER)
(Dutch consumer
organization)
Postbus 3757
1001 AN Amsterdam
Netherlands
Email: info@pint.nl
Internet: www.pint.nl

RETAILERS
DE BIERKONING
Paleisstraat 125
Amsterdam
1012 ZL
Tel: +31-20-625-23-36
Fax: +31-20-627-06-54
Email: info@bierkoning.nl
Internet: www.bier.nl

D'OUDE GEKROONDE BIER EN
WIJNWINKEL
Rosmarijn Steeg 10
1012RP Amsterdam
Tel: +31-20-623-77-11
(tasting room upstairs)

THE BEER SHOP
Gier Straat 70
2011GG Haarlem
Tel: +31-23-53-14-180
Fax: +31-23-52-47-868

VERSLUIS DRANKENHAND
35a Conradkade
Den Haag
Tel: +31-70-345-3682

NEW ZEALAND

WEBSITES

www.brewing.co.nz
The most comprehensive site
covering the New Zealand
beer scene. Carries extensive
listings and reviews, as well as
information about many local
beer festivals and events.

www.nz-beer-awards.co.nz
Covers the New Zealand
International Beer Awards, first
held in 1999 and primarily an
industry event but may be of
interest to consumers.

RETAILERS

The retailers in this section are
listed from north to south.
THE BEER CELLAR
158 Garnet Road
Westmere
Auckland
Tel: +64-9-360-7251

MASONIC TAVERN
29 King Edward Parade
Devonport
Auckland
Tel: +64-9-445-0485
Email: fist@ihug.co.nz

HAVELOCK WINES & SPIRITS
Donnelly Street
Havelock North
Hastings
Tel: +64-6-877-8208
Fax: +64-6-877-5223

REGIONAL WINES & SPIRITS
15 Ellice Street
Basin Reserve
Wellington
Tel: +64-4-385-6952
Fax: +64-4-382-8488

Email:
wine@regionalwines.co.nz
Internet:
www.regionalwines.co.nz

LIQUORLAND
Cnr. Clyde & Ilam Roads
Ilam
Christchurch
Tel: +64-3-351-9285

MEENAN WINES & SPIRITS
750 Great King Street
Dunedin North
Dunedin
Tel: +64-3-477-2047
Fax: +64-3-477-2049

NORWAY

ORGANIZATIONS

NORØL (NORSKE
ØLVENNERS LANDSFORBUND)
(Federation of Norwegian Beer
Consumers)
Postboks 6567 Etterstad,
N-0607 Oslo
NORWAY
Email: nor-ale@interpost.no
Internet:
www.interpost.no/nor-ale

WEBSITES

BRYGGERI – OG
MINERALVANNFORENINGEN
www.nbmf.no
Site from the Norwegian
Brewers and Soft Drink
Producers. Good statistics about
consumption, etc. In English.

FESTIVALS

Since 1994 NORØL has
arranged a small
CHRISTMAS BEER FESTIVAL
("JULEØLFESTIVAL") in Oslo
in the second weekend of
November. Here you can taste
all the traditional "strong"
(about 6.5 percent abv)
Christmas Beers. It also
arranges a tiny BOCK BEER

FESTIVAL ("BOKKØLFESTIVAL")
in February/March to support
the four existing traditional
Norwegian (dark) Bock Beers.
(Info can be found at
NORØL's website.)

RETAILERS

The Norwegian state
monopolizes the sale of beer
with an alcohol content higher
than 4.75 percent abv, through
the agency Vinmonopol.
Beer with an alcohol content
lower than 4.7 percent abv
may be bought from
supermarkets, grocery shops,
and specialist beer and beverage
shops including:
ØLEKSPERTEN BEMA100
Sandsværvn 221
3615 Kongsberg
Tel: +47-32-73-18-50

BRYGGERIMESTERN A.S.
Cappelensgt 12
3718 Skien
Tel/fax: +47-35-53-10-99

OLE SIMON AS
Vågsg. 43
4306 Sandnes
Tel: +47-51-66-20-84

ULTRA
Bryn Senter
Østensjøv. 79
0667 Oslo
Tel: +47-22-75-79-00

SWEDEN

WEBSITES

www.stockholmbeer.se
The principal website for
information about beer in
Sweden is produced by the
organizers of the Stockholm
Beer Festival (see below).
Text in English and Swedish.

www.swedbrewers.se
Site with information about
Swedish breweries.
Text in English and Swedish.

PUBLICATIONS

APÉRITIF
A magazine specializing in alcoholic beverages including beer.
Box 15
S-101 20 STOCKHOLM
Tel: +46-8-545-120-00
Fax: +46-8-545-120-11
Email:
m.ljungstrom@tidningsmakarna.se

FESTIVALS

THE STOCKHOLM BEER FESTIVAL is the largest beer exhibition in the Nordic European countries with around 1,000 different kinds of beer, cider, and whiskey from all over the world. Established in 1992, this annual event takes place over the last two weekends every September.

RETAILERS

Sweden has a monopoly retail system for alcohol, the Systembolaget. There are 403 shops runned by the Systembolaget and details can be found at www.systembolaget.se
The three shops with the largest beer selection are found in the three largest towns in Sweden.

SYSTEMBOLAGET BEER SHOP
Norra Stationsgatan 58–60
S-113 33 Stockholm
Tel: +46-8-31-73-49
Fax: + 46-8-32-69-04
Email:
butik.0140@systembolaget.se

SYSTEMBOLAGET
Lilla Klädpressargatan 8–16,
Östra Nordstan
S- 404 22 Göteborg

Tel: +46-31-25-80-09
Fax: + 46-31-15-25-59
Email:
butik.1409@systembolaget.se

SYSTEMBOLAGET
Baltzargatan 23
S-211 36 Malmö
Tel. +46-40-611-68-45
Fax: +46-40-12-20-63
Email:
butik.1201@systembolaget.se

UNITED KINGDOM

ORGANIZATIONS

CAMPAIGN FOR REAL ALE (CAMRA)
A consumer organization dealing with traditional UK beers. Publishers of the monthly *What's Brewing*, the annual *Good Beer Guide* (which lists pubs selling good beers throughout the UK), and organizers of the Great British Beer Festival (usually held in early August, at Olympia, London).
230 Hatfield Road
St. Albans
Hertfordshire AL1 4LW
Tel: 01727-867201
Fax: 01727-867670
Email: camra@camra.org.uk
Internet: www.camra.org.uk

WEBSITES

THE BEER HUNTER®
www.beerhunter.com
Michael Jackson's own website. News, articles, tastings, reviews and extensive archive of The Beer Hunter's® writings.

THE REAL BEER PAGE
www.realbeer.com
The most extensive worldwide web publication

for beer-lovers. Links to many other sites.

www.breworld.com
Largest European beer and brewing internet site (text in English).
info@breworld.com

FESTIVALS

THE GREAT BRITISH BEER FESTIVAL averages around 300 British cask-conditioned beers (see CAMRA above). Most of the local beer festivals in the UK are listed in the CAMRA monthly newspaper *What's Brewing.*

ENGLAND

RETAILERS

Among local wine merchants, Oddbins has in recent years paid particular attention to speciality beers, but there are growing ranges in supermarkets such as Asda, Morrisons, Safeway, Sainsbury, Tesco and Waitrose. In London, the department store Selfridges has a good range.
* Indicates a UK mail order service available.

CUMBRIA

BEERS IN PARTICULAR
151 Highgate
Kendal
Cumbria LA9 4EN
Tel: 01539-735714
Fax: 01539-724686

THE MASONS ARMS
(also a brewpub)
Strawberry Bank
Cartmel Fell
Grange-over-Sands
Windermere

Cumbria LA11 6NW
Tel: 015395-68486
Fax: 015395-68780
Email: stevensonwalsh@.aol

LANCASHIRE

THE REAL ALE SHOP
47 Lovat Road
Preston
Lancashire PR1 6DQ
Tel: 01772-201591
Fax: 01772-558717

LEICESTERSHIRE

THE BOTTLE STORE *
77 Queens Road
Leicester LE2 1TT
Tel: 0116-270-7744
Fax: 0116-270-7744

LINCOLNSHIRE

SMALL BEER
199 Grimsby Road
Grimsby
Lincolnshire DN35 7HB
Tel: 01472-699234
Fax: 01472-594182
Email:
dave@sbclle.freeserve.co.uk

SMALL BEER
91 Newland Street West
Lincoln LM1 1QF
Tel: 01522-528628

LONDON

THE BEER SHOP AND
PITFIELD BREWERY *
14 Pitfield Street
London N1 6EY
Tel: 020-7739-3701
Internet:
www.pitfieldbeershop.co.uk

NORFOLK

THE BEER CELLAR *
31 Norwich Road
Strumpshaw

Norwich
Norfolk
Tel: 01603-714884

YORKSHIRE

BEER RITZ
17 Market Place
Knaresborough
Yorkshire HG5 8AL
Tel: 0142-386-2850
Fax: 0142-386-2850

BEER RITZ
Arch Z
Granary Wharf
The Canal Basin
Leeds, Yorkshire LS1 4BR
Tel: 0113-2427400
Fax: 0113-2426417
Email: sales@beerritz.co.uk
Internet: www.beerritz.co.uk

THE ARCHER ROAD
BEER STOP *
57 Archer Road
Sheffield
Yorkshire
Tel: 0114-2551356

BARRELS & BOTTLES *
3 Oak Street
Heeley Bridge,
Yorkshire
S8 9UB
Tel: 0114-2556611
Fax: 0114-2551010
Email:
sales@barrelsandbottles.co.uk
Internet:
www.barrelsandbottles.co.uk
(International mail order
service available)

THE DRAM SHOP
21 Commonside
Sheffield
Yorkshire
S10 1GA
Tel: 0114-2683117

M&D HOMEBREW
Fernades Brewery
Beerhunters Paradise
The Old Malt House
5 Avison Yard, Kirkgate
Wakefield
Yorkshire
WF1 1UA
Tel: 01924-369547

YORK BEER SHOP
28 Sandringham Street
(off Fishergate)
York, Yorkshire, YO10 4BA
Tel: 01904-647136
Fax: 01904-647136

SCOTLAND

RETAILERS

VILLENEUVE WINES
1 Venlaw Court
Peebles, Edinburgh
EH45 8AE
Tel: 01721-722500
Fax: 01721-729922
Email:
wines@villeneuvewines.com

PECKHAM & RYE
155–159 Bruntsfield Place
Edinburgh, EH10 3DG
Tel: 0131-229-7054
Internet: www.peckhams.com

PECKHAM & RYE
21 Clarence Drive
Glasgow, G12 9QN
Tel: 0141-334-4312

OCTOPUS AT FENCE BAY
Fence Foot Farm
Fairlie (Southwest of Glasgow,
on the coast at Fairlie)
Ayrshire, KA29 OEG
Sells specialty beers,
smoked and organic foods.
Tel: 01475-568918
Fax: 01475-568921
Email: fencebay@aol.com
Internet: www.fencebay.co.uk

INDEX

Note: As the beers are listed alphabetically in the book, the beers in this index are listed under their country of origin. Some are also listed under their common names.

W

ACKNOWLEDGMENTS

Author's acknowledgments: Most of the beers in this book were chosen by the author on the basis of past tastings. The brewers were then requested to supply current bottles for re-tasting and photography. The author and publishers would like heartily to thank all of the brewers who supplied beer, especially those whose products for one reason or another did not make the final selection. In the longer term, we hope to produce further editions, in which some of these beers will feature. Many of the glasses were supplied by the brewers but a large number were provided directly by the Rastal company, of Höhr-Grenzhausen, Germany; special thanks to them. For this book and over the years, the following have all offered great help:

Larry Baush, Stephen Beaumont, Eugene Bohensky, Andrew Bonner, Kathleen Boyen, Ian Burgess, Sonia Charbonnier, Jennifer Colosi, Vince Cottone, Tom Dalldorf, Stephen D'Arcy, Erich Dederichs, Jürgen Deibel, René Descheirder, Alan Dikty, Sarah and Phil Doersam, Jim Dorsch, Pierre-André Dubois, Anders Evald, Drew Ferguson, David Furer, Gary and Libby Gillman, Geoff Griggs, Chuck Hahn, Thomas Halpin, Erik Hartman, Dr. Alfred Haunold of Oregon State University, Bob Henham, Hans J. Henschien, Graham Howard, Miles Jenner, Vidar Johnsen, Eric Källgren, Nirbhao Khalsa, Alan Knight, Konishi Brewing, Jim Krecjie, Michiko Kurita, Graham Lees, Lars Lundsten, Rob Maerz, Peter McAuslan, Ed McNally, Franz Mather, Carl Mathys, Bill Metzger, Steve Middlemiss, Mikko Montonen, Richard Morrice, Mathias MüllerMultilines, Father Ronald Murphy of Georgetown University, Professor Doctor Ludwig Narziss of Weihenstephan, Hans Nordlov, Lynne and Don O'Connor, Ryouji Oda, Darren Peacock, Barrie Pepper, Chris Pietruski, Portugalia Wines (UK), Hélène Reuterwall, Bernard Rotman, John Rowling, Rüdiger Ruoss, Silvano Rusmini, Margarita Sahm, the late Dr. Hans Schultze-Berndt, Professor Paul Schwarz of North Dakota State University, Conrad Seidl, Todd Selbert, Willie Simpson, Simpson's Malt, Ritchie Stolarz, Peter Terhune, Unto Tikkanen, Anastasy and Jo Tynan, Mike Urseth, Marianne Wallberg Sämsjö, De Wolff Cosijns Malt, Derek Walsh, Sabina Weyerman, Przemyslaw Wisniewski, Kari Ylane...

...and everyone else who has helped me or shared a beer on the road.

Publisher's acknowledgments:
Photography: Steve Gorton, Ian O'Leary, Sarah Ashun
Editorial assistance: Jill Fornary, Tracie Lee Davis
Index: Margaret McCormack   *Hop illustration:* Ruth Hall
Home economist: Ricky Turner

FURTHER READING

GENERAL
Beer, Michael Jackson, Dorling Kindersley, New York, 1998
Beer Companion, Michael Jackson, Running Press, second edition, Philadelphia, 1997
Pocket Beer Book, Michael Jackson, Running Press, eighth edition, Philadelphia, 2000

USA
The Beer Lover's Guide to the USA: Brewpubs, Taverns, and Good Beer Bars, Stan Hieronymus & Daria Labinsky, St. Martin's Griffin, New York, 2000

BELGIUM
The Great Beers of Belgium, Michael Jackson, Running Press, third edition, Philadelphia, 1998
The Beers of Wallonia, John Woods & Keith Rigley, The Artisan Press, Bristol, 1996

Good Beer Guide to Belgium, Holland & Luxembourg, Tim Webb, CAMRA Books, St. Albans, 1998

CZECH REPUBLIC
Good Beer Guide to Prague and the Czech Republic, Graham Lees, CAMRA Books, St. Albans, 1996

FRANCE
The Beers of France, John Woods & Keith Rigley, The Artisan Press, Bristol, 1998

AUSTRIA
Unser Bier, Conrad Seidl, Deuticke, Vienna, 1996

GERMANY
Good Beer Guide to Munich & Bavaria, Graham Lees, CAMRA Books, St. Albans, 1994